Conversations
with Natasha Trethewey

Literary Conversations Series
Peggy Whitman Prenshaw
General Editor

Conversations
with Natasha Trethewey

Edited by Joan Wylie Hall

University Press of Mississippi   *Jackson*

Books by Natasha Trethewey

Domestic Work: Poems. Saint Paul, MN: Graywolf, 2000.
Bellocq's Ophelia: Poems. Saint Paul, MN: Graywolf, 2002.
Native Guard: Poems. Mariner Books. Boston: Houghton Mifflin, 2006.
Best New Poets 2007: 50 Poems from Emerging Writers. Edited by Natasha Trethewey. Charlottesville: University of Virginia Press, 2007.
Native Guard: Poems. Gift edition, with CD. Boston: Houghton Mifflin Harcourt, 2007.
Beyond Katrina: A Meditation on the Mississippi Gulf Coast. Athens: University of Georgia Press, 2010.
Thrall: Poems. Boston: Houghton Mifflin Harcourt, 2012.
Memoir under contract. Ecco Books. New York: Harper Collins, 2014.

www.upress.state.ms.us

The University Press of Mississippi is a member of the Association of American University Presses.

Copyright © 2013 by University Press of Mississippi
All rights reserved
Manufactured in the United States of America

First printing 2013

∞

Library of Congress Cataloging-in-Publication Data
Conversations with Natasha Trethewey / edited by Joan Wylie Hall.
    pages cm. — (Literary Conversations Series)
  Includes index.
  ISBN 978-1-61703-879-2 (cloth : alk. paper) — ISBN 978-1-61703-880-8 (ebook) — ISBN 978-1-61703-951-5 (pbk.) 1. Trethewey, Natasha D., 1966– —Interviews. 2. Poets, American—21st century—Interviews. I. Hall, Joan Wylie, editor of compilation.
  PS3570.R433Z46 2013
  811'.54—dc23
  [B]   2013008041

British Library Cataloging-in-Publication Data available

Contents

Introduction vii

Chronology xxvi

An Interview with Natasha Trethewey 3
Jill Petty / 1996

A Conversation with Natasha Trethewey 18
David Haney / 2003

Natasha Trethewey—Decatur, Georgia 33
W. T. Pfefferle / 2004

Interview: Natasha Trethewey on Facts, Photographs, and Loss 37
Sara Kaplan / 2006

An Interview with Natasha Trethewey 45
Pearl Amelia McHaney / 2007

Interview with Natasha Trethewey 61
Remica L. Bingham / 2007

Natasha Trethewey Interview 77
Jonathan Fink / 2007

An Interview with Natasha Trethewey 87
Wendy Anderson / 2008

Conversation between Natasha Trethewey and Alan Fox in New York City, January 31st, 2008 92
Alan Fox / 2008

Because of Blood: Natasha Trethewey's Historical Memory 106
    Lisa DeVries / 2008

An Interview with Natasha Trethewey 113
    Christian Teresi / 2009

Interview with Natasha Trethewey 126
    Ana-Maurine Lara / 2009

A Conversation with Natasha Trethewey 136
    Marc McKee / 2010

Outside the Frame: An Interview with Natasha Trethewey 150
    Regina Bennett, Harbour Winn, and Zoe Miles / 2010

Southern Crossings: An Interview with Natasha Trethewey 156
    Daniel Cross Turner / 2010

Jake Adam York Interviews Natasha Trethewey 168
    Jake Adam York / 2010

Report from Part Three: Rita Dove and Natasha Trethewey, Entering the World through Language 174
    Rudolph Byrd, Rita Dove, and Natasha Trethewey / 2011

An Interview with Natasha Trethewey 196
    Jocelyn Heath / 2011

Index 205

Introduction

Poet Laureate Natasha Trethewey and her father, Eric Trethewey, have shared the platform for several poetry readings; and their relationship as biracial child and divorced Caucasian parent is a subject of *Thrall* (2012), her latest book. Shortly after her selection as Consultant in Poetry to the Library of Congress for 2012–2013, both authors were interviewed by Mike Allen of the *Roanoke Times*. Roanoke, Virginia, is home to Hollins University, where Eric Trethewey has taught since 1984, and where his daughter—a Hollins M.A. graduate—served as 2012 Louis D. Rubin writer-in-residence. Citing the active laureateships of Robert Pinsky and Billy Collins, Natasha Trethewey told Allen she hopes to follow their example by finding "something that best suits my abilities to bring poetry to a larger audience."[1] Her father predicts, "We'll hear a lot from her in this position" because she "has a powerful sense of having a responsibility as a poet, a moral and political responsibility to speak out about important things."

Reacting to the selection of a poet in her forties, *New York Times* interviewer Charles McGrath comments that Trethewey "is still in midcareer and not well known outside poetry circles."[2] Although her immediate predecessors, laureates W. S. Merwin and Philip Levine, began publishing before she was born, Trethewey has, in fact, received considerable attention, particularly in the years since *Native Guard* won the 2007 Pulitzer Prize for poetry. Thanks to her heavy schedule of reading tours, her invitations to national and international literary events, and her presence on National Public Radio and the Internet, many academic and general audiences have learned about Trethewey's four poetry volumes and her prose book, *Beyond Katrina: A Meditation on the Mississippi Gulf Coast* (2010), published on the fifth anniversary of Hurricane Katrina. Her long list of honors includes Guggenheim, Rockefeller, Bunting, and National Endowment for the Arts fellowships, as well as an endowed professorship at Emory University in Atlanta, Georgia, where she has taught creative writing since 2001. Many of the awards have brought her into contact with writers and researchers whose work has the same moral and social dimensions noted by Eric Trethewey.

Interviewers frequently ask Natasha Trethewey about the influence of other poets on her work. In the *Times* interview with McGrath, she answers that Seamus Heaney's poems about 1970s violence in Ireland helped her "understand my own relationship to history."[3] Trethewey elaborates in her conversation with Christian Teresi of the *Writer's Chronicle*. She is struck, she says, by the way both Heaney and the poet Eavan Boland "claim Irish history and their places in it—their relationship to homeland and to ideas of exile showed me a way into my own material, not in Northern Ireland, but in Mississippi, in the Deep South. Reading Heaney's *North* helped me to understand my relationship to my South." In Sara Kaplan's *Fugue* interview, Trethewey adds that Emory University houses Seamus Heaney's papers, which shaped the writing of "South," the final poem in Trethewey's *Native Guard*. Reading copies of the *North* drafts, Trethewey says she "could see Heaney's thought process, what he was doing"; his title poem "spoke to me so much that I started writing 'South' after reading it."

Trethewey tells her Emory colleague Bill Chace that she identifies with the African American "family history" in Rita Dove's *Thomas and Beulah* (1987), a volume in which "the individual struggles within a larger historical context."[4] The significance of Dove—a Pulitzer Prize poet and former poet laureate—as a model and mentor is evident throughout their 2011 videotaped discussion with Emory professor Rudolph Byrd, "Report from Part Three: A Creativity Conversation with Rita Dove and Natasha Trethewey." Trethewey observes that, "like Rita, I feel like I began getting interested in history because of what I saw as those glaring absences and omissions. I also wanted to use history as a way to understand my place in the world." This hour-long dialogue is full of insights into the work of both poets.

As the eighteen interviews in *Conversations with Natasha Trethewey* make clear, intersections of the personal and the historic have always been at the heart of her writing. This collection brings together material from an array of sources, including an Internet journal of southern culture, an English department newsletter, university-sponsored literary magazines from different regions of the country, a premiere journal of African American arts and letters, journals for women's writing, poetry journals, a humanities council publication, a book on poets' geographies, the journal of the Association of Writers & Writing programs, and a litblog. Segments of a *Southern Spaces* interview are transcribed for the first time, and the transcript of Trethewey's Creativity Conversation with Rita Dove appears here in print for the first time. At least fifteen additional interviews are cited briefly in this introduction and footnoted for the reader's further reference. Trethewey told Daniel Cross Turner of *Waccamaw: a journal of contemporary lit-*

erature that she will always be "a fan of the book," but she is interested in "poetry as new media" because "these are different ways to bring poetry to audiences." Interviews with Trethewey are available in these newer formats. Perhaps her quickest interview is Erika Thomas's two-minute YouTube clip for Think Talk Networks. Recorded between sessions at the 2010 National Book Festival in Washington, D.C., Trethewey tells Thomas that "Every word is a poem in itself" and laughs about her "love affair with my *OED*," the indispensable dictionary she mentions to many interviewers.[5]

Because the Literary Conversations series reprints interviews in full, certain questions resound like a refrain or leitmotif, but Trethewey often responds with variations on persistent themes. Thus, in Teresi's interview, she suggests that personal understanding is not her only goal in reading and writing poetry. Her memories of growing up in the South, with its many Confederate monuments, remind her that Civil War history books have typically excluded the African American presence in battle. In her *Native Guard* poems about black soldiers, Trethewey not only reclaims a missing part of her history, but she gives a fuller picture of every American's history. She tells Teresi: "If I can remind people that what I'm writing about is a shared history, not merely a personal history, that my personal stake in it can resonate and connect across time and space to other people and their personal stakes in history, then I think I'm able to avoid the trap of my own personal ideology."

In her first major interview, with *Callaloo*'s Jill Petty in 1996, Trethewey says she felt "compelled and responsible to speak about the connection" she had with early twentieth-century workers whose pictures she saw in an exhibition gallery. She included her poems about these African American laundrywomen and other laborers in her first book, *Domestic Work* (2000), to commemorate forgotten lives, just as she has more recently featured black Civil War soldiers in *Native Guard*. The domestic workers in the gallery photos, says Trethewey, are reminiscent of generations of black women, including her seamstress grandmother.

A showcase for young authors, *Callaloo*'s "Emerging Women Writers" number printed several of Trethewey's poems along with Petty's interview. Although she had previously published in *Callaloo* and other journals, the *Callaloo* special issue placed her in the company of rising stars in various genres, including Suzan-Lori Parks, Edwidge Danticat, and Elizabeth Alexander. *Callaloo* identified Trethewey as a member of the Dark Room Collective, an African American writers' group based in Boston. In her dialogue with Petty, Trethewey praises the Dark Room as "one of the greatest things that happened to me coming north and being at UMass for my MFA.... As a collective, we are always influencing each other. There isn't a member that I can't learn something from." She recalls an exchange of poems with Sharan Strange, whose "Still Life" reminds Trethewey of her own "Hot Comb," an earlier version of *Domestic Work*'s "Hot Combs." Both poets wrote about their mothers and "beauty and suffering"; but the differences in their work remind Trethewey that "there is room in the collective for different experiences, different voices, different styles."

Trethewey's appreciation for the diversity of her colleagues' work is mirrored in the variety of authors she mentions to interviewers, a range that has already been suggested by her allusions to Seamus Heaney and Rita Dove. Among her many other references are Toni Morrison, Yeats, James Baldwin, Ellen Bryant Voigt, Robert Frost, Camille Dungy, Anne Frank, W. H. Auden, Shelley, Richard Hugo, Langston Hughes, Yusef Komunyakaa, Mark Doty, Elizabeth Alexander, Shahid Ali, Sharon Olds, James Tate, Terrance Hayes, Robert Hass, Kevin Young, Agi Mishol, Robert Hayden, Gwendolyn Brooks, and Theodore Roethke. Most of these are poets, and Trethewey tells *Atlanta Journal-Constitution* journalist Teresa K. Weaver that "poems captivate me in a way that nothing else does. It's so much more than just pleasure reading."[6] Bill Chace wonders if "the writers evoked in *Native Guard*—Charles Wright, Walt Whitman, Allen Tate, Robert Herrick (and perhaps Nina Simone)—form a constellation of muses, provocations, or allies, in your poetic mind?"[7] Trethewey emphasizes that her choices were "careful," and she cautions Chace not to overlook Robert Penn Warren because "he's there, too. I wanted to situate myself as a poet, a Southern poet, within a larger tradition. I wanted to connect to a place that I both love and hate." She tells Ana-Maurine Lara, "Growing up in the Deep South, I was confronted constantly with the absence of narratives about who I was and the people that I felt closest to." In the *Native Guard* poem "Pastoral," Trethewey pictures herself "in blackface" in a crowd of Southern Agrarian poets headed by Warren; yet she boldly asserts her right to stand among these white male forebears (*Native Guard* 35).

Trethewey's allusion to Warren is much different in a *Smartish Pace* interview with Jocelyn Heath, where she regards his book *Segregation: The Inner Conflict in the South* (1956) as a model for her *Beyond Katrina*. Like the Katrina volume, Trethewey explains, its predecessor is a "literary hybrid" that blends different forms to produce "not a memoir, but somehow clearly an investigation of the self" as well as a type of "investigative reporting." Both authors interviewed a spectrum of southerners in response to events that brought drastic change to the Deep South: for Warren, the Supreme Court's 1954 *Brown v. Board of Education* ruling; for Trethewey, the devastation of Hurricane Katrina in 2005. Even more than the *Segregation* volume, Warren's 1965 book, *Who Speaks for the Negro?*, separated him from his more conservative poet colleagues in the alliance of Vanderbilt Fugitives. In 1986–1987, a few years before his death, he served as the first Poet Laureate Consultant in Poetry, the only southern writer in the position before Natasha Trethewey.

Daniel Cross Turner studies Trethewey and fourteen other contemporary poets in his *Southern Crossings: Poetry, Memory, and the Transcultural South* (2012); and, in his interview for *Waccamaw*, he asks her about the "nature of 'Southernness'" in her work. Pointing to her *Native Guard* references to Tate's "Ode to the Confederate Dead" and Faulkner's *Light in August*, Turner is curious about her sense of her place among such stereotypically regional authors. Trethewey laughs, "I am the quintessential Southern writer! Quintessentially American too!" For her, "The story of America has always been a story of miscegenation, of border crossings, of integration of cultures, and again, I embody this in my person." Her *Native Guard* allusion to the orator and author Frederick Douglass underscores this statement.

Son of an unknown white father and a slave mother, fugitive from South to North, colleague of white abolitionists, Douglass is a nineteenth-century embodiment of the "story of America." He provides the epigraph to *Native Guard*'s sonnet sequence, narrated by a black federal soldier who guards Confederate war prisoners in the Union Army's Ship Island fortress, off the Mississippi Gulf Coast. "Ms. Trethewey's great theme is memory," interviewer Charles McGrath concludes; and Douglass urges his audience to remember the Civil War in the right way.[8] Trethewey quotes from his 1871 Decoration Day speech near the monument to the "Unknown Loyal Dead" in Arlington National Cemetery. Rejoicing in the end of slavery, Douglass praises the triumph of the republic over the forces of rebellion: "If this war is to be forgotten, I ask in the name of all things sacred what shall men remember?" (*Native Guard* 25).

Trethewey tells Sara Kaplan that the "elegiac quality" of *Native Guard* is often overlooked: "everything" in the book, she says, is "a way of making sense of what's buried. And what has no marker. No inscription on the landscape to remember. My mother doesn't have a tombstone. She is like those Native Guards." In several interviews that followed the publication of *Native Guard*, Trethewey draws similar parallels between her mother's unmarked grave and the absence of any physical evidence of the black guardsmen's presence on Ship Island; but the scope of the book was not apparent to her from the start. "For a long time I thought the main thing was the Native Guard," she told *Bookslut*'s Wendy Anderson. She discovered their story by chance. "When I took my grandmother to a restaurant on the beach on Ship Island, someone heard our conversation and told me this history that I hadn't learned my whole life"—even though she had spent much of her childhood in Gulfport, Mississippi, a ferry-ride away from Fort Massachusetts.

Trethewey uses the term "historical erasure" twice in the Anderson interview, emphasizing her determination to recover forgotten histories. Native Americans are among those whose "narratives" are "covered over" in the South, although their names remain in the names of states and rivers, she tells W. T. Pfefferle in his *Poets on Place: Interviews and Tales from the Road*. As Trethewey stresses in conversation with Maria Browning of *Chapter 16*, Tennessee's Internet writing community: "Historical erasure and amnesia is an ongoing problem that society faces. This is always a danger. We have to recover, inscribe, and guard the memory of events as much as we can."[9] In *Native Guard*, the guardsman's sonnet sequence and several other elements of prosody constitute "an important technique for addressing historical erasure," Trethewey tells Christian Teresi. "The use of repetition was a formal decision I made early on in the writing because what I was trying to do was to reinscribe what had been erased, what was lost or forgotten—it was not necessary just to say a thing, but also to say it again," she elaborates. In her *Five Points* interview with Pearl McHaney, Trethewey shows just how crucial the pantoum verse form is to her poem "Incident": "What is exciting about the pantoum or the villanelle, some of those forms, is the kind of mathematical way that they work. They allow you to see other possibilities."

As several interviews report, the poet gradually saw that her mother's history demanded a place in the *Native Guard* collection. Trethewey was at the end of her freshman year at the University of Georgia when Gwendolyn Ann Turnbough was murdered outside her Atlanta apartment by her estranged second husband; their son, waiting for his school bus, was a witness. Trethewey's brother went to Mississippi to live with their maternal grandmother. Their mother was buried in Gulfport without a headstone because her name at death was that of the man who shot her; Trethewey refused to allow this name on the grave. On the other hand, "I didn't want my father's name because of my brother," Trethewey explained to Wendy Anderson. Years later, she realized that the inscription could record their mother's name at birth instead of a surname from marriage.

When she joined the Emory faculty and returned to Atlanta from teaching in Alabama, Trethewey lived near the courthouse where her stepfather had been sentenced. "I think it was impossible for me not to return," she told Anderson. "I not only was approaching the anniversary of her death, but also my own fortieth birthday. She died just short of her forty-first birthday. And I reached the midpoint where I'd crossed over, where I had lived more of my years without her than with her. All of that converged, and I started writing." Interviewed by Jake Adam York for the Internet journal *Southern Spaces*, Trethewey says that her return to Atlanta "became something I had to do in order to reclaim so much of myself and her that I had lost."

After *Native Guard* won the 2007 Pulitzer Prize for poetry, commentator Terry Gross conducted an emotional interview with Trethewey for the National Public Radio program *Fresh Air*. The forty-minute radio dialogue was the first interview that detailed at length the facts of her mother's abusive second marriage and death, as well as her own tense relationship with her stepfather, who taunted her for years. In the essay "Southern Erasures: Natasha Trethewey's *Native Guard*," scholar Pearl McHaney states that "Gross's interview followed a lengthy discussion with the program's producer to review Trethewey's willingness and preparation to respond to direct questions about the murder of her mother, the subject with which Gross opens. The first half of the interview concerns this aspect of *Native Guard* with Trethewey answering brutal questions with direct honesty and obvious sorrow."[10] Toward the end of the interview, Trethewey's sorrow encompasses the guardsmen as well as her mother. She tells Gross: "It wasn't until I was, I think, far along into writing the book, the book that's the part about the Civil War and that history, that I realized that these other poems that I was writing, the poems that are elegies for my mother, were also connected." Neither her mother nor the black soldiers "had a monument—not on my mother's grave, not on Ship Island—that would tell us they've been there."[11]

Speaking with Savannah journalist Robin Wright Gunn about the name of her book, Trethewey describes herself as both a native guard and monument-builder: "The title comes quite literally from the name of the regiment, but figuratively it's about being a native guardian to these historical memories, a native guardian of Mississippi that will tell a fuller version of this story, tell the parts left out and create a living monument to the lesser known parts."[12] As Trethewey told Lisa DeVries after a reading and book signing at East Carolina University, her research on the military men "led me back inward to the thing that was really driving me—a desire to create a monument to my mother." Her mother's death, she says, "has shaped everything I've done. If I think about the things that have defined who I am as a poet, and what I feel it is my duty to write, such as being born of mixed race in 1960s Mississippi, it was losing my mother." Trethewey explains to Remica Bingham that *Native Guard* is such an "emotionally raw" book that "in order to write it, I had to really restrain myself. I think if I didn't—if I didn't use formal constraints, if I didn't allow for silences around certain things in the book—the pages would be dripping wet, soaked with my tears when a reader picked them up."

Trethewey's poetry addresses the loss of her mother most directly in *Native Guard*, but her interview with DeVries indicates that her sense of loss has informed her writing from the start. Her first book, *Domestic Work*, is divided into four sections. The first two sections are primarily about the labors of African Americans—strangers in photographs and family members—from the start of the twentieth century through mid-century, when her maternal grandmother's generation was working and raising children. Poems like "Speculation, 1939" and "Signs, Oakvale, Mississippi, 1941" recall lost possibilities for employment and romance. Trethewey told National Public Radio's Angela Elam, of *New Letters on the Air*, that the book makes a statement on the limited opportunities for both black and white poor southern women; she includes specific dates, she says, to identify her grandmother's work through the decades.[13]

Leretta Dixon Turnbough reappears later in the book, as do Trethewey's great-uncle Son Dixon and her great-aunt Sugar (her "muse," Trethewey told Jill Petty); but the last two divisions of *Domestic Work* mainly concern the speaker (born in 1966), her mother, and—to a lesser extent—her father and stepfather. This poetry outlines the growth and loss of love and the end of childhood innocence. Several titles in the final section reinforce themes of loss, especially the poems "Accounting," "Gathering," "Give and Take," and "Collection Day." In the closing poem, "Limen," the first-person speaker identifies with a woodpecker whose persistent tapping at a catalpa tree is "a hinge, a door knocker" to thoughts of her dead mother, "the cluttered house of memory" (*Domestic Work* 58). Trethewey tells *Callaloo* editor Charles Henry Rowell that she regards "Limen" as "a way of not simply shutting down the collection, but also as a way of circling back to the opening and commenting on the poet's work as well—that work of memory and inscription."[14]

In the same conversation with Rowell, Trethewey clarifies that the title of *Domestic Work* applies not only to sewing, laundering, and sweeping but also to "the everyday work that we do as human beings to live with or without people that we've lost, the work of memory and forgetting, and of self-discovery—not simply the work of earning a living and managing our households, but that larger, daily, domestic work that all of us do."[15] In residence at Yale University as the James Weldon Johnson fellow in African American Studies, Trethewey spoke to Ana-Maurine Lara on the relevance of photography to her poetry of loss: "For me, something is always gone. I started writing about photographs because it was the way that I could locate that feeling I had of constant loss: the loss of a moment that is gone from us." When Jonathan Fink asks her about discovering the subject matter for *Domestic Work*, Trethewey recalls the UMass gallery she visited with Margaret Gibson, one of her MFA professors. The exhibit featured images of black southerners who came north during the Great Migration, as well as Clifton Johnson's photographs of African Americans from his travel narratives of the South. Gibson urged Trethewey to examine the pictures carefully. "Until that moment," says Trethewey, "I hadn't thought that, as I was writing my grandmother's story, that I was writing a larger narrative of a people, that her story (that seemed so personal and so family) was also a story that spoke to the larger condition of people in the Jim Crow South."

Trethewey tells Marc McKee of the *Missouri Review* that visual art played an even larger part in the books that followed *Domestic Work*: "The more I've gotten interested in writing about history and making sense of myself within the continuum of history, the more I've turned to paintings, to art. I look to the imagery of art to help me understand something about my own place in the world. By just beginning to contemplate a work of art, I find myself led toward some other understanding." The cover of Trethewey's second poetry volume, *Bellocq's Ophelia* (2002) reproduces one of E. J. Bellocq's most elegant photographs of a prostitute from Storyville, the red-light district of New Orleans at the start of the twentieth century. In her title poem, Trethewey compares a different Bellocq photo to Millais's pre-Raphaelite painting of Shakespeare's Ophelia, drowning herself in a lush landscape. Trethewey gives Ophelia's name to this "nameless inmate in Storyville"; the prostitute's naked body is "limp as dead Ophelia," but there is "a dare" in her expression, and her lips are "poised to open, to speak" (*Bellocq's Ophelia* 3).

Although *Bellocq's Ophelia* is Trethewey's least autobiographical book, she tells David Haney of *Cold Mountain Review* that the "idea of observation" is "really personal" to her because she—like her biracial protagonist—is "constantly 'passing,'" either deliberately or unintentionally.[16] The fictitious Ophelia "tries to pass for white, because she thinks, well, that's what I look like, but she's constantly talking about how that's different than what's on the inside, and how those two finally come together." Trethewey adds, "I think that I'm drawn to thinking about seeing in that way because it's been in my life." Similarly, she suggests to Charles Rowell that, with Ophelia, "I was searching for a persona through whom I might investigate aspects of my own mixed-race experience growing up in the Deep South."[17]

Bellocq's pictures provided copious details for the poems of *Bellocq's Ophelia*, and interviews indicate that Trethewey conducted extensive research on New Orleans, photography, prostitution, and art. But she tells Ana-Maurine Lara that she "knew I had to create Ophelia as if I was remembering. As much as I used photographs in that project to bring what I was seeing to life, I spent a lot of time in New Orleans. I had spent a lot of time there growing up, so it felt like a landscape that was part of my development." Returning to the city, Trethewey walked again on Dumaine Street, "trying to imagine what my grandmother saw or heard or felt walking through that place" when she lived in the French Quarter, where Trethewey's mother was born. "Knowledge of the lives of other people" is what Trethewey gained from her poetry about Ophelia and the photographed laborers in *Domestic Work*. "I think that I write for that reason," she says in Lara's *Torch* interview: "in order to know something about the lives of other human beings across time and space. And that's why I think of poetry as a social practice, not just an aesthetic one."

Trethewey was introduced to Bellocq's Storyville portraits in a UMass graduate course, Materials for the Study of American Culture. Citing culture critics Roland Barthes and Janet Malcolm, her conversation with Rowell reflects her familiarity with such terms as "punctums," "framing," and "the gaze." At the end of the book, however, Ophelia is no longer subjected to the staring eyes of Storyville patrons or even the sympathetic lens of Bellocq's camera. "In the final poem," Trethewey tells Rowell, "I wanted to find a way for her to exit all of the frameworks that I had created for her, so I have her stepping out of the frame of the photograph, and she steps out of the frame of the book itself and goes out into her own life, no longer shaped by someone else's gaze."[18] Trethewey's Ophelia also found new life in another artistic setting. An Emory Creativity Conversation between Trethewey and composer Steve Everett, moderated by Emory vice president and secretary Rosemary Magee, describes the collaboration between poet and musician for Everett's 2008 chamber opera, *Ophelia's Gaze*.[19]

Even though *Bellocq's Ophelia* traces the fairly cohesive narrative of a young woman's life in New Orleans between the fall of 1910 and the spring of 1912, Trethewey complicates the story by dividing most of the poems into fourteen of Ophelia's "Letters from Storyville" and ten sonnet entries in her "Storyville Diary." These parallel accounts reveal "contradictions between the two stories," Trethewey tells Marc McKee. The poet deliberately aims to "subvert" her "tendency to be linear." In *Bellocq's Ophelia*, her subversive strategy is "to tell the story and then to tell it again." In both *Bellocq's Ophelia* and her next poetry volume, *Native Guard*, says Trethewey, "So many of the formal decisions I made are about circling back, so the narrative circles back in on itself and simply can't proceed in a linear fashion."

Beyond Katrina, the mixed-genre book that followed *Native Guard*, is also circular in many ways, as the section headings "Cycle" and "Redux" announce. Terry Gross, who interviewed Trethewey after *Native Guard* won the Pulitzer Prize, spoke with her again on NPR's *Fresh Air* when *Beyond Katrina* was published. Like the earlier radio program, the 2010 interview places more emphasis on family crisis than historic context. As the fifth anniversary of Hurricane Katrina approached, Gross asked Trethewey about her brother's imprisonment for transporting cocaine when employment opportunities almost disappeared on the Mississippi Gulf Coast. The rental properties he had repaired and supervised for the family were severely damaged by the storm, and he was not eligible for loans to rebuild. Trethewey tells Gross that she feels she has failed as a surrogate-mother, and her grandmother's death three years after the hurricane further intensifies her sense of loss. She says she chose to include the family's post-Katrina struggles in her book because she hoped that her brother's story "would be useful, not only to give voice to his own experience, but actually as a way of allowing his story to speak for the countless people whose stories aren't being told."[20]

Before she wrote *Beyond Katrina*, Trethewey told Frank Stasio of WUNC's *The State of Things* that the hurricane made her reflect on her *Domestic Work* poetry. Stressing the urgency to "inscribe and reinscribe" what is lost, she hopes that her approaching trip to the Mississippi Gulf Coast in spring 2006 will produce "at least one poem" as she re-sees her old home through her grandmother's eyes.[21] The following year, Remica Bingham asked if Trethewey would "breach any of the political/ social significance of the storm and the events surrounding it in your work." Trethewey's reply was, "Well, not in the poems"; but the early twentieth-century bulldozing of "all the natural landscape" to make a twenty-six-mile beach stands as "a sort of metaphor for these ideas about historical erasure and remembrance." With the landscape "erased yet again" by the hurricane, Trethewey speculates whether the coast's new "narrative" should be "the narrative of the Redneck Riviera or the high-rise condos that the people who are from there can't necessarily afford? How will we memorialize not only what happened, but also what was there before that and what was there before that?" *Beyond Katrina*, based on Trethewey's Page-Barbour Lectures at the University of Virginia in November 2007, develops the environmental and social concerns raised in Bingham's interview, including the impact of tourism and the gaming industry. In Lindsey Alexander's *Sycamore Review* conversation, Trethewey says her book manuscript once contained "all the kind of scholarly footnotes you would expect a historian to include in a book"; but adds, "Publishers who do creative nonfiction don't want that sort of thing and you get rid of them." [22]

Although Trethewey includes many family photographs and much of her maternal family's Gulf Coast heritage in the book, she describes *Beyond Katrina* not as a memoir but as "lyrical meditation" in an interview with Billy Watkins of the Jackson, Mississippi, *Clarion-Ledger*. She adds that writing the Katrina "essays" was "a lot harder" for her than writing poetry.[23] Because *Beyond Katrina* called such attention to the suffering of Mississippians after the storm, the state's media were eager to speak with Trethewey. She told Ezra Wall, of Mississippi Public Broadcasting's *Mississippi Edition*, that she originally thought she would never write another prose book after *Beyond Katrina*; but she soon realized some things can be said better in prose. She compares the book to her poetry volumes, however, in the way that they all "circle around and come at the subject from a different angle," instead of proceeding chronologically.[24]

A 2008 interview with Alan Fox is one of several occasions on which Trethewey cites Philip Levine's "I write what is given me to write." In the conversation for *Rattle: Poetry for the 21st Century*, the reference is prelude to Trethewey's closing comment: "I was born 100 years to the day that Mississippi first celebrated Confederate Memorial Day—the daughter of miscegenation. I know I was given that to write." In *Thrall*, her fourth poetry volume, Trethewey gives fullest expression to her destined theme. She tells Christian Teresi that the book began with her "historical investigation of the language and iconography of eighteenth-century casta paintings in colonial Mexico that showed the mixed blood unions and the offspring of those unions in the colonies." Many of the groupings portray a white father, mother of color, and mixed-race child. Trethewey found that "the difficult thing I've learned is that these poems are about my father, and the history of colonization, and who the colonialist is, and who the colonial bodies are."

Trethewey tells Jake Adam York that her father figures "more prominently" in *Thrall* than in her earlier books "because now is the time to turn my attention there." When she wrote the first of her casta poems, however, "I didn't know where they were leading me." Yet she discovered that "ideas of knowledge and dominion and colony and empire" are "not so far from me thinking about my relationship to Mississippi and its history." Trethewey describes a lifelong "sense of exile" to Ana-Maurine Lara, acknowledging that "a great number of people" might share the condition; but her own "feelings of exile are rooted in the duality of the mixed-race body and are rooted in the laws of the state of Mississippi, in the laws of the U.S. that rendered a person like me illegitimate and rendered my parents as law breakers." The dominance of the white father in *Thrall* complicates these issues of race and oppression.

Trethewey tells Daniel Cross Turner that, "in many ways," *Thrall* is "the book that is actually most about race that I've ever written. Race always appears in my work because I have a racialized experience of America. But in this new book I'm fully examining race as such, as a category itself, and its relation to that vexed issue of blood." In a similar discussion with Lindsey Alexander, Trethewey qualifies: "Even when I say that it's me taking on race in a more direct way, I realize what I'm still taking on is not even exactly that. It's more about knowledge."[25] Philosophers of the English Enlightenment, for instance, developed a "codification of racial difference" that has been "made natural" over the generations. In a conversation for *Oklahoma HUMANITIES Magazine*, Trethewey illustrates by reading her *Thrall* poem "Knowledge." Her father used "the language of zoology, natural philosophy" in calling her his "crossbreed child" in one of his early poems, she tells interviewers Regina Bennett, Harbour Winn, and Zoe Miles. Eric Trethewey's poem is "really loving, it's sweet," she says; even so, "There's still an edge and a blindness." Trethewey worked on *Thrall* for six years, she tells Lindsey Alexander, "revising it all along and changing the order, and deciding to take things out, and writing new things that got put in it."[26] But six years "almost didn't feel like enough time to me," possibly because the book feels "so different than what I've done before." While the *Native Guard* elegies arose from "very old grief," a grief that was "twenty years old by the time I wrote those poems. This was not; this is very new."

When Remica Bingham asks Trethewey about the role of women writers, "especially writers of color, as artists in this millennium," the poet proposes: "I think our duty is to learn to reckon with the human experience across time and space. We should create language that churns up that connection, language that looks at our relationship to other human beings within the web of history." She tells Penne Laubenthal that she has always loved words and that her father "used to encourage me on long car trips, if I got bored, to write a poem. He used to say that it is a problem if you don't have inner resources."[27] In *Oklahoma HUMANITIES Magazine*, Zoe Miles wonders if Trethewey sees her "wordsmith abilities as innate or as something that you caught on to as you grew up," and Trethewey suspects her father "would probably want to claim responsibility for my wordsmithing abilities." Eric Trethewey was "one of my earliest teachers"; yet, "the other people that I spent a good deal of my life with were amazing at idiom and metaphor and the cadences of language and the richness of sound and figurative language." At her grandmother's house, she recalls, she listened to churchwomen "talking about the Bible, chanting hymns and psalms. I was surrounded by the lovely cadences of different human voices. So, while much might come from a natural talent that passed to me from my father, a great deal passed to me from my mother as well."

Trethewey tells Sara Kaplan that she thinks of herself "as a poet who writes not collections of poems, but books of poems." As early as graduate school, Trethewey was driven by her "obsessions" and "wanted to envision a work as an integral whole." She compares each book to a plexiglass picture cube (a familiar image from her childhood), with every poem "trying to connect to the others to create a whole." Yet, poetry's appeal is not limited to its artistry and craftsmanship. Engaged in a lively "Q & A with Natasha Trethewey" at Eastern Connecticut State University, she told her student-audience that she loves "the elegant envelope of form," the "lyricism and musicality" of poetry; but poetry, more than short stories or novels, is "perhaps the most powerful way to reach both the intellect and the heart."[28] At an interdisciplinary forum sponsored by the *Journal of American History*, Trethewey describes her efforts to reach her readers: "I try to make the poems engaging aesthetically, and I want imagery vivid enough to invite them into the world of the poem as participants who experience the emotional context of it rather than as distant observers who are told what to think or feel about the historical material I am presenting. This is, of course, all about empathy."[29] Summing up her *Five Points* conversation with Pearl McHaney, Trethewey could be charting a course for her poet laureateship: "History belongs to all of us and our one charge is to present it well with all the complexity and humanity that peoples' lives deserve and that art requires."

My thanks to my students at the University of Mississippi, who have been reading and admiring Natasha Trethewey's poetry since the publication of *Domestic Work* in 2000. Several years ago, the Center for the Study of

Southern Culture invited me to present a lecture on Trethewey; former associate director Ann Abadie and the late Sue Hart gave major encouragement for my work on this volume. Thanks to the CSSC's Kathryn McKee, Charles Reagan Wilson, Ted Ownby, Jimmy Thomas, and Mary Hartwell Howorth for all they do to promote southern studies on our campus and beyond. At the Sarah Isom Center for Women and Gender Studies, former director Mary C. Carruth was especially supportive of *Conversations with Natasha Trethewey*. Ivo Kamps, English Department chair, provided travel funds for presentations at the Society for the Study of Southern Literature Conference and the Southern Women Writers' Conference. Meeting Natasha Trethewey and her brother Joe at Berry College's SWWC was a highlight of that outstanding weekend.

MFA program director Beth Ann Fennelly and poet Ann W. Fisher-Wirth invited Trethewey to the University of Mississippi for a memorable reading in the Grisham Visiting Writers series. The most essential help on this campus came from the J. D. Williams Library. *Conversations with Natasha Trethewey* benefited tremendously from the labors of Julia Rholes, Dean of Libraries; Jennifer Ford, head of Archives and Special Collections; Alex Watson, reference librarian; and—above all—interlibrary loan librarian Judy Greenwood and senior assistants Lisa Harrison and Anne Johnson.

Shirley A. James Hanshaw, editor of *Conversations with Yusef Komunyakaa*, gave good advice and was warmly supportive of adding a Trethewey volume to the Literary Conversations series. Rosemary Magee, vice president and secretary of Emory, helped secure this book's most unusual interview: a Creativity Conversation between Natasha Trethewey and Rita Dove. The late Noel Polk, editor of *Mississippi Quarterly*, and Jay Parini, editor of *American Writers Supplements*, showed early interest in my research on Trethewey and published my essays. I greatly appreciate the support of *Southern Quarterly* editor Philip C. Kolin, who has published Nastasha Trethewey's work in the journal and who invited me to serve as guest editor of a special issue on the poet laureate.

Natasha Trethewey's interviewers, along with their editors and publishers, made the timely publication of this volume possible with their prompt communications and their strong support for the Literary Conversations series. I am especially pleased to include thoughtful selections by scholars and creative writers who are friends, colleagues, and former students of Natasha Trethewey, including Remica Bingham, Rita Dove, Jonathan Fink, David Haney, Pearl Amelia McHaney, Daniel Cross Turner, and the late Jake Adam York. Dan Turner, Jake Adam York, and especially Pearl McHaney gave repeated assistance. Most interviewers generously waived permissions fees in allowing University Press of Mississippi to reprint their work in *Conversations with Natasha Trethewey*. Correspondence with the contributors was a special pleasure. I am also grateful to those interviewers whose work is represented very briefly in this collection; because of space constraints and budget restrictions, some valuable material is cited in the introduction and listed in the Notes for further reading. Nancy Crampton's photographic portrait of Natasha Trethewey beautifully enhances the volume. At University Press of Mississippi, the advice of acquiring editor Walter Biggins was crucial. I am also grateful to director Leila W. Salisbury, assistant director Craig Gill, director emeritus Seetha Srinivasan, and Literary Conversations editor Peggy Prenshaw for promoting the Literary Conversations series. Managing editor Anne Stascavage provided generous support in preparing the manuscript for publication. Without the design and production, marketing, and business staff at UPM, these interviews would not have become a book.

All of the following deserve more than short mention for their scholarship, correspondence, friendship, and other contributions: Colby Kullman, Jack Barbera, Barbara J. Butler, William R. Ferris, Barbara C. Ewell, Christina Bucher, James Watkins, E. Ethelbert Miller, Robert West, Laura West, Bill Chace, J. Janice Coleman, Justin Hall, Christine Dyott Hall, Ralph Eubanks, Allen Tullos, James Everett, Anne R. Gowdy, Thadious Davis, H. C. Porter, Lauchlin Fields, Betty Conway, Penne Laubenthal, Timothy Green, Shannon Jackson, Michael Spooner, Lindsey Alexander, Susanne Balke, Timothy Green, Michael Nye, Anne Gilliam, Sarah Vitorino, and Carla Walker.

My husband, J. R. Hall, and my daughter, Jennifer Hall, have helped in countless ways. Jennifer's skills as transcriber and proofreader were particularly important in preparing the manuscript. My greatest thanks go to Natasha Trethewey, whose support of this collection has been as constant (from Latin: standing firm) as her poetry—and the North Star.

JWH

Notes

1. Mike Allen, "New U.S. Poet Laureate Is Hollins University Alumna," *Roanoke.com*, 8 June 2012, http://www.roanoke.com/news/roanoke/wb/309927. Web. 24 July 2012. Poet Kyle

Dargan's forthcoming article for *Shenandoah: The Washington and Lee University Review* 61.2 (2013) will be one of the first major interviews conducted after Trethewey's appointment as poet laureate.

2. Charles McGrath, "New Laureate Looks Deep into Memory," *New York Times*, 7 June 2012, C1. After *Native Guard* won the Pulitzer Prize in 2007, Deborah Solomon conducted a brief interview for the Mother's Day issue, "Questions for Natasha Trethewey, Native Daughter," *New York Times*, 13 May 2007, http://www.nytimes.com/2007/05/13/magazine/13wwln-Q4-t.html. Web. 3 August 2012.

3. McGrath, C1.

4. Bill Chace, "Considering *Native Guard*: Bill Chace Interviews Natasha Trethewey," *Loose Canons* (Emory University English Department) 10.3 (Summer 2007), 3.

5. Erika Thomas, "The Blank Page: Natasha Trethewey," Think Talk Networks, Career TV for College, 2010 National Book Festival, Washington, D.C. 2 minutes, uploaded 8 February 2011, YouTube, http://www.youtube.com/watch?v=nAdmmItLou8. Web. 1 August 2012. One of Trethewey's best taped conversations is a fifty-minute discussion with students for Eastern Connecticut State University's Visiting Writers Series, "Q & A Session: Natasha Trethewey, April 15, 2010," moderated by Daniel Donaghy, broadcast by Eastern Television, http://infxapps.influxis.com/apps/xhnphplay7hd7cpijtlm/InfluxisPlayer_20101013083252/InfluxisPlay. Web. 1 August 2012. See also n. 28 below.

6. Teresa K. Weaver, "Q&A / Natasha Trethewey, Pulitzer Prize–winning Poet and Emory Professor," *Atlanta Journal-Constitution*, 29 April 2007, 1B.

7. Chace, 3.

8. McGrath, C1.

9. Maria Browning, "Making a Necessity of Memory," *Chapter 16: A Community of Tennessee Writers, Readers & Passersby*, 28 October 2009, http://www.chapter16.org/content/making-necessity-memory. Web. 3 August 2012.

10. Pearl A. McHaney, "Southern Erasures: Natasha Trethewey's *Native Guard*," *The (Un)Popular South*, ed. Marcel Arbeit and M. Thomas Inge, Proceedings of the Southern Studies Forum Biennial Conference, 6–9 September 2007 (Olomouc, Czech Republic: Palacky University, 2011), 93. See also, on the Pulitzer Prize–winning book: Giorgia De Cenzo, "Natasha Trethewey: The Native Guard of Southern History," *Annali di Ca' Foscari* 46.1 (2007), 101–26.

11. Terry Gross, "Poet Natasha Trethewey, Hymning the Native Guard," *Fresh Air*, WHYY, National Public Radio, 16 July 2007, http://www.npr.org/2007/07/16/12003278/poet-natasha-trethewey-hymning-the-native-guard. Web. 3 August 2012.

12. Robin Wright Gunn, "Books: When the Historical Is Personal," *Connect Savannah*, 18 March 2008, http://www.connectsavannah.com/news/archive/6976/. Web. 3 August 2012.

13. Angela Elam, "U.S. Poet Laureate, 2012–2013, Natasha Trethewey," *New Letters on the Air*, KCUR-FM, National Public Radio, encore interview July 2012, originally broadcast April

2008, http://www.prx.org/pieces/43611-u-s-poet-laureate-2012-2013-natasha-trethewey. Web. 3 August 2012.

14. Charles Henry Rowell, "Inscriptive Restorations: An Interview with Natasha Trethewey," *Callaloo* 27.4 (Fall 2004), 1027.

15. Rowell, 1026–27. On the theme of work in Trethewey's first three volumes, see Joan Wylie Hall, "'I shirk not': Domestic Labor, Sex Work, and Warfare in the Poetry of Natasha Trethewey," *Mississippi Quarterly* 62.2 (Spring 2009), 265–80.

16. The *Domestic Work* poem "White Lies" shows how the poet in childhood presented herself as white in certain situations to avoid embarrassment: "But I paid for it every time" (*Domestic Work*, 37).

17. Rowell, 1027. On Trethewey's second book, see Annette Debo, "Ophelia Speaks: Resurrecting Still Lives in Natasha Trethewey's *Bellocq's Ophelia*," *African American Review* 42.2 (Summer 2008), 201–14; and Debora Rindge and Anna Leahy, "'Become What You Must': Trethewey's Poems and Bellocq's Photographs," *English Language Notes* 44.2 (Fall–Winter 2006), 291–305.

18. Rowell, 1030. Although prose works are her focus, Katherine Henninger is among the first scholars to discuss *Bellocq's Ophelia* in the context of other literature by southern women; see *Ordering the Façade: Photography and Contemporary Southern Women's Writing* (Chapel Hill: University of North Carolina Press, 2007). Henninger says that Trethewey's Ophelia "takes up a camera to represent what's missing from the southern picture" (158).

19. "Steve Everett, Natasha Trethewey, and Rosemary Magee: Emory Professors Everett and Trethewey Talk about Artistic Collaboration," *Creativity Conversations*, Creativity & Arts Initiative, 5 November 2008. Audio, http://itunes.apple.com/us/itunes-u/creativity-conversations-audio/id422850039. Web. 4 August 2012. See also "Dorothy Allison, Natasha Trethewey, and Michael Elliott: Visiting Professor Dorothy Allison Talks about Writing with Faculty Trethewey and Elliot," *Creativity Conversations*, Creativity & Arts Initiative, 15 April 2008. Audio, http://itunes.apple.com/itunes-u/creativity-conversations-audio/id422850039#ls=1. Web. 4 August 2012. Trethewey and Allison, author of *Bastard Out of Carolina*, discuss tragic family narratives and both writers' interest in the domestic, extending to the intrusion of violence.

20. Terry Gross, "Mississippi Meditation: A Poet Looks 'Beyond Katrina,'" *Fresh Air*, WHYY, National Public Radio, 18 August 2010. Audio, http://www.npr.org/2010/08/18/129252666/mississippi-meditation-a-poet-looks-beyond-katrina. Web. 4 August 2012. Terry Gross also spoke with Trethewey on the inauguration of President Barack Obama: "Natasha Trethewey: If My Mom Could See Us Now," *Fresh Air*, WHYY, National Public Radio, 20 January 2009. Audio, http://www.npr.org/templates/story/story.php?storyId=99474984. Web. 4 August 2012. On the radio program, Trethewey read and commented on her *Native Guard* poem "My Mother Dreams Another Country," as well as Langston Hughes's short poem "I, Too, Sing America." She regrets that her mother and her grandmother did not live to see America's first biracial president.

21. Frank Stasio, "Author Interview, Natasha Trethewey," *The State of Things*, WUNC, National Public Radio, 1 May 2006. Audio, http://www.ibiblio.org/wunc_archives/sot/?cat=9. Web. 4 August 2012.

22. Lindsey Alexander, "Dissection and Other Kinds of Love: An Interview with Natasha Trethewey," *Sycamore Review* 24.1 (Winter/Spring 2012), 43.

23. Billy Watkins, "Books: Q&A Natasha Trethewey," *Clarion-Ledger* (Jackson, MS), 29 August 2010, 3E.

24. Ezra Wall, "Pulitzer Prize–Winner Natasha Trethewey's 'Beyond Katrina,'" *Mississippi Edition*, Mississippi Public Broadcasting, 28 September 2010.

25. Alexander, 33.

26. Alexander, 34–35.

27. Penne J. Laubenthal, "Natasha Trethewey: Winner of the 2007 Pulitzer Prize for Poetry," *Swampland.com*, http://swampland.com/articles/view/title:natasha_trethewey__winner_of_the_2007_pulitzer_prize_for_poetry_. Web. 4 August 2012.

28. "Q & A with Natasha Trethewey," Eastern Connecticut website. See n. 5 above.

29. Robert Begiebing et al., "Interchange: Genres of History," *Journal of American History* 91.2 (September 2004), 581. In fall 2003, the six participants in this forum exchanged comments online about "genres of history," from cartoons and poetry to museum exhibits.

Chronology

1966   Born April 26 in Gulfport, Mississippi, daughter of poet Eric Trethewey and social worker Gwendolyn Ann Turnbough Trethewey, who married in Cincinnati, Ohio, because interracial marriages were illegal in Mississippi.

1969   Hurricane Camille makes landfall in Mississippi on August 17. Trethewey describes the event in the poem "Providence" and in *Beyond Katrina*. In the late 1960s, the Ku Klux Klan burns a cross in front of her grandmother's house in Gulfport.

1972   After her parents divorce, Trethewey moves to Atlanta with her mother, who remarries.

1973   Birth of Joel (nicknamed Joe) Grimmette, her only sibling.

1985   Trethewey's mother is shot to death by her second husband, from whom she was divorced.

1989   Graduates from University of Georgia, B.A. in English. Becomes a caseworker in Augusta, Georgia.

1991   M.A. in English and creative writing from Hollins College (later University), Roanoke, Virginia.

1994   As a graduate student at the University of Massachusetts Amherst, Trethewey becomes a member of Boston's Dark Room Collective, a group of young African American writers founded in 1987.

1995   M.F.A in poetry from the University of Massachusetts Amherst.

1996   Fourteen of Trethewey's poems appear in *Callaloo*, along with Jill Petty's interview with Trethewey.

1997   Reads at Charter Oak Cultural Center in Hartford, Connecticut. Hired by Auburn University in Auburn, Alabama, as an assistant professor of English.

1998   Marries historian Brett Gadsden. Reads at Hill-Stead Museum's Sunken Garden Poetry Festival, in Farmington, Connecticut. Trethewey and other Dark Room Collective poets appear in the video anthology *Furious Flower: African American Poetry 1960–1995*.

1999   Trethewey's "watershed year," according to the *New Georgia Encyclopedia*. Rita Dove picks her "Domestic Work" manuscript for the Cave Canem Foundation prize. Grants from Alabama State Council on the Arts and National Endowment for the Arts. Margaret Walker Award for Poetry, Grolier Poetry Prize, and Jessica Nobel Maxwell Prize.

2000   *Domestic Work* published by Graywolf Press. "Limen" selected for *The Best American Poetry 2000*. Julia Peterkin Award from Converse College, Spartanburg, South Carolina. Alabama State Council on the Arts poetry fellowship. Distinguished Young Alumna of the Year Award from University of Massachusetts Amherst. A Bunting Fellow for 2000–2001 at Radcliffe Institute for Advanced Study, Harvard University.

2001   Trethewey becomes assistant professor of English at Emory University in Atlanta. *Domestic Work* receives the 2001 Lillian Smith Award for Poetry and the Mississippi Institute of Arts and Letters Poetry Award. Fellow at Middlebury College (Vermont) Bread Loaf Writers' Conference.

2002   *Bellocq's Ophelia: Poems* published by Graywolf Press. Finalist for both the Academy of American Poets' James Laughlin Prize and the Lenore Marshall Prize.

2003   Mississippi Institute of Arts and Letters Poetry Award for *Bellocq's Ophelia*, which is also a 2003 Notable Book of the American Library Association. John Simon Guggenheim Memorial Foundation fellowship. "After Your Death" selected for *The Best American Poetry 2003*.

2004   National Book Festival reading in Washington, D.C., sponsored by the Library of Congress. Rockefeller Foundation fellowship for residency at the Bellagio Center in Italy. Reading at Newcomb College, Tulane University, in October as Florie Gale Arons poet.

2005   Hurricane Katrina strikes the Mississippi Gulf Coast on August 28, causing major damage to uninsured rental houses owned by Trethewey's family. With Allen Tullos, Trethewey produces the Poets in Place series for the interdisciplinary Internet journal *Southern Spaces*. On sabbatical from Emory, Trethewey is Lehman Brady Joint Chair Professor of Documentary and American Studies at the University of North Carolina at Chapel Hill and at Duke University.

2006   *Native Guard: Poems* published by Houghton Mifflin. "Miscegenation" is reprinted in *Gathering Ground: A Reader Celebrating Cave*

Canem's First Decade. Poetry reading at the Beinecke Library, Yale University, in November.

2007 Pulitzer Prize for Poetry for *Native Guard*, which also receives the Mississippi Institute of Arts and Letters Poetry Award and the Lillian Smith Award for Poetry. Coeditor, with series editor Jeb Livingood, of *Best New Poets 2007: 50 Poems from Emerging Writers*. Trethewey is named Phillis Wheatley Chair of Poetry at Emory. Bread Loaf Writers' Conference faculty member. Reading with Stephen Dunn, 2001 Pulitzer Prize–winning poet, at Margaret Mitchell House & Museum in Atlanta in October. Trethewey delivers the Page-Barbour and James W. Richard Lectures at the University of Virginia: "Beyond Katrina: A Meditation on the Mississippi Gulf Coast: Present, Past, Future," in November. Honorary doctorate from Delta State University in Cleveland, Mississippi.

2008 Mississippi Governor's Award for Excellence in the Arts for *Native Guard*. 2008 Georgia Woman of the Year. Readings with former U.S. poet laureate Robert Pinsky in New York and Pulitzer Prize–winning poet Claudia Emerson in Virginia. Creative writers' exchange at U.S. Embassy in Cyprus and Calabash International Literary Festival in Jamaica, both in May. Kathleen Carlin Justice Seekers Award from Men Stopping Violence. Inaugural Distinguished Artist Award at Hambidge, Georgia's oldest residential program for artists. Intergovernmental literary program in Belfast, Northern Ireland, in October. World premiere of an opera based on *Bellocq's Ophelia* in November at Emory. "On Captivity" is selected for *Best American Poetry 2008*.

2009 James Weldon Johnson Fellow in African American Studies at the Beinecke Library, Yale. Inducted into the Fellowship of Southern Writers in Chattanooga, Tennessee. Attends President Barack Obama's inauguration. Richard Wright Excellence Award, Natchez Literary and Cinema Celebration in Natchez, Mississippi. Gives the Ralph Ellison Lecture at Tuskegee University, Tuskegee, Alabama, in March and the Sheth Distinguished Lecture at Emory in April. Reading and discussion for Fulbright grantees and alumni in South Korea in May. Trethewey records two multimedia "documentary poems" with photographer Joshua Cogan and producer Lu Olkowski.

2010 *Beyond Katrina: A Meditation on the Mississippi Gulf Coast* published by University of Georgia Press. Trethewey participates in the Key West Literary Seminar in January. Distinguished Faculty Lecture for Emory's Life of the Mind Series in February. Reads with poet Terrance Hayes in New York at the 92nd Street Y's reading series in April. Delivers graduation speech and is awarded an honorary doctorate at Hollins. Reads at the 2010 National Book Festival in Washington, D.C. Trethewey and poet Kyle Dargan launch Spelman College's first Creative Writing Series in October in Atlanta. Grisham Visiting Writer at the University of Mississippi, Oxford, in November. Serves as Southeast Representative, Association of Writers & Writing Programs, 2010–2014.

2011   Inducted into the Georgia Writers Hall of Fame. Mississippi Institute of Arts and Letters Nonfiction Award for *Beyond Katrina*. Trethewey is named Charles Howard Candler Chair of English and Creative Writing, an endowed professorship at Emory. Spring 2011 poet-in-residence at Bucknell University. Keynote address, "Beyond Katrina: A Meditation on the Mississippi Gulf Coast," for the 2011 Lozano Long Conference in February, University of Texas at Austin. Autobiography panelist at the University of Mississippi's Oxford Conference for the Book, with Ralph Eubanks, director of publishing at the Library of Congress, in March. "Another Country" is included in the anthology *44 on 44: Forty-Four African American Writers on the Election of Barack Obama, 44th President of the United States*. *Best American Poetry 2011* selects her "Elegy."

2012   Librarian of Congress James Billington names Trethewey nineteenth United States Poet Laureate for 2012–13. Appointed Robert W. Woodruff Professor of English and creative writing at Emory, where she directs the creative writing program. Louis D. Rubin Writer-in-Residence for 2012 at her alma mater, Hollins University. Stage production of *Bellocq's Ophelia* debuts in February at Hollins. Trethewey is named State Poet Laureate of Mississippi (2012-2016) by outgoing Governor Haley Barbour. Presents the Robert Chasen Poetry Reading at Cornell University in February and reads with Indian poet and translator Yuyutsu Ram Dass Sharma at New York University in March. Featured reader with poet Jake Adam York for the Nancy K. Smith Distinguished Visitors Series, Coastal Carolina University, in March. Reads with other Dark Room Collective alumni on a reunion tour. Featured reader at Hill-Stead Museum's Sunken Garden Poetry Festival, Farmington, Connecticut, in July. Faculty member at Middlebury College's Bread Loaf Writers' Conference in August. *Thrall* is published by Houghton Mifflin Harcourt. Keynote address at the Decatur Book Festival in August. Reads in October in Newark at the Geraldine R. Dodge Poetry Festival, North America's largest poetry event. Keynote address, "War and Remembrance," at the annual Georgia Literary Festival, Jekyll Island Convention Center, Veterans Day weekend.

2013   In residence in Washington, D.C., from January to May, the first poet laureate to work from the Poetry Room at the Library of Congress.

2014   Memoir on growing up biracial in the 1970s and 1980s South, to be published by Ecco, an imprint of HarperCollins.

Conversations
with Natasha Trethewey

An Interview with Natasha Trethewey

Jill Petty / 1996

From *Callaloo* 19.2 (Spring 1996), 364-75. © 1996 Charles H. Rowell. Reprinted with permission of The Johns Hopkins University Press.

JILL PETTY: Photography figures a lot in your work—often you're in the heads of black people while they're being photographed, or speaking to whites who are taking those pictures. What does that allow you to explore? What are you saying about visibility or spectatorship?

NATASHA TRETHEWEY: I actually think about both, but I'm especially interested in absence. Every photograph represents a moment that is no longer, passed, as well as ways of being that have disappeared. I've always been a little obsessed with the way photographs hold and create an object out of that moment. And I've often thought if you look at a photograph, if you really study the gestures and expressions that the people have in the photograph, you could see the rest of their lives, everything that's to come. I think my interest in photographs started after my mother died. I started looking at old photographs of her, trying to see if it was all there in the photographs, what was going to happen to her and to us and our lives. Is it here, or do I, as the poet, put it there? That's part of my fixation with photographs. Recently, I've been reading *On Photography*, Susan Sontag's book, and she says the very act of taking a photograph is somewhat cruel and mean. The first part of my poem, "Three Photographs," is from the point of view of the photographer, and the next part of the poem is from the point of view of one of the subjects in the photograph. She has a voice that's not usually heard—she talks about the reality that is imposed on her, as a subject in a photo. The persona in the poem tries to turn that around with language while looking back at the photographer at the same time. The third section of that poem is more or less in my voice. I'm in a gallery, seeing these photographs, feeling the gaze of the photographer, which I share as I view these images on the wall. But I am overwhelmed by their—the subject, the black people's—gaze that comes out of those photographs through time to look at me. And I feel compelled and responsible to speak about the connection that I have to them.

PETTY: That's a powerful moment when you make that connection between the subjects and yourself. But something you said about Susan Sontag made me think about the nature of poetry, too. You frame your poems like photos, with dates, certain language, metaphor. If photography is cruel, is poetry cruel also? Your poems read like sepia snapshots to me, too. They are very much, as you said, a way into somebody's life

TRETHEWEY: At the same time Sontag mentions photography as a cruel practice, she makes the distinction between the photographer as artist and the poet. Poets turn themselves inside out, search for the substance of their own lives and their own pain, but photographers voluntarily go out seeking other people's pain. Now, that's how she puts it, and I guess in many ways I would agree. But are my poems cruel? I think there's a little bit of cruelty and introspection, because I certainly dig down. Say we were to talk about the series of poems about my grandmother's work and her life. I chose her work to be the thing that I was going to narrate her life through; I was going out and looking for her particular pains or her particular sufferings and using the stories she's told me to create this framework. At the same time, she became a character for me. I'm not separate from that character, and I don't think I would have been able to write those poems if each feeling expressed and what her character goes through in every poem wasn't something that was close to home, something I knew very well. So it's still my pain, but I have taken someone's life and made a picture out of it. And that can be cruel.

PETTY: It's also interesting how photography functions in your work in terms of memory. Here you are, a Generation X kid, a child born towards the end of the Civil Rights Movement, and you return to the Depression-era South consistently. You're able to access a time and place that you can't remember. Do you sometimes sit down with photographs, or did you start with your grandmother's stories, or does a combination of all these things get you back there? All writers do this, but you're mediating a lot of different distances.

TRETHEWEY: You started off by placing me in the twentysomething set, but I think of myself as so "old timey." I think a lot of my friends do, too. I grew up in Mississippi, and my community was really on the cusp of major change. I get together with my cousin occasionally, and we walk around the neighborhood and talk about this. We talk about how we are the last generation in that community that still played marbles, that had pigs rooting under our houses, that had chickens running around, where people still had cows in their yards. Really old school. The way this community was—which has been black since the turn of the century—we still lived like our parents and grandparents to a large degree. Now my brother, who's seven years younger than me, and others who are just separated by a couple of years don't have the same experiences. And I think that was because I was a part of that time when the stories of my grandmother's life were more accessible. That's when people still told stories a lot more. I was always around the old women in the neighborhood who were doing that. So I had that, and I had those photographs, and I had something else, too. August Wilson said that he doesn't really do any research for any of his plays—he just kind of picks the time period and maybe he does some superficial research. But he used what he called "blood memory" to transport him to that other place. I can connect with a particular feeling that my grandmother talks about from that time. It relates to something I've experienced. As a younger writer, I wrote poems that were narrative, and they were about me. I was always traveling around and experiencing this and seeing that, and I had some other issues that I wanted to write about. I felt that I had to get out of using the "I," so I decided that I was going to create a character and do these poems third person. I was going to make myself do it like that. That forced me to learn a lot about narrative and to do different things to tell stories and relate experiences. I'm remembering in some of those poems memories that aren't mine immediately but ones that are given to me, and I think those become part of who you are, too. I really can't distance myself from my mother's life growing up in the 1950s and 1960s or my grandmother's life growing up in the 1920s and 1930s. They feel like part of my life. It's all in there now with me growing up in the 1970s and 1980s, and it all makes that a part of who I am.

PETTY: Wouldn't you call your poems nostalgic?
TRETHEWEY: Well, I think I am a tremendously nostalgic person. I love the artifact that a photograph is. I cherish objects—I've got my grandmother's old hot combs in my house—I'm just in love with artifacts. I'm sentimental in many ways, which is definitely a danger for anyone trying to write, but I think, as Richard Hugo says, that if you're not risking sentimentality then you're not really writing. So I think that I risk it every single time I go into a poem. I hope that I overcome it, but I definitely risk that.

PETTY: You mentioned the fact that you write about your grandmother's life through her work. The world of black women in your poems seems inextricably tied to the world of labor and employment. What makes that realm compelling for you?

TRETHEWEY: Mostly it was my grandmother's life that I was interested in, but I also write other poems about work and labor that are not only about "women's work." I am fascinated with work and with labor and the objects of work and labor and with hands. Students in one of my creative writing classes had a running joke that I would love any poem that had hands in it, and in a way that's true! You can look at hands just like you can look at photographs and learn so much. Hands play a big role in the work that I do.

PETTY: There's something dignified about them?

TRETHEWEY: There is something dignified about them. I think it's cliché to say they tell a story, but in many ways they do. [Laughs] They're just a part of humans that are very beautiful to me. And if you're trying to make art or trying to make poetry, it's not just about taking traditionally beautiful things but finding beauty in anything. So the calluses on my grandmother's hands from sewing where she doesn't need to use a thimble are beautiful to me.

PETTY: Tell me more about her and how she has influenced your work.

TRETHEWEY: I'd like to talk about her, but I'd also like to talk about my Aunt Sugar. She is a subject of a few of those poems, and sometimes I don't make a distinction. There's just an old woman who is there. My grandmother, I got a lot from just watching her work, because she was a seamstress the entire time I lived with her. I got to watch her sew all the time, and she would also tell a lot of her stories. My Aunt Sugar was a different sort. I've even tried to write about her in an essay, because she really seems to be a muse. Aunt Sugar lived next door to my grandmother and is ten years older than my grandmother. She actually raised my grandmother after my great grandmother died young and after my great grandfather . . . well, he left first, and then my great grandmother died. So my Aunt Sugar was one of the two older children who raised the rest, and she became a school teacher. She started a church in an arbor just around the house. She later went on to migrate to Chicago and become a medical technician, but she came back home and built a house to settle back in Gulfport next to my grandmother. She was someone who was in love with objects. Aunt Sugar had what you might call "trinkets"—she had more trinkets on shelves in her house than anyone I've known. She used to collect them; I mean she was always finding something and holding onto it and rubbing it in her hands for the way that it felt, how heavy it was, if it was rough or smooth. And as she got older, she developed Alzheimer's, and she had gathered up the little objects she had collected. Each time I visited her house, I had to leave with one of them. So I began, then, to have a collection. I took on all those objects and all her ways of seeing things with hands and touching things, you know, holding them up and looking at all their sides. And even now, you know, in the rest home, she is still collecting things—bits of paper, food. You'll find anything stuffed in her pockets. She doesn't let go of anything, and I know that's just an extreme result of her Alzheimer's, but it's very metaphorical to me. From her, I learned to love objects. I want to hold onto them.

PETTY: What does that represent to you in a larger way, her love of objects and your inherited feeling for them?

TRETHEWEY: I think that she did something that was very meaningful to me as a poet. After all, objects can really write a poem for you. Sandra McPherson talks about that, as have a lot of other writers, but they can really write a poem for you. One of the most important things about how you use objects in a poem is juxtaposition, and Aunt Sugar really had a way of juxtaposing some of the objects she would give me. I remember one time that she knocked at the back door of my grandmother's house, and I answered it. She had three very hard figs in her hand, and she held them out to me just in the strangest way—if you didn't know her, you would think it was ominous. But she handed them to me, and it was like she was handing me something that was precious. What she gave me, again and again, was knowledge about how to juxtapose one object against another. That's really where you get tension, I think, in a poem and where you can work on its various levels of meaning.

PETTY: Hearing how important your family is to your writing and understanding how your life was distinctly rural, I wonder if you identify as a Southern writer?

TRETHEWEY: I am not bothered when someone says they see landscapes or ways of life in the South represented in my poems because, I think, yeah that's a whole huge chunk of who I am. I'm not bothered; I don't feel limited or pigeonholed by people just because they happen to find that in my work. Of course, it's not happenstance—it's there because that's who I am, and I'm writing out of a particular consciousness. So yeah, I'm not bothered by that, although there's gonna be other things in there, too, that represent other pieces of my consciousness.

PETTY: What things do you think play the largest roles—I'm not sure you'd quantify it—in terms of what you choose to write about and who you feel you're writing for?
TRETHEWEY: Well, certainly being black, but also I think being mixed, having had a biracial experience, that's also important. The fact that I come from a very matrilineal family is very significant and influences what things get played out in the work. And I've talked about growing up with chickens and all that, but at the same time my grandmother's house sits right on Highway 49—the Highway 49 of all the blues songs—so we've got this big highway running right through this neighborhood that has been rural for the longest time. And some big company talked her into allowing them to put in a billboard, so the billboard is half in our yard and half on government property. My father is a poet who comes from a rural atmosphere, and he writes about that a lot; but anything that's rural for me is always undercut by a highway, undercut by this other world being smashed right up against it. In many ways, I guess this understanding hearkens back to being a mixed person. There are pieces of identity that you know fit together and everything's fine, but at the same time you know there might occasionally be some opposition going on, and so opposition is probably something really important in my work. One of the ways it's physical for me is my parents having a mixed marriage and living right there, straddling, you know, this rural community and a highway at the same time . . .

PETTY: And also straddling two different eras, before and after Jim Crow . . .
TRETHEWEY: Yeah, I think I do that in my work, too.

PETTY: What other writers influence you?
TRETHEWEY: I read *Thomas and Beulah* upside down and back and forth when I was trying to write the poems about my grandmother's life and trying to get away from being the first person narrator in all my poems. I really looked at how delicately Rita Dove works a story, how she styles a fragment of a story that might not even strike you if you just heard it, you know, floating around as some anecdote or something. But she really knows how to craft that fragment and find the right narrative, structure, and language to turn it into something really beautiful. I think I was at one point too worried—as I think a lot of our young writers are—too worried with sticking to

the story. Like, "this is how it happened, this is how I'm gonna tell it, and this is the order it's gonna be told in." It was from her that I learned the whole story may not be the whole poem. I mean the whole story may not be the poem. That may not be what the poem needs, and so I began to see there are moments in any story that can make up the whole world of a poem.

PETTY: And Dove certainly writes a lot about being a mother, about having a daughter, about matrilineage, about race.
TRETHEWEY: Yes. And another writer that has influenced me is Sharon Olds. She can attach meaning to the smallest details in a photograph, and I think that for any poet that's a wonderful thing. She's able to look at the smallest things, and all of a sudden the picture almost moves, begins to have motion. I can see a whole story, a whole swirling narrative, going on around the way that she presents the photograph. That was one thing I studied in her work.

PETTY: Sharon Olds is obsessed with her father—she writes so much about her father and the men in her life. How are men and your father's side of your family expressed in your work?
TRETHEWEY: Well, being from a very matrilineal family, knowing the stories about how women in my family have dealt with men, and thinking about my own dealings with men—you know, my father, my uncle, whoever that may be—men do make their presence known in my work, often by their absences. Again that's the reason for the photographs a lot of times. I have one poem where I'm talking about how my grandmother can almost remember or barely imagine what her father looked like—just that he left. My grandmother's first husband had another wife at the same time that he was married to her—which becomes the basis of a poem although bigamy doesn't get mentioned in the poem—and she had to leave him. My father takes on, I think, sort of mythical proportions to me because he was absent in some way. Because he was divorced from my mother, I could create a whole mythology around who he was; it's only when you get older and you actually start to fill in some of those absent spaces that your view of a person can change. In terms of how the other side of my family is represented, they are in Canada first of all, so knowing them is something I've not done all my life. I spent a year there when I was an infant and then have only gone back since I've been in my mid-twenties to visit and to meet them again. I've always known that they were there, but in many ways they were the periphery, the part of a photograph that from a particular angle you won't

get to see. But they are there. I think that perhaps the more that I begin to story parts of my own life and delve into other parts of my consciousness, the circle will get wider—the camera's angle will be a wide-angle lens, and I'll be able to include more. But right now in terms of binary oppositions of some sort there's what's there and what's not there. And what's not there really can make its presence known by its absence. I'm reminded of a time that I walked in to find my grandmother sitting at a table cutting some old photographs. She was actually cutting them up, cutting a certain person out of the photograph. It's as if she felt that by cutting them out she could really remove them; but, you know, I hold up that photograph, and the lightbulb in the top of the ceiling shines through that space. And you see the absence and feel the person's presence through their absence even more.

PETTY: It's interesting, the way men and women operate in your poetry. Women work together in the workplace and the family, working in communion despite the elements of competition between them. And then there are poems where men are working, talking and relaxing with each other. When you get the two together, even in a potentially loving situation, there's a tension. I was intrigued by that.
TRETHEWEY: I don't think I can escape that tension, and it flows from all those senses, all the ways I've seen men make their presences known by the women in my family's lives. I really believe that men and women need each other, but those needs are good and bad, and they get manifested in both positive and negative ways. I am fascinated by those desires and needs, and by how the lack of a common language sometimes prevents a successful union.

PETTY: How do you mean?
TRETHEWEY: One of my poems, "At the Station," shows a woman who's decided to take charge of her relationship by leaving it. Yet she faces him as she rides away on the train. She's so drawn to him and to what was there, I think, and she might stay if he had some way of speaking to her. But the man in that poem can't say anything. A line from a Robert Johnson song is the epigraph for that poem: "The blue light was my blues and the red light was my mind." I think of that line as an indication that he has found some language, that he's singing this blues song, saying something, but the man doesn't seem to be able to say anything to her. He just follows her with her suitcases basically to see her off. Being there is a sign that he doesn't really want her to go, but he doesn't have the right language to ask her to stay

or the language that will communicate something to her. He has his own language, and he's able to communicate something with it, but it may not reach her.

PETTY: That's sad. Do you think that men and women write differently as a result?

TRETHEWEY: I don't want to generalize about that, but I've been reading a lot of stuff from a class I teach, a writing class, and we read a lot about connected knowing vs. separate knowing and the ways that women communicate. We read one article by Deborah Tannen called "Talk in the Intimate Relationship," a he-said/she-said kind of thing, and really you see that women are saying one thing and men are saying something else. Women also read a meta-message into what men say, but men aren't trying to say that. There's a place where men and women just break down, because they just don't have the same way of communicating. I think that I say that in a poem of mine called "His Hands." A man comes in at the end of the poem, and the woman just takes his hands and removes splinters and just works with the hands. That is the best moment of communication those two have, and it comes through something else, through a language of the body not of the spoken word.

PETTY: I was thinking about your poem "Flounder" when you were talking about the ways that the camera widens and takes in different oppositions. I think it's as much about passing wisdom between women in a family as it is about racial identity.

TRETHEWEY: That actually is one of those that comes . . . it was one of my earliest poems, and it was published in *Callaloo*, too. It really came from a real fishing trip with my Aunt Sugar. We were catching a flounder, and, you know, obviously the story changes when you have adult wisdom, adult perspective to look back on what happened to you as a child. But we were on the fishing trip, and she actually did say that flounders are black on one side and white on the other. You know, when I think about that years later, I ask myself whether Aunt Sugar was on the sly trying to tell me something? Was that her metaphorical way of signifying, of letting me know this is part of what you're going to have to experience?

PETTY: Right, and this is part of nature.

TRETHEWEY: Yes, it's an opposition that exists in nature, but it's not an opposition because it's all one fish. So what do you do with that.

PETTY: I want to talk a little more about how you work, why you work, and what it's like to participate as a student in a creative writing program. How do you find your space, find people to mentor you? And how do you work out questions about audience when you're workshopping in a predominantly white class?

TRETHEWEY: I have one story that I have told so many times about this. It was really my first encounter with institutionalized racism—if you don't want to go that far, you could call it institutionalized blindness to other people's culture. Let's start with that. I was getting my MA in writing at Hollins College, and I was actually writing fiction at this point. In this particular story, I had a scene that I thought was a piece of the finest writing in the entire story. The scene was about a woman and her daughter sitting at the kitchen table together eating neck bones and rice. The scene was supposed to represent how this mother feels towards her daughter and how she guides the daughter in terms of teaching her how to do things—this is a very little girl. If you've ever eaten neck bones, you know there ain't a lot of meat on them and you got to pick them up with your hands and suck on them, if you going get anything, and there's gravy and everything else. And the little girl, you know, she can use her fork and get the rice and all—that's because she's old enough to do that—but she really has a hard time with the slippery bone. Her mother helps her draw whatever little bit she can from these bones. It was an important scene for me, metaphorically and everything else. One person in my class, and you know I was the only black person in class, writes on the story when she gives it back to me—she doesn't say this in class, which is really what annoys me because there might have been discussion about it—she writes on my paper, "this scene is unbelievable and almost silly." Perhaps she'd never heard of eating neck bones and rice; she didn't know what it was or how anyone could pick up anything dressed in brown gravy and hold it to their mouth and suck meat out of it? I was really hurt. Since then I've had an agenda.

It's also happened to me in workshops while getting my MFA, and I've talked to other black writers who seem to have the same frustration in the workshops. They say that the white students put obscure literary references in their poetry, or some piece of language, or anything, and you're expected to do some homework, some research to go find out what it means. But if I put something in there that is culturally related that they don't understand, I just get a big question mark or "what does this mean?" written in a really condescending manner across my paper. No one makes the effort to try to understand it as a piece of language that is working within the whole of the poem. That is frustrating. In terms of voice and audience—oh, that's a big one, too—my audience, though I expect it to be very wide, can be both broad and narrow at the same time. I can remember a good example. I had the phrase "Quiet as it's kept" in my poem. Now most black people know what the phrase "Quiet as it's kept" means, but a lot of white people don't. In this one particular class the workshop leader—this was very good—she said, "I don't know what this means, but as a piece of language it works so well right there." Now that's how I expect it to work—if you don't know what it means, if you are not part of the community, if I'm doing my job as a writer, that piece of language is still going to have some meaning for you within the context of the poem. But if you are also a member of that community, and you know what that phrase or word means, it takes you to yet another level. So that's why my audience can be so broad and narrow at the same time.

In other classes I try to have a range of voice, of what I can do. In one class I may be working in a particular vein of my narrative abilities in a poem. I've been turning workshop after workshop to one thing that I'm working on. People kind of get used to you like that. Those poems seemed more like family stories and were told in the language of my grandmother, so they were filled with metaphors, idiomatic phrases that had to do with black southern culture, black English. They decided that's who I was, that's what I should be writing. So if I came in with a sonnet or some other thing that had a language so different from what they had come to expect from me, they didn't know what to do with it.

When I was talking about audience earlier, I meant to mention something a teacher actually said to me about this question of cultural references. When I made that statement to her that I just repeated to you a moment ago—about how a phrase can mean something to your audience on a deeper cultural level or as a piece of language, and that's fine, but if they don't know the history of this phrase or what it means, then that's fine with me, too—when I said that to her, she responded, "No, I don't think that's fine; it's your responsibility to educate us, to tell us." Now how often have we heard that phrase—as feminists?

PETTY: This is a classic situation. If you're presented with a poem and the poet is from Ireland and it lapses into Celtic or they start to talk about County Cork, you're supposed to be able to make that leap with them, when they are bringing in cultural references or turns of phrase. But as a black artist you are supposed to stop and educate. That's very interesting, that people don't always want to make that leap with you.

TRETHEWEY: They don't want to make that leap of faith, you know; they won't just go with it, see where it takes them. They're stopped immediately by it and will not read further or try to engage with what the poem is doing. That has affected my writing so much. When I was a younger writer coming through workshops and having to face that, it bothered me so much when people would do that to me. I decided that I was going to be beyond reproach in terms of clarity in my poetry. I was going to make it so clear that you would have to be totally dense to not understand the reference in the context of the narrative. I think I've done that a lot.

People have said that I am really accessible and that that is a good thing. I think so, too, because I have an agenda about that. I want to write in language that, if I go and read in my grandmother's church, all of those old ladies I have known all my life are going to understand; they'll know exactly what I'm saying. And so people who are literary-minded can see that beyond being accessible other things are going on in the poem. That's important to me because so often I have students in workshops who come to the table with this idea that the more obscure the poem is, the better it is.

PETTY: Do you think if you had studied and workshopped in more integrated settings that your writing would have turned out differently?

TRETHEWEY: You know, I used to wonder if I'd made the right decision about choosing UMass to do an MFA. But I think that the biggest lesson I learned and one that I try to convey to my students is that learning some rules, giving yourself some rules, is a really good thing. Richard Hugo talks about this in *The Triggering Town*, that some of the rules, as arbitrary as they may sound, are necessary. Once you have rules, then you can start breaking them. And once I decided to use this technique or that effect and learned to build on that, I could switch that up a little bit, break that rule. And I still grew and hope to keep growing like that, to keep breaking each new set of rules that I make for myself.

PETTY: I want to come back to what you were talking about as far as your students' first impressions of how to write poetry. But I want to return to what you were saying earlier about going into workshops and writing in a different voice, and about the response you get from people when you start to move away from the expected voice or content you've been using.

TRETHEWEY: I talked about making rules for myself. I need to learn how to do other things with narrative and not always be the first-person narrator. So I made it a rule for myself that I was going to write these poems using this "she" who became my character. And my "she" was going to be filled with all sorts of characteristics that are my own, but she was going to be living in a different time and having different experiences. It freed me up to imagine the possibilities of what she could be like, and what happened in her life. I didn't have to stick to the kinds of "real" events that you sometimes get caught up trying to duplicate just because it really happened that way. Just because it happened doesn't mean it's going to make a good piece of art. I tell my students that what happened to you, what traumatic thing you've been through, is never so interesting as it is once you reimagine it. My father always tells me, "You have to stick to the truth, you have to tell truth in a poem." I believe that, but I think the truth for me is different than it is for him. He might mean some literal, factual, this is-how-it-happened truth; but when I write my poems, if those stories become true, they really do become yet another piece of the story. I've listened to chunks of my grandmother's stories, and I've gone and written a poem that I've just created, out of my imagination. I come back to my grandmother, and I read it to her. And she says, "That's just how it was; it happened just like that." Now that's impossible, but it just becomes the truth for her and me. I mean, it's so convincing. I've convinced her of so much about her own life, yet it's all made up. That really tells me—if she says I've done it right—that I've done it right.

PETTY: Do you think you're interested in moving at some point away from writing about people that you know?
TRETHEWEY: My teacher John Wideman asked me that same question—when do I plan to move on and have the kind of eye that can just be walking out there in the world and see things and write poems about them? I want to be able to do that. I'm worried that I'm so fixated about things I've known that my eye is always going to draw me back to those old places. But I want to be able to write a poem like that poem of Rita Dove's—I think it's called "Vacation"—where she's sitting in the airport before leaving and just talking about how she loves the moment before vacation. She can just sit in the airport before takeoff and write a poem about that. I want to be able to do that.

PETTY: I'm curious about the ways that your teaching has informed your writing. You've mentioned earlier talking to your students about the ways you write and what they bring to the table when they come into a classroom. What have you learned about your own writing and about writing in general from teaching?
TRETHEWEY: I think one of the great things about an MFA program is

that you're in workshop and you learn a lot about what kind of teaching you'd like to do, what kind of teacher you would like to be, and what kind of teacher you'd absolutely not like to be: you think to yourself, "I would never run a workshop like that." I think that teaching and trying to deal with students throws issues of respect back in your face. I could always remember being the person sitting there and not wanting to go through this long, pregnant silence that some workshop leaders allow. Because other students perhaps haven't done their homework, haven't done a close reading of someone's work, no one has anything to say. The teacher, in my opinion, has the responsibility to save the student from that excruciating silence. I try to do that by asking questions that lead the students into discussion. To do that, I've got to read the person's work as closely as possible. I think anybody's poem deserves that, especially in a workshop. Once you're in a workshop setting, you're committed to a community. Part of your responsibility is to write and turn in your poems, but that's not the only thing you're doing in there: you're also supposed to be a really good reader, a half of the workshop responsibility that a lot of people forget, I think. I would like to be a workshop teacher who is constantly reminding us of that half of our commitment and responsibility in being a part of a workshop community.

PETTY: I wanted to ask you a little bit about the Dark Room. How does that feed you as a writer of color? What type of balance does that help create as you move from writing in a majority white program to working and talking with other writers of color at the Dark Room?
TRETHEWEY: One of the greatest things that happened to me coming north and being at UMass for my MFA was hooking up with the Dark Room. It was really funny the way that it happened.

A friend of mine, who lived in Boston and was commuting a lot of the time, brought a newspaper to me that had an article about a collective of young black writers. He stuck it in my mailbox one day. When I read it, I thought, "Wow, something like that sounds so great!" And then several coincidences later I met up with them and joined the Dark Room. There's been a real peace of mind in knowing that, when I was sitting in those workshops, there were other people out there who were trying to do the same thing that I was doing, other people who believed, as Tom Ellis has said, that clarity is revolutionary. Once I started getting together and doing readings with the Dark Room, I saw how attentive everyone was to each other's work. We started choosing a poem by another collective member and reading it first—that's how we opened our readings. At one in particular, Sharan Strange and I swapped poems, and I read her "Still Life"—a poem I love about her mother, beauty, and suffering. A few weeks later she had a reading without the collective and realized she still had a poem of mine, "Hot Comb," instead of her own poem. My poem was also about my mother, beauty, and suffering—so she read it. When she told me that story, I was honored. It made me think of our similarities; and because I really respect her work, I was happy to make that connection, to know we were trying to do some of the same things. At the same time, our work is different, and I really pay attention to that. As a collective, we are always influencing each other. There isn't a member that I can't learn something from. This attests to what I consider a major strength of the Dark Room. Cornelius Eady talked about it in an introduction he gave for us at a reading not too long ago. Instead of us presenting an essentialized notion of blackness or black experience, he pointed out that the collective shows many different black experiences. So there is room in the collective for different experiences, different voices, different styles.

PETTY: How has your perception of your own work, of what poetry is, grown because of your association with the Dark Room?

TRETHEWEY: Again, it's about difference. Within the collective, the diversity of our voices is respected and nurtured in so many ways. I feel safe to try new things because I know I'll get a close and careful reading, an honest response. A few years ago Tom Ellis chose a poem of mine for a special emerging writers issue that he was editing. The poem was experimental for me. I thought no one would publish it. When he did, I said, "OK, I can do this." I realize that I was a little afraid to take risks in my work—in many ways I still am—but in the collective I feel encouraged to do so. This means I can continue to grow, and right now, that's exactly what I hope for.

A Conversation with Natasha Trethewey

David Haney / 2003

From *Cold Mountain Review* (Appalachian State University) 33.1 (Fall 2004), 19–34. Reprinted by permission.

This interview took place March 28, 2003, in the office of *Cold Mountain Review* at Appalachian State University, during Natasha Trethewey's visit as part of Appalachian State's Visiting Writers Series. Trethewey, who teaches creative writing at Emory University, is the author of two collections of poems, *Domestic Work* (2000) and *Bellocq's Ophelia* (2002), both on Graywolf Press. Poems in the latter collection are inspired by early twentieth-century photos taken by E. J. Bellocq of New Orleans prostitutes. Trethewey not only imagines the life of "Ophelia" in poems that re-create the life of a mixed-race prostitute forced to negotiate among different racial, cultural, and economic worlds, but she also raises many practical and theoretical issues about the relationship between photographic and poetic representation. Those issues served as the starting point for the following conversation.

Haney: Let's talk a little about, especially with *Bellocq's Ophelia*, how you see the process of moving from the photo to the poem. What I'd like for you to think about is the intersection of the theoretical issues you face as someone thinking about that problem and the practical issues you face as a poet writing.
Trethewey: I think whenever I approach the photograph I always approach it as a moment of loss. You know people have talked about the ways in which a photograph really is all about loss because it represents a moment that is no more. We've moved on from it, we can't ever get back to it. That seems to be the nature of poetry as well, something about that moment of loss, something about nostalgia, the things that we would like to return to through

imagery. So whenever I look at photographs I'm always thinking about a couple of things; the moment just before it, the moment after it, and what the subjects of the photograph could or could not have known about what was to come. It's a wonderful given image to begin as a starting off point for a poem, and then I am always reminded that it is a one-dimensional representation of the world, and so I'm also thinking about what's immediately outside the frame. That becomes the theoretical thing I am most interested in: what it is we can't see versus what it is that the photograph gives us. I think often of one of the epigraphs that I use from Susan Sontag: "Nevertheless the camera's rendering of reality must always hide more than it discloses." I'm interested in trying to disclose something else beyond the limitations of the photograph.

H: I'm looking at Martin Jay's book here, *Downcast Eyes*. This is Jay quoting Barthes: "[The photograph] establishes not a consciousness of the being there of the thing (which any copy could provoke) but an awareness of its having been there. What we have is a new space time category: spatial immediacy, and temporal anteriority, the photograph being an illogical conjunction between the here-now and the there-then."[1] Particularly in photographs like these, how do you think about that spatial immediacy in the same breath as the ongoing temporal anteriority?
T: Well I think it again goes back to Barthes when he talks about the "punctum": that little thing within the photograph that strikes you and makes you begin to contemplate all that's not there, all that you can't see. I think it's that little part that becomes an entrance into seeing the photograph as just a frame in a longer, ongoing narrative or a sequence of events. So I see it as that captured moment, but, for example, in one of *Bellocq's* photographs of the woman in the black and white striped stockings that's sitting next to the bottle of Raleigh Rye—the fact that she's sort of twirling her shot glass, that's the punctum for me in that photograph because she refused to hold still and thus the blur that occurs right there reminds us that this is not simply a moment that can be frozen and captured but that it is representative of an ongoing sequence of events. The photograph's just one frame, like in a film.

H: You take that to a metalevel sometimes with characters who refuse to do what they are supposed to do in a photograph. Then you have the *tableau vivant*, freezing a moment that's very staged and unnatural.
T: Right, drawing attention to itself because it's unnatural. I wanted to say I also have a moment of punctum that appears in *Domestic Work*, in the

very first poem in *Domestic Work*, which is kind of an *ars poetica* for that book for me; it's the one gesture of a woman in process. In that poem, "The Woman," there are two women posing or being photographed, and one of them, again, refuses to be still, and she's got an apron on. And so she must have done something with her hand that makes the apron fluff out in front of her. It actually looks like a swirl of white as if she was churning her hands, and it's that refusal to be trapped in that moment, to be trapped in history. I think that I see the agency of these characters, these subjects of photographs. Their agency is that they insist on inserting themselves into our contemporary imagination by refusing to be still.

H: So the past really speaks.
T: Yes, and it refuses to simply be the past. It's ongoing as representative in that movement, that unwillingness to be totally still.

H: One of the things that my favorite philosopher, Hans-Georg Gadamer, talks about is the way history works as a conversation between the past and the present. You have to see the past as a living partner in that conversation. Do you see yourself as creating that conversation or recording that conversation?
T: Isn't it William Faulkner who says, the past isn't dead, it's not even in the past, it's not even past? And that's what I think, that it constantly lives all around us. My project has been and continues to be to try to find a way to restore lost narratives to our collective and public memory; things that are left out of authoritative histories. There are gaps that are there, there are these erasures that are just waiting to be filled in. I think in some ways I'm trying to record those things, but in the act of trying to do that I'm bringing that past to bear on this moment.

H: You've used the word "narrative" a few times, and this has been pointed out in the blurbs to your books, that there is a narrative content. *Bellocq's Ophelia* has been referred to as a novella. If you are interested in recovering lost narratives, why are you writing poetry instead of novels?
T: Well, the easy answer would probably be that I don't think I could write a novel, I really love the elegant little envelope that is a poem. For example, there are photographers who photograph. You can look at it, and there seems to be within the photograph a sequence of events. Carrie Mae Williams, for example, can do that. I am drawn to that particular moment for what the moment stands up and can do more than simply what seems to be

captured within that frame. And so I lean toward that rather than the space that I would be given if I were making a film or writing a novel. I think there's something about the restraint of a poem. Sometimes the things I write about are so deeply important to me that if I didn't have the constraints that a poem places on me, I might fill up a whole page with stuff that's not necessary. And I want to distill it, and so maybe that's why I give myself less space.

H: That issue of restraint shows up in the content too, doesn't it? In the photographs of the women, we almost forget that what we're talking about here is a brothel and even though there's evidence of brutal sex and everything else, we have these photos that are elegant and restrained. If you are writing a novel, you have to put in all of the details that those photographs specifically refer to but exclude.
T: Right, I'd talk a lot more about VD than I did.

H: Right. What's your theory of seeing? Martin Jay's book is about the history of vision in Western thought at least. And one of the things that Jay says is that we use sight, we use it in terms of speculation, the association of sight with rationality. What you can see is rational. We use it in terms of observation, whether that's the gaze that reduces the other to an object or whatever. But we also use it as a kind of metaphor for visionary illumination. Depending on what century you're in, you might think about vision and sight differently. How do you see those ideas, those different versions of possibilities for the visual working themselves out in your work?
T: I'm glad you explained it like that because now I think I can see a way to answer your question. All three of them, and I'm probably going to ask you the names of them again, so I'm making sure that I'm talking about each one.

H: Speculation, observation, and visionary illumination.
T: Observation, I'll start with the middle one, that's the one that you said sort of reduces the other person to an object. Speculation was about . . .

H: The association of the visual with the rational. In other words, that there's a tradition, particularly in the eighteenth century of clear and distinct ideas. You can get a handle on something if it can be seen clearly. As long as it's a visual metaphor, not a hearing metaphor or . . .
T: Well, okay, I'll start there instead. I think that in my attempt to make poems that are imagistic, it is seeing that I think most about because I want to create a kind of seeing or vision that goes along with the speculative, or

the rational as you said. I'm drawn to doing that but also drawn to undercutting that because of the second one. The idea of observation. And that's a really personal one for me, and one that Ophelia deals with a lot because people believe that what they see is what is indeed there, and that there are signifiers or clues that should alert them to exactly the nature of the thing that they are looking at. And that's something that's bothered me so much, and it bothers Ophelia because, you know, I've grown up biracial and so I'm constantly "passing." Sometimes, when I was a child, intentionally. Most of the time now, inadvertently. And what I realize is that what people are seeing when they see me is always different. It's always changing, and it doesn't necessarily mesh with what I think is going on in the inside. And that's the thing she comes to realize. Ophelia doesn't have any sense of herself that's not rooted in the gaze of someone else. And so she doesn't realize how to construct an identity that's removed from what everyone else sees of her. So she tries to do a *tableau vivant* in order to be what it is that people want to see or think they're seeing. She tries to pass for white, because she thinks, well, that's what I look like, but she's constantly talking about how that's different than what's on the inside, and how those two finally come together. And I think that I'm drawn to thinking about seeing in that way because it's been in my life.

H: But many of your characters, especially the ones looking at Ophelia, also come to her . . . looking at her through their own glasses, obviously.
T: Yeah, when someone goes to the brothel that she's in, for example, they already expect to see a certain kind of person. They expect her to be a certain skin color, but at the same time, they expect her to have a sense of who she is because of that as well. Because they know she looks like this on the outside, but I know very well that on the inside she's black. And it's that invisible presence of blackness that Joseph Roach talks about that marks her flesh as a commodity even as it changes her value. Some of Storyville's houses were better situations to be set up in. The Octoroon houses, the really high class ones, like Countess Willie Piazza's house, are the kinds of places that one would want to get into even if one weren't an Octoroon. So imagine white women passing for Octoroon. Imagine a white woman passing for having black insides just to be at that house. What we're seeing is that that kind of decision-making about who someone is based on outward signifiers is dangerous.

H: The big question then, and I guess this is a question of how postmodern are you, is: is there a possibility that she will come out at the end of this with an authentic self?

T: I don't know about the word "authentic." I guess that's the dangerous word, but I would like to say that she has a little more of a sense of herself and that she can look inward and not always through someone else. She's not going to go have an out-of-body experience where she looks through the eyes of someone else into her own self. I think she may not need that lens anymore when she takes up the camera and all of a sudden she's directing her vision outward at someone else. There is that moment early on where Countess P—— says, "Train yourself not to look back." She is not in any way participating in the gaze by looking at someone else in the way that she is being looked at. Only when she starts to look through that lens does she look outward at others. And then at the very end, in the second to the last poem, "Self Portrait," she mentions that mistake of leaving the lens cover on. And so she sees the reflection of her eye, which is, of course, a metaphor for the eye being turned inward to the self. That's the moment that she first is able to do it. And it's probably not any grand authentic self, because I think she is constantly changing. The letters are an attempt to show the constantly changing self because they are written in different stanzas and lines and the forms are different. I almost felt like she was trying out different selves each time she wrote a letter to Constance. But I like to imply with the diary that there is perhaps some tiny little core of self that she didn't even realize she had, which is why the diary is written in very uniform fourteen lines.

H: There are a few ethical theorists who argue that's the way we find whatever authenticity we can find in the self. The way we do it is by imitation. It strikes me that one of the reasons she gets to be able to look at herself without going through the gaze of the other is precisely that she can't follow the advice. Or she can't ignore the gaze. She's just constitutionally incapable, she's too aware to do that.

T: She tries. She turns away from it, but she is aware that it's there. And she begins to be aware also, both of looking and also of signifiers and outward appearances. She thinks clothes are going to do it, she thinks manners will. She thinks she can say to the other girls, you are what you look like, which is not true. She thinks that she can dress up and go out into the street, but then she's recognized by someone as being from the brothel, so that sort of destroys that. "March 1912—Postcard, en route westward," is a tiny little postcard, and it's little haiku stanzas. So there's a kind of internal form being placed on her by the time she gets to the end. And it's in this poem that she is thinking that she can cast off the limitations of her own skin in some ways.

H: I was going to ask about her literary education and to what extent is she a poet, because you do talk about her in that way.

T: When I was embarking upon writing this character, I actually encountered lots of people who did not want to believe that such a character could exist. Because people sometimes have limited ideas about what's possible for the human spirit. So, for example, someone might say how could a black woman in 1912 be so literate? Well, how was Frederick Douglass? I mean, we forget that there are people who got enough of a start of some learning from someone, and then just because they wanted it so much and because they could find books here and there, that they continued to do it. So I set her up as someone who really has that desire, because that's the only way to the life that she can imagine. Her relationship with Constance is all about that. Constance is someone who does have an education, a black woman who went to a teacher's college like Tuskegee who would have been teaching in one of those small town schools that they had around the South at that point. I did a lot of research to make sure that it was feasible. Ophelia could have gone, as could whites in the South in Alabama and Mississippi, up until ninth grade. She chose to continue going and builds a relationship with Constance. I also read a book called *The Maimie Papers* that Ruth Rosen edited.[2] Maimie is the name that Rosen gave to protect the identity of a woman who was a Jewish prostitute around the same time living in Philadelphia. And as it happens, Maimie had the exact same amount of formal education, up until ninth grade, because her father was murdered then. She had to start working in the department stores, which in Philadelphia were sort of the gateway into prostitution for a lot of young girls. That's where they would meet young men. They had access to nicer clothing because they could buy things, and that's where it begins and that's sort of what happens to Maimie. But I even told this to someone once who said, "Well, you know, a Jewish woman could have been educated but not a black woman." So it's as if the person who said that was trying to be sympathetic. But it also really limits people in terms of their agency. It's as if there are certain people in history who have only been victims, never agents. And what I want to say is Ophelia has been victimized, but she is an agent, and she is making choices to get to where she wants to go.

H: The radical thing that you do is not buy into a rhetoric of absolute agency or absolute victimization.
T: Where would you go if you did that? There would be nothing to explore.

H: Basically what you are telling us as we try to be sympathetic, politically correct readers is that we're limiting her if we read her totally through that notion of victim.
T: You asked whether or not she was a poet. Even though she's writing letters and keeping a diary there is the artifice of the poem that I'm imposing on what she's saying. I do think, however, that Maimie's letters are very lyrical and poetic and she seemed to be someone who naturally made metaphor. And I think a lot of people do. There are a lot of country folks who speak metaphorically, and I grew up around those people. Within Black English and Black idiom, there is a lot of metaphor. So it occurs to me that that metaphorical, poetic speech that people have is natural for someone like Ophelia. And her level of diction is a little higher because she reads a lot: It's not so farfetched to imagine that we could have seen a letter from such a woman in a nice prose paragraph that was lyrical and imagistic and metaphoric.

H: So I gather from what you say that you would not like to have someone say that your poetic voice becomes identical with hers.
T: That wouldn't bother me. What would bother me is that someone see as a shortcoming of the book that Ophelia begins to be poetical in ways that are just not feasible, unbelievable for her as a character.

H: You have talked about what appears to be a fairly complicated relationship between your own voice and hers. And so I wondered if you could talk about that a little bit. You've touched on it already.
T: Well, I think that if I were to look at poems which are clearly closest to my own voice those would be the poems that are directly about looking at a photograph. So in the title poem, "Vignette," the last poem, I'd like to believe that I sound a little different from her. I mean there's a little bit more contemporary edge, I think, a language in those and in hers. I've tried to place her diction and some of the syntax and the tone of her speech in a different historical moment. And I think, if there's a possibility for the separation of her voice and mine it occurs in those things. It's funny, I don't know how this happened, but the first time I saw a review, someone said the only time Bellocq speaks in the whole book is in "Photograph of a Bawd Drinking

Raleigh Rye." So this poem was attributed to Bellocq, which I had not intended. But then I realized I was sending poems out individually before the book was a book. When I put his name right there, what I meant was that I was attributing the photograph to him, but because I've done it differently in other places, what happens is readers have attributed this to Bellocq's voice. I think it seems to have worked just fine, but I'm talking to myself in some ways in this poem and also to the reader who becomes implicated as reader, as viewer in the gaze. But of course it would make sense that Bellocq implicated himself in looking too, so it kind of works.

H: That's one of the many things that is so interesting about these poems. There is all this shifting back and forth between you looking at the photograph, Bellocq looking at the photograph, Ophelia looking at herself being photographed. You have all these gazes intersecting and sometimes switching. So we all seem to be involved in the same dynamic here somehow.
T: Right, all looking.

H: In my literary criticism class this morning we were serendipitously discussing an essay on the history of representations of Ophelia. We concluded with a brief discussion of your extension of this history, the title poem, "Bellocq's Ophelia," and one of my students pointed out that "unlike many feminist writers that deliberately conflate art and life, and by that I mean who see it as patriarchal to separate the aesthetic in a separate realm, Trethewey separates art and life only to reorient them in a new relation." If you could talk about that in terms of writing as a woman, as an African American woman, as a multiracial woman—how do you treat the aesthetic?
T: I kept focusing on the difference between art and life. And I think that's, of course, exactly the dichotomy that the poem "Bellocq's Ophelia" is about, because the poem begins with two still kinds of images, one in the painting by John Everett Millais and then the photograph by Bellocq. And it really is the kind of poem that I think people write a lot. I mean we might even say to students "Do a poem that is rooted in a comparison." But it also is rooted in a contrast. So I'm looking at the two photographs, the two images, the painting and the photograph, for the ways in which they are alike, and that's the first thing that I am struck by. But I also, because of research, know a little bit more, and so that's always where I enter. I can't simply look at any piece of art without thinking about its historical and social contexts, how it was made. You can't go and walk around Monticello and think, "Ooh how lovely," without thinking that there's something else here, and they're always bump-

ing up against each other. And there are ways in which they try to make you see only one part of that. I know that the woman who posed for Millais died of pneumonia afterwards. So she just becomes a mention in history books, but he was the artist. He made this thing that's lasting. Maybe you know about her, maybe you don't. Historically, women's roles in the service of art is clear in how mad people were at Victorine Meurent, who was the model who posed for Manet's "Olympia." Rather than really getting mad at Manet, people got mad at her because she was this brazen hussy who dared stare out of Manet's painting. With Bellocq's photographs, it just seemed natural then to imagine the circumstances of the woman who posed for him, because we don't know the names of those women. And not that Bellocq was trying to render them nameless or anything, but history has in some ways. So we don't know the conditions that she labored under in order for him to make this photograph. That became the comparison and then the difference, however, between the two of them. Of course, the third layering of imagery or story is that of Ophelia in *Hamlet* who at some point didn't have a furtherance of her own voice. She's cut off from that as is the woman who posed for Millais because she dies. So then there's the fourth layering, the next woman Ophelia, who is my character Ophelia, who actually can then speak where there has been no voice before.

H: Let's talk about language a little bit, because you do seem to have a thread of really being interested and having Ophelia be interested in language as a material thing. There just seems to be a strain of imagery that sees words as things. Am I right about that?

T: She does believe there's a tangible quality to words because you do actually feel the shape of them when you speak them. And she's really attuned to that, and she's attuned to it because she understands that in this whole idea of the making of the self, what words we own and how we own them and how we speak them has everything to do with who we might be or who we might become. So she's very much wanting to remember as many words as she can by making them an image—she wants the mnemonic device of an image—but also to feel the shape of each one. She practices sounding like her teacher, which is about how to shape the words in such a way to make them be a signifier for who you are. She is in the process of acquiring not only a sense of self in terms of seeing, but also a sense of self by having a voice. Which is why at that moment when she's asked to speak, to say what she wants, she's not yet seeing herself as someone who speaks, someone who has a voice at that moment. And so it startles her. She only has a voice to herself in letters, in her communication with Constance and then in her diary but not one that we think of as a larger voice that's going to be heard.

H: I was going to ask you just to talk about memory and forgetting a little bit, because one of the things that Nietzsche says is that the only way we have culture is by forgetting what's not there, and there's a lot of that rhetoric in photography as well.
T: I've been reading an historian named David Blight. He's got a book called *Race and Reunion*,[3] and it's all about the kinds of things that are forgotten, that are left out of the public, cultural memory. He says that certain kinds of remembering and willed forgetting are the stuff of historical memory. I've always been disturbed by historical memory as it was given to me in my high school and college history books, as it is given to me with the monuments that dot the landscape of my home, and the monuments that could be there but are not there. I'm interested in what is forgotten, what's willfully forgotten, those gaps within stories. It's about restoring some of the things that have been left out of even public records.

H: So talk more about what you are doing now.
T: Well, right now I'm working on a collection that's tentatively titled *Native Guard*, and *Native Guard* has both literal and figurative meanings. The literal is that the Native Guard refers to the Louisiana Native Guard who were the first officially sanctioned regiment of African American soldiers in the Civil War, the second regiment of which was stationed off the coast of my hometown of Gulfport, Mississippi. And out there on Ship Island they were primarily responsible for manning the fort, and the fort was run as a prison for Confederate soldiers. So many of these Native Guard, most of whom had been slaves only months before, were now charged with the duty of guarding these white Confederate prisoners. And it struck me that the irony is there may have been white soldiers who were invalids because of injury or even illiterate; that this African American soldier might have ended up writing letters for [them], much like Whitman did when he visited New York. By this time in the Civil War the Union army was taking on the responsibility of having someone write home to the families of deceased Union soldiers, letting them know that they had died. So this would be the soldier who would have that job, who might then begin to also write for these other people who want to send word back home. And it occurred to me that so much of history and what gets remembered is about who has that documentary power,

who's actually writing it down. That's who makes what we remember. Whoever erects the monuments makes the history. What happens if the person who's making it is someone who's part of the group who's not usually making it? There's a fear of dictating to someone if you can't check it, because you don't know what they're really going to say. At the same time, the guy who's writing it might want to embellish a little bit and to add some comfort for the people that he's writing home to. So I've envisioned that kind of relationship. Now the figurative part is that I see myself in some ways as a Native Guard of Mississippi. I'm thinking of the term "Native Daughter" that C. Vann Woodward uses when he talks about the early part of the twentieth century. It was the Daughters of the Revolution who were Native Daughters, and they were the ones responsible for making a lot of the public memory about the Civil War. They were erecting monuments, they were hosting events, remembrances, and non-Daughters were excluded from this act of public memory making. So, of course, I'm a non-Daughter because I'm not a Daughter of the Confederacy but I'm also a non-Daughter because in 1966 in Mississippi I would have been illegitimate because my parents' marriage was illegal. They weren't legally married. They broke the law by leaving the state to get married. When they came back, they were still breaking the law because you can't then come back having been married somewhere else. I was born there, so in terms of the law, I would not even be a true daughter of the home to which I am a real native. My birth certificate reads, "Race of Mother: Colored. Race of Father: Canadian." It's just so funny to think that someone, for whatever reason, decided to sort of skirt the truth a little bit. So even in documentary records, it's not written down. There's something left out of the historical record of my birth.

H: It's only the written record that gives legitimacy.
T: Right. So I have to write my way in, and it's also about asserting myself as part of one of the many traditions of poetry to which I belong. Southern poetry is indeed one of them. I have a poem called "Southern Pastoral" that I've worked on that's a dream poem. It's pretty tongue-in-cheek, but in it I'm dreaming that I'm taking a picture with the Fugitive poets and I'm right in the middle of the photograph, which would not have been the case, of course. There's the Fugitive sidestepping of race, as if we can just forget or ignore it, and it's not there. They've created a hole that I feel it is sort of my goal, my duty even, to fill. And it's not an antithetical relationship at all. I don't see my work as antithetical to a tradition of Southern poetry, but very

much a synthesis because those spaces are there. It's not like I'm creating them, I'm fitting something in. The spaces are there for what we will re-remember.

H: Filling in the gaps.
T: That same thing.

H: What do you read?
T: Right now I'm reading *Race and Reunion*. I'm also reading a collection of essays called *Jumpin' Jim Crow*. I'm reading Andrew Hudgins or I've just finished reading *After the Lost War*, because that's in the voice of Sidney Lanier who is a Confederate soldier and a poet that Hudgins imagines himself into. And, let's see, lots of books of poems. I read Robert Penn Warren's *Segregation* recently. I've been reading *The Mind of the South*. Oh, Eric Foner has a book called *Who Owns History*? I'm reading a lot of history right now, collections of letters from Civil War soldiers.[4]

H: It sounds like you keep a pretty rigorous reading and research schedule.
T: I struggle with it all the time, because I think there are some people who just sit down and write poems and they pluck them out of the universe. And I wish I could do that. But I don't. That happens to me occasionally, but mostly I have obsessions and things that I have to make sense of. And I think about James Baldwin saying, "This is the only real concern of the artist, to re-create out of the disorder of life that order which is art." What's pretty disorderly is how much willed forgetting is out there. And so I'm just trying to remember.

H: That art is creating order out of disorder is a fairly traditionalist formalist statement. At the same time, the way you define order as restoring what's been forgotten puts it into a whole different cultural register.
T: I was interested in an essay by Joel Brewer, "Cleo Rising," and he mentions Davis McCombs in it too, who, at the same time, was one of the editors for *Poetry* magazine. They got so many poems that were about the idea of "I look out of the window, and I am important," those lyrical poems that are really prevalent in contemporary poetry with some notable exceptions. I'm really interested in that, and I really do think there is a way to move beyond what might be narcissistic subject matter. I mean, Ophelia's exploration of mixed race identity and being looked at and all of those kinds of things are my issues, but how much different might it have been if I wrote all those poems just from my point of view. I think that somebody would really get

sick of it. I would too, that sort of lyrical self-investigation that we like to do so much. But I can't imagine doing it without a social and historical context. That actually influences all of our lives.

H: Reuniting the public and the private. You are doing both. Do you think things have changed in terms of the way poets show current events?
T: Well, I don't know how to answer that except to say I know that there are more and more people who are interested in research and historical research and in locating the poem or the poem's speaker within an actual historical moment. I was on a panel at AWP [Association of Writers and Writing Programs] about research in the creative writing classroom. And you would think that recent events would make it even more important to find a way not to see the self in a vacuum. How can you?

H: I guess one of the things that was surprising with the whole Laura Bush business was the idea that someone would say that poetry has nothing to do with politics.
T: Well, a lot of people think that. Poets are just supposed to be on the quest for beauty, right? And that doesn't really encompass the ugly of everyday.

H: But it has to do with those people outside, people who don't read contemporary poetry, who see poets as people that are isolated in universities, rather than public figures. And if you are isolated in the university, you should have nothing to do with politics.
T: Right. I read something recently about that, about the proliferation of creative writing programs, of MFAs, and it was around that time that poets became these people isolated within universities who weren't connected to anything else. My father is also a poet, a very working-class kind of poet from Canada, but also a full professor at Hollins. But for the longest time he's been teaching a class at the Roanoke City Jail, and several of the guys that had been inmates have gone on to publish some things here and there. You know, I've gone and done classes in the jails in Alabama. I think that there are people who would say that "The poet's job is only to the language, to making, to words and the service of that." But there are poets who are different than that. Phil Levine doesn't want to write a poem in which the words draw any attention to themselves, but instead he wants to write a poem in which they become transparent or a window through which you might clearly see the people. I do a lot of outreach as a poet, just myself going places and talking to schoolchildren and all kinds of people. And I hope that the poems do that too. What I really like is when someone who doesn't

read poetry because of some of the reasons we are talking about says, "You know, I read that, I read your poems and I actually liked them. I actually sat down and read the whole thing." One woman is a former vice-cop, someone who wouldn't pick another book of poems. She read *Bellocq's Ophelia*. She was a vice-cop, and that's why she liked it.

H: She probably was able to see some things that a non-vice-cop wouldn't see.

T: And you know, I don't think that poems are just pretty little things that don't do anything. Now I don't think they are changing the world, or doing anything like that, but I think that here and there you might change one person's mind about something. And I know that this must be true because of the numbers of people who seem to have been angry with me in their remarks on Amazon.com. They say things like they see *Domestic Work* as just being about race, that I'm constantly throwing up these race narratives in your face. But that's because they can only see them that way. The moment that they know that this is a black writer, they are not going to see anything but that. So the fact that I've made some people mad means . . .

H: . . . you've done something.

T: I'm not afraid when someone says there's a political content. We don't like to use the word "agenda" because that sounds bad, but "obsession" sounds like what all poets have. So I use that word instead of agenda.

Notes

1. Roland Barthes, "Rhetoric of the Image," *Image Music Text*, 44, qtd. in Martin Jay, *Downcast Eyes: The Denigration of Vision in Twentieth-Century French Thought* (Berkeley: U of California P, 1993), 443.

2. Ruth Rosen, ed., The *Maimie Papers: Letters from an Ex-Prostitute* (Bloomington: Indiana UP, 1985; rpt. New York: The Feminist Press: at CUNY, 1997).

3. David W. Blight, *Race and Reunion: The Civil War in American Memory* (Cambridge, MA: Belknap P, 2002).

4. Jane Daily, et al., ed., *Jumpin' Jim Crow* (Princeton: Princeton UP, 2000); Andrew Hudgins, *After the Lost War* (New York: Houghton Mifflin, 1989); Robert Penn Warren, *Segregation: The Inner Conflict in the South* (New York: Random House, 1956); W. J. Cash, *The Mind of the South* (New York: Vintage P, 1991); Eric Foner, *Who Owns History?: Rethinking the Past in a Changing World* (New York: Hill and Wang, 2003).

Natasha Trethewey—Decatur, Georgia

W. T. Pfefferle / 2004

From W. T. Pfefferle, *Poets on Place: Tales and Interviews from the Road*, foreword by David St. John (Logan: Utah State University Press, 2005), 163—65. The interview was conducted on 5 March 2004 in Decatur. Reprinted with permission from Utah State University Press.

No city offers a more stunning transition from its ring of highways and interstates to its inner hub of suburban plots. Coming into Atlanta is like driving on the Ugly Highway to Ugly Town. The gray slabs extend to four and five lanes in every direction. Cloverleaf after cloverleaf—almost all of them under construction—web together endlessly. The pines that line the road obscure everything else that might resemble a place where one would want to spend some time; and the cars just hurtle onward, onward, deadeye stare, smoldering tires, eighteen-wheelers pinning you in one lane or the other.

But once you leave that behind—and in our case, skirt the southern bypass and then slip into Avondale Estates—large sweeping yards and one-story ranch houses line each road. Businesses cluster at intersections; but as soon as you leave them behind, you are back in another pleasant neighborhood. They all have churches with towering steeples, small parks with grinning kids. Houses are brick, surrounded by bushes and trees.

We find Decatur, another beautiful suburb. Natasha Trethewey has told us there's a church parking lot near her, and we find it easily. I stroll across the street to a two-story, weathered-brick building. It's from the '30s, was a boarding house for years, and is now a set of small but cozy condos. I poke my foot in the black dirt along a walkway and straighten some pink and yellow pansies that look like they're fixing to go across the road. When they're back in place, I go to the front door.

Natasha buzzes me up, and I meet her and her husband. We stand in their glittering kitchen—not just spectacularly clean, but ringed with stainless steel appliances—and then Natasha and I go and sit on two overstuffed couches in the living room.

She was born in Mississippi and now makes her home next door in Georgia. While she's spent time elsewhere, she's back home in a sense here in suburban Atlanta. She feels totally at ease in this pretty New South suburb.

W. T. Pfefferle: Do you think the places of your life had an impact on the poet you're becoming?
Natasha Trethewey: I do. I think that it's true for so many people who come out of Mississippi. If you're born into a place like that with that landscape and that history, because it's so troubled, it fuels you, trying to grapple with that beautiful and troubled history. The landscape where I'm from—Gulfport, Biloxi, Ocean Springs—has the longest man-made beach in the world—twenty-six miles. It used to be a mangrove swamp, so they bulldozed that and dumped sand there to make it more like a beach resort you'd see in Florida. And that seems so metaphorical for me, because there's so much buried history—people's lives who have been left out of the public record and people whose lives have been erased. And if you look at the landscape, it suggests that. There's so much of the natural and man-made landscape of my home that reveals and conceals at the same time. For example, they've gotten rid of the swamp, put all this sand there, and then put all these sickly looking palm trees, trying to make it look like a different kind of beach. They point to and suggest something else that is beneath the surface. They point to a kind of evidence or a way to dig below and see below the layer of sand that's been dumped there.

WTP: You spent a great deal of your life in the South; has there ever been the thought in your head that you might not remain here?
NT: I went to the Northeast for graduate school, and I lived in Massachusetts for six years. I often thought that I could have stayed. I didn't expect to come back to the South. When I did come back every year to see my grandmother, I came with a weird chip on my shoulder. After having been in the Northeast for a while, you begin to internalize ideas that Northerners have about the South; and I came down here with the same ones. *(Laughs.)* Not that there's nothing to complain about.

I think about the monuments. How the narrative that they have tried to impose upon the landscape is of the Confederacy. You see it in the town squares and public buildings that are named for Confederate heroes. The monuments, the graveyards, the flag still flying. That's the narrative that's been inscribed upon the landscape, and I think it takes a different kind of narrative to reveal what has been covered over. Narratives of Native Americans, for whom many of these states are named, the rivers. It's a weird contrast of the naming of those things and, say, the naming of roads. Jeff Davis Highway.

WTP: In your second book, *Bellocq's Ophelia*, you write about the life of a New Orleans prostitute from the turn of the twentieth century. Obviously you had to do a fair amount of research, not just into Bellocq's photographs, but also into the time period.
NT: I did a lot of research. Gulfport is only about an hour from New Orleans. My father did his PhD at Tulane, so as a child I spent a lot of time in New Orleans. I had a certain image of it in my head and a certain idea of what things were like there. The climate, the way the air smells there. It has a scent that's different from anywhere else.

One thing I did was actually go and spend a month there, because I wanted to be reminded of all of that and to be reminded of that little thundershower that happens at the same time every day. And then it's gone, and it's sweltering. The photographs were my main documents, but I read actual published letters of a real prostitute who lived in Philadelphia—but at the same time—renamed "Maimie" for the collection. I read lots of histories of New Orleans, histories of prostitution, theories of prostitution. Histories and theories of photography. I also read the kind of thing you might find in almanacs, stuff about the mosquitoes in a certain year. Stuff about sewage, the cisterns, stuff about rats in New Orleans. And the cockroaches!

WTB: Are there elements of the natural world that have a role in your work as a poet?
NT: My landscape was always the natural world sliced or divided or undercut by a highway. The first place that I called home, and the place I return to the most, is my grandmother's home. Her house is in an area of North Gulfport that for a very long time was very rural. Highway 49 runs through it, but it was just a tiny little highway that blues singers would sing about. There were still lots of people who had farm animals around. I remember pigs underneath the house and chickens from someone's yard. Cows in the yard. And that changed rapidly when they built the new Highway 49. The old highway was on one side of her house, a few blocks away, but they built the new one right next to her house. Some men came and asked her—this must have been in the early '70s—if they could put up a billboard, and one of the big poles was going to be right in her yard. I think they paid her a hundred dollars a year for that.

That's what it was like for me. There was this rural world with fig trees, pecan trees, and persimmon trees, turtles. But there were eighteen-wheelers zooming through at the same time.

Interview: Natasha Trethewey on Facts, Photographs, and Loss

Sara Kaplan / 2006

From *Fugue* (University of Idaho) number 32 (Winter–Spring 2007), 66–74. The interview was conducted in October 2006 in Moscow, Idaho. Reprinted by permission.

Sara Kaplan: Poets find their inspiration from any number of sources—paintings and songs, for example. American history, or more specifically, southern American history, seems to be from where you draw much of your inspiration. Your poems reinterpret our history, however, not from the stance of an historian; rather, history allows you to create new language. In terms of your writing process, how much and how often do you commit yourself to researching your subjects? When does the research end and, you, the poet, begin?

Natasha Trethewey: I spend a lot of time doing research. In *Native Guard*, I had a historical question in mind about historical erasure. I began my research by reading American historians and looking at letters from soldiers during the Civil War, now housed at the Library of Congress.

In my second book, *Bellocq's Ophelia*, I looked in archival blue books as well as photographs. I feel, though, that there is a real danger in absorbing too much of the history and, in effect, the poems could risk sounding like history essays. Ezra Pound uses the term "luminous details" to describe how we extract from history, from our reading in history, and how those details become transcendental. The details help the poem to be more than a little essay in history. I think of those luminous details. A visual equivalent is Roland Barthes's theory of the punctum in a photograph. This is the spark, the thing that makes you begin to think of what's outside of the frame, and beyond what's captured in the photograph. I start with what's not there. The photograph shows everything that I can see, but there's also everything I can't see. What I can't see is what really interests me.

37

SK: And from there you begin to create a poetic story?

NT: Yes, from that absence, those gaps in history—those spaces that are yet to be filled in.

SK: Do you ever feel as if the research overwhelms the poems? How do you know when and where to omit facts or history?

NT: This was a problem when I was writing *Bellocq's Ophelia*. I learned a lot about the balance of historical facts and prosody during that time. I read not only history while researching for that book, but also theory. This got me into trouble. When thinking theoretically about photography and the gaze, I would sit down sometimes and write poems that sounded like theory. At a certain point, I realized I had absorbed as much theory as I could. I also don't have a great memory. However, I had read and underlined and I hoped that I would be able to recall the theory and facts. I pushed all the history and the theory aside and didn't look at it again until I began to revise and needed to fact-check. I don't want to misrepresent something, make it anachronistic. Therefore, when revising, I try to use whatever I've absorbed from the facts and theory, but also focus on the imagery. For example, I was trying to write a poem and it was sounding like an essay in theory about photography and I finally scratched through it and I wrote, "Stop it! Stop trying to write this theory and look at the photographs again." All I would allow myself to do was to look at the image.

SK: Dates appear frequently in your poems, particularly in *Bellocq's Ophelia*, but also in *Native Guard*. The dates in *Bellocq's Ophelia*, for example, evoke a journalistic quality since the poems are also letters. When you're writing, does the accuracy of dates and history and facts interfere with your creative energies? As poet, what kinds of liberties do you take with historical data?

NT: When writing *Domestic Work*, I felt the need to use dates because the poems are about my maternal grandmother and her life and work in Mississippi beginning in 1937. It occurred to me that her opportunities, the possibilities that existed in her life, had everything to do with a particular historical moment and her life as a domestic worker. The dates provide a very important context for the poem that should point readers to that historical moment that exists outside of the poem. This is why I started using dates. For example, in "Speculation 1939," I felt I could be flexible because the poem needed to be connected to the historical moment, the New Deal, which connects to the speaker's idea of imagining a better life for herself.

In *Native Guard*, I had a difficult time with dates because of the title poem, the sequence, "Native Guard," which is heavily annotated in the back of the book. Even though the speaker is an imagined character, the events surrounding him were real. There are moments that I discovered that I had written something and the date that I had assigned to the poem wouldn't make sense with the historical events occurring in the poem. Therefore, I had to go back and make sure when the speaker is talking about one thing, it is what the speaker could have known. I don't know that I felt limited by it. I think it was an important way of getting at truth. Even though dates suggest a factual kind of truth, my desire to inscribe these stories of soldiers who were often forgotten or lesser known onto our landscape of our cultural memory, I needed to adhere to some of the facts so the imagined voice could take on the weight of a historical document.

SK: And the dates and the facts start to resonate with the poems. I like your idea of recalling the truth.
NT: If an audience wonders if the poems are true and asks, "Did it happen?," I say, "Maybe (pauses). Is it true? Yes." Because I'm interested in historical memory, I don't feel like I can contribute to that by being historically inaccurate. I want to get as close to what is plausible or what could have been.

SK: *Bellocq's Ophelia* and *Native Guard* are cohesive as books, but the poems also stand alone. When you compose poems, do you consider a larger manuscript or do you write poems and then see how they might work together?
NT: I like to think of myself as a poet who writes not collections of poems, but books of poems. I have always been this way. When I was in graduate school, I wanted to envision a work as an integral whole, and I remember talking to my thesis advisor who said to me, "Just who do you think you are? You just need to go in your little apartment and gather up every single poem you've ever written and throw them up in the air, and wherever they land, scoop 'em up and that's your book of poems." That bothered me so much because I felt like the books I had admired, the things I had read seemed to be whole because they weren't simply made up of disparate parts. And I think they were whole because we have obsessions. My obsessions are driving every individual poem I write. I like doing research. I like setting my mind to some new thing I want to find out about. I like occupying my time with reading history about this or that, so I tend to set myself a goal with some question I am asking. In my mind, all the research I do is swirling around trying to answer that question I've given myself.

Another way of thinking about what I do—do you remember in the 1970s they made these picture cubes of plexi-glass and you could slide a photograph in every surface of the cube and you could look at each individual photograph, you could hold it up and turn it around.

SK: Like a kaleidoscope? I was born in the 1980s. Are you referring to one of the Fisher Price camera toys?
NT: Well, no, it's just a plexi-glass cube where you could see each part that made up the whole of the cube. At the center of that cube, there is the question, that obsession, that thing that's driving me and each facet of the cube, each surface. Each poem is trying to connect to the others to create a whole. Each poem is like a separate answer and they're all necessary. And if you take out one of them, there's going to be a blank space. Because I write like that, I can very easily see what's missing so that the book becomes a whole.

SK: The stillness of the body seems to be important in all of your books. In "What the Body Can Say" in *Native Guard*, you write, "What matters is context—" Can you speak about how you bring context to the stillness of a body—whether it's in a photograph or someone dying?
NT: I think you're right to point to the idea of the stillness of the body in photographs, or the stillness of a body represented in a statue. I always look at those things and then desire to animate them at the same time. The very first poem in *Domestic Work* is about a photograph where the woman wasn't holding as still as you're supposed to be and she moved. There's a white swirl and this made me think that there is that photographic stillness, but there's also something in her gesture that animates her. This doesn't trap her in time and space so much as it allows her to enter into our own time and space interactively. What matters are how things are juxtaposed.

SK: Your lines are beautifully metered and this musicality lends the poems to being read aloud. You also employ a lot of forms. However, in your series of sonnets in "Native Guard" and the villanelle, "Incident," you also play with these forms. Can you speak about the benefits as well as the difficulties of using regular meter and form in terms of composition, but also reading poetry aloud?
NT: I'd like to believe that I have a good ear, but an intuitive ear, and that's perhaps a blessing and a curse. I can remember being in New Orleans years ago with my father when I was just starting out and thinking of myself as someone who wanted to write poems seriously. My father and I were walk-

ing through the quarter and through some open doors we could hear strains of music coming out and when we walked by one door there was a woman singing. We could hear her and I remarked that she sounded beautiful, but that I hated that I couldn't sing. My father said, "You can't sing? How can you be a poet if you can't sing?" I carried that around with me for a long time asking myself that very question, "How can I be a poet if I'm not musically inclined in that way?" And that's when I began to realize I was musically inclined but it manifested itself differently.

I think of myself as someone who has a hard time with meter and scansion, with my own or other people's. It doesn't come naturally to me. I have to work at it very, very hard because I don't hear that way. I'm definitely a foot-tapper. When I read I'm tapping my feet because there is a music that I'm hearing. Writing sonnets in syllabics is one way that I think that I have harnessed whatever my own music might be or my connection to meter. I decided that I would first focus on a ten-syllable line and then I was hoping that being an English-speaking person who had read a lot of literature in English, the natural cadence of iambic pentameter might come through. But it was training myself to think in a ten-syllable line that allowed me to do that and once I did it, once I became comfortable in it, it was there.

I wish that prosody had been part of my M.F.A. experience. I think there are probably some places where they do teach classes in prosody; I just didn't go to one of them.

SK: Who are the poets you find helpful or influential and why?
NT: For *Native Guard*, in particular, I modeled my work after writers whose work was very important as a way of showing me into my own. Primarily I read Irish poets like Seamus Heaney and Eavan Boland because of their connection to place and to their geographies. The histories of those places for Boland, in particular, helped me discover what's left out or what needs to be given voice. I wrote my poem, "South" after spending a lot of time reading "North," the title poem of Heaney's book, *North*. I have a colleague who had helped to get Heaney's papers at Emory and he knew that I liked him, so he gave me copies of all of the drafts of "North" and I could see Heaney's thought process, what he was doing, and that poem spoke to me so much that I started writing "South" after reading it.

SK: I've noticed that photographs appear in all of your books. But you do more than translate an image. In *Domestic Work*, the first poem addresses a photograph, but there is movement beyond the photograph as you write, "the white blur of her apron/ still in motion." Bellocq's photographs of prostitutes inspired your second book, *Bellocq's Ophelia*. *Native Guard* begins with a photograph: "the photograph—who you were—." What is your relationship to photographs? Have they always fascinated you? How do you think they inform your poetry?

NT: I think I have always been obsessed with photographs for a couple of reasons. First, I never liked being in them, which is odd because I love them so much. I love them for their narrative possibilities, I love how they both reveal a version of something, but also conceal countless other versions. They speak most to me about absence, about what's not there, what's outside, what's behind. I thought for a long time that because the way people appear in photographs, because they're gestural, because we see people's bodies in a still motion of some sort that we can read into photographs who people are and where they're going. They carry so much figurative meaning.

A good example of this is a photograph that I have of my family when I was about ten years old. It's a photograph of my mother, my stepfather, me, and my brother. My brother is probably not even two years old. In the photograph it's obviously summertime because we're in shorts and my mother was wearing a little shorts jumpsuit-thing that was so '70s. We're at a relative's house, sitting on the sofa. This is not long after my mother had married my stepfather and then had my brother. It was around the same time that my stepfather told my mother that he wanted to adopt me so that I would have his name. I remember telling my mother that I didn't want to do that, and I wanted to keep my last name, my father's last name. Nothing was ever said about it, but I think that my stepfather resented that. Because I had a different name I was, in many ways, outside of the family. In this photograph, I am sitting on the far end of this eight-foot sofa on the right and they're all down on the left side. My mother and stepfather were both wearing big afros at the time because it was the 1970s and they're leaning toward each other looking at my brother who is standing up and balancing on the coffee table in between them. Their afros are touching and it creates this little triangle above him while I'm way down at the other end of the sofa. I think that photograph said everything about what it was like in that house at that time. And my position in it.

SK: What advice would you give to poets trying to publish individual poems as well as full-length manuscripts?

NT: To echo what a lot of editors would say, and perhaps you would say this too, Sara, it helps to read the journals you intend to submit your poems to. It sounds like bland advice, but it's true. I've actually had experiences of reading a journal and being so taken by a poem that they've published that it inspired me to write a poem of my own, and indeed that journal took it. There's a conversation that journals are having and you get to know something about the kind of work they're publishing if you read it before submitting your own work. I think that's very necessary. I'm not an experimental poet and it might be a waste of my time if I'm only sending my work to journals that are very interested in experimental poetics. To be familiar with the journal is very important.

I also think that even as you're sending around a manuscript it's good to be sending individual poems out too because you are developing an audience that way too. If your poems are appearing in different journals you begin to develop a large audience of people out there who have encountered your poems and they might actually go and buy your collection when you have it. I also think when you read particular poets you admire whose work is the kind of work that you want your work to be like or you see some kind of connection between your work and that poet's work, I think it's good to read the acknowledgments page and see where they've published those poems. That can help give you a sense of where you might send your poems.

You also know how it is these days. Most first books get published through those contests. Few places still have open reading periods for unsolicited manuscripts, but there are some of the contests that wonderfully will not only publish the winner of the contest but some of the runners up too. You almost get more for your money by paying their reading fee because there's more of a shot of being published.

SK: You write, "in my native land, this place they'll bury me" in "South," the final poem in *Native Guard*. Oftentimes we search endlessly for a place to call our own, through our memories, through photographs, a place to live and finally die. Sometimes we struggle against the very place that we love even though that's what we know the best. How do you think poetry can help us find our place in a land we may not fully understand?
NT: In dealing with my particular place, my South, my Mississippi, I have always felt exiled. It's psychological more than physical. I live in the Deep South, I'm still there. I know that it's my place, but it's also not my place because of its history. There are things that would seek to make it not mine. But the poems allow me to own it. To call it mine. To love it and hate it very publicly and the poems create a space in which to reenter the site of exile

and be home inside it. It's the poem that's the thing that we're in home inside of, all of us exiles in some way. Inside the poem I am most at home.

SK: If there's a question that you haven't been asked in this interview or other interviews, what would you like to be asked and what would your response to that question be?
NT: The things that come to my mind are things that I get upset about because I feel that many aspects of my poetry are being overlooked. I don't always feel like my work is taken as whole or that I'm taken as a whole. Perhaps this is a condition of being biracial. I feel that there is often a fragmented perception of my work and people can only focus on some part of it. If you listen to some people, you'd be misled to think that this book is only about history or you'd be misled to think that this book is only about my experience growing up mixed race in Mississippi.

People tend to speak less of the elegiac quality of the book, that the book is about my mother, that everything in it, actually, is a way of making sense of what's buried. And what has no marker. No inscription on the landscape to remember. My mother doesn't have a tombstone. She is like those Native Guards. I want someone to say, "Natasha Trethewey is an elegiac poet." But people say I write only about race. That's what they say about black writers all the time. I'm just writing about the people I know about, the people to whom I belong. Nobody says any white poets are writing about the white race because whiteness isn't a race to people, but it just so happens that people in my poems are black, so people say I'm writing about race. But, no. I'm writing about loss, history, and what's forgotten. However, it's always seen through some lens of blackness or race and I think that is a barrier to some readers, but not all of them. Some will only read through that lens and not see I'm many things at once: black, mixed, southern, woman, a daughter, a motherless child, all at once. If I didn't have blackness, people would go to the next thing, the next thing to focus on, but blackness just stands out there like the eight-foot gorilla in the room.

SK: Or a white elephant.
NT: Or one of each.

An Interview with Natasha Trethewey

Pearl Amelia McHaney / 2007

From *Five Points: A Journal of Literature & Art* (Georgia State University) 11.3 (2007), 96–115. Reprinted by permission.

Natasha Trethewey's subject is history: hers; her mother's—Gwendolyn Ann Turnbough; her mother's tragic death at the hands of a divorced second husband; the Louisiana Native Guards—freed slaves serving the Union by guarding Confederate soldiers imprisoned at Fort Massachusetts on Ship Island in the Gulf of Mexico; the Fugitive Poets and the canon of Southern poetry; and the South—its continuing struggle to accept its story. In poems both elegiac and elegant, Trethewey tells these stories and writes the forgotten into history. She is the author of *Domestic Work* (Graywolf 2000), winner of the inaugural 1999 Cave Canem poetry prize selected by Rita Dove, and *Bellocq's Ophelia* (Graywolf 2002), which received the 2003 Mississippi Institute of Arts and Letters Book Prize and was a finalist for the Academy of American Poets' James Laughlin and Lenore Marshall prizes.

Moving from outside to inside, from tea to prosecco, from Indie Bookstore to Café Lily in Decatur, Georgia, we talked together on May 14, 2007, one month after the Pulitzer Prize award for Trethewey's third book, *Native Guard*, a quintessentially American book.

McHaney: Congratulations on winning the 2007 Pulitzer Prize for Poetry for *Native Guard* (March 2006). It is a book so deserving that your readers are thrilled for the thousands more readers who will be drawn to these poems. Several years ago, maybe in 2002 at the Society for the Study of Southern Literature in Lafayette, Louisiana, after reading from your second book, *Bellocq's Ophelia*, you answered a question about your next project saying that you wanted to discover your own voice, that having written from Ophelia's point of view, you wished to see the world through your own lens. Then you read "Miscegenation," a poem about your white father and black

mother, about your naming, essentially about who you are after telling us so much about Ophelia, who is partly you even though you directed us away from yourself, unlike in *Domestic Work* and unlike in *Native Guard*.
Trethewey: Right, because a persona poem, like any poem, has a mask, but the mask seems somehow thicker. I think you are allowed to investigate the self a little bit more comfortably behind the thicker mask, the distant historical mask of a persona.

McHaney: I like that idea of masking. Tell us about the genesis of *Native Guard*, about the first poems that became part of the book, and about its organization.
Trethewey: When I first started thinking about writing *Native Guard*, it was my interest in the history of the Louisiana Native Guards that got me going. I had gone out to visit my grandmother in Gulfport, right after I started my first job at Auburn University. I took her out to lunch at a restaurant on the beach, and I was talking to her about a creative writing assignment that I was going to give my students in which you get them to write about a time when a relative met someone famous. I was telling her that I was going to do this assignment, too, about her story, about the time her brother, my great uncle, met Al Capone. Uncle Hubert was a bellhop at a hotel on the beach, and he shook Al Capone's hand. Al Capone used to go down there when he was running a gambling joint out of the fort at Ship Island. As I am telling my grandmother this, there's a woman who is listening the whole time to our conversation. And I think it is particularly important to mention because of what she said that this is a white woman listening to our conversation. And as she gets up to leave the restaurant, she leans over and she says, "I think there is something else you need to know about Ship Island." It was very much like she was saying, "There's this other history about these black soldiers that you should know as part of your history as well," and so she told me about them. I went right away to the Gulfport Public library to try to look up something about them. And the first thing I found was a small mention in someone's M.A. thesis. And then later on of course I found the full length monograph by James G. Hollandsworth that I mention in the notes in the book as well as the published diary of the colonel who was stationed there that C. P. Weaver edited. But I was interested in this because I had been going out to that island my whole life and the park rangers don't mention anything about the black presence on the island. There isn't any marker mentioning the Native Guards or their presence the way there is for the Confederate soldiers who were imprisoned there. And that suggested to

me a kind of historical erasure from the manmade monumental landscape. I was interested in telling that story, telling a fuller version of our story as Americans in this pivotal moment in history.

McHaney: You said that originally you thought you were working on poems that would lead to two separate books, about the Louisiana Native Guards and then the ones that become the elegies for your mother Gwendolyn Ann Turnbough. When did you realize the confluence of the two projects? When did you realize that these personal poems could successfully frame the public poems about the Louisiana Native Guards?

Trethewey: That took a long time for me to recognize. When I went to Radcliffe on a Bunting Fellowship in 2000, I was still thinking about the soldiers. And I was doing a lot of the research about historical memory, the Civil War, and the idea of what gets memorialized in the form of monuments. It seems to me that should have alerted me to something that was on my mind, but it didn't. I was writing, at the same time as these poems, about my mother. Sometimes they would be just a portion of a poem that I wouldn't finish until years later. But I started writing some of them and putting them away in a drawer because I thought, well that's for another thing, another time. I couldn't see how, at the time, they would have anything to do with this larger project that was only about something historical. And maybe because I was coming off the heels of *Bellocq's Ophelia*, still thinking only about a kind of public history, I didn't see the connections, even though what I do in *Bellocq's Ophelia* is to find a way to weave a personal history into what is my imagined history for her.

McHaney: Ophelia moves from in front of the camera, being objectified, to behind the camera, choosing what she takes a picture of, what she sees. It is a similar kind of movement.

Trethewey: Right, the same kind of journey I was taking, but I didn't know that. I did start publishing a lot of those elegies, but I was still thinking they didn't belong. I think I remember at one point feeling that I was coming close to having a new book, and there I was writing all of those things, and I started to think, well, could they go together? But I still didn't know.

McHaney: Didn't know that you would be able to have a first section that were the elegies to your mother and that at the same time they were leading to the Native Guards poems and then that they would be so interwoven by the third section?

Trethewey: Well, I started thinking that a poem like "Miscegenation" and some poems that I was writing about my own personal history as a biracial person growing up in the Deep South had a connection to the history of the Native Guards because I saw that the umbrella over them was something about the South. I still hadn't connected those elegies for my mother. In the meantime, I was living here in Atlanta. Returning to the landscape that was haunted by the tragedy of my mother's death made me write these elegies. I wrote a poem for the book early on called "Graveyard Blues" after jogging through the little Decatur cemetery and being overwhelmed by all the names of the dead. I am one of those people who can't just walk through a graveyard. I feel like I have to read every single name that presents itself to me, and it seemed like a good metaphor for the insistence of history, or for the insistence of people to be heard or their stories to be told, or even their names to be registered or spoken. And so even seeing those names, I was still thinking: this is about history. But the poem I wrote was about the memory of the day we buried my mother. The final image in the poem, the final two lines, reads:

> *I wander now among names of the dead:*
> *My mother's name, stone pillow for my head.*

That's an image of hard, or cold comfort. I might want to lie my head down on my mother's stone and that would be a kind of comfort, but one that was stone and cold. A few months later, I could not, I could not simply deal with the fact that I had written those two lines in that poem because I felt that whatever obligation I have to truth was being sacrificed by the poem. So I started writing another poem to undo the lie that I told in "Graveyard Blues." My mother does not have a stone or any marker at all. There's no marker, no memorial at her grave, and so I started writing the poem "Monument" because I wanted to tell the reader that I had lied about this. It was stunning to me when I realized that I had, for the sake of one poem, told a lie and needed to fix it in another one. But it was the realization that I needed to fix the lie that made me realize exactly why those elegies to my mother should be in the same book with the Native Guards. Like them, she had no marker.

McHaney: You arrived at it through a kind of journeying; it evolved in a very natural way. Maybe that is one aspect of your genius, the weavings and stitchings and cross-hatchings all together. That was the work that you had to do.
Trethewey: Well, perhaps it is the genius of poetry. Robert Frost said, "No

surprise for the writer, no surprise for the reader." It is absolutely true that I didn't set off knowing exactly what I wanted to say, and when I figured it out, it was because the writing of the poems led me to it. It was stunning for me, too, and painfully so.

McHaney: You dedicate *Native Guard* to your mother, in memory, and the book is the elegies for your mother, the weaving together the personal and the public histories, the erasures and the monuments and the memorial. And then, moving backward, you dedicated your second book *Bellocq's Ophelia* to your husband, Brett Gadsden, historian, professor of African American studies at Emory University. And your first book *Domestic Work*, going back further, you dedicated to your father, Eric Trethewey, a poet, who teaches at Hollins University. In *Domestic Work*, the second section of four is dedicated to your mother's mother, your grandmother: "For Leretta Dixon Turnbough, born June 22, 1916," who is still living. Yet, Rita Dove introduces *Domestic Work* saying, that you "resisted the lure of autobiography . . . weaving no less than a tapestry of ancestors." In *Domestic Work*, reading it now again, I see many autobiographical seeds.
Trethewey: Oh, absolutely.

McHaney: But they are masked just as you said earlier. In "Tableau," for example, the beautiful line "—sees for the first time,/the hairline crack/that has begun to split the bowl in half." And there are poems about your father, your Uncle Son and Aunt Sugar. So what changed? Even though you've explained how *Native Guard* came about, what changed even in those jottings and those poems that you would so explicitly write about the private anxieties and grief experienced by your family, so that you were no longer passing, in a sense, when you were addressing your biraciality, your grief, the tragedies?
Trethewey: Rita did a wonderful thing for me in writing what she did about the larger public history that is represented by the poems in *Domestic Work*, particularly "Domestic Work" the section. When I started writing those, I really just wanted to write about my grandmother who has lived an extraordinary life. So I thought I was doing a very personal family history. But early on I started placing the events of her life within the context of a particular historical moment. Without understanding the depth of my obsessions, I was already, by using dates or other historical events within the poems, working to blend personal or family stories with collective history. Maybe her taking note of that helped me to see it as a long term obsession of mine.

McHaney: You said a little bit about how being back here in the physical landscape where the tragedies happened didn't let you escape them. Did your studies at University of Massachusetts, Amherst, influence your shift to the autobiographical?

Trethewey: James Tate once said to me to unburden myself of my mother's death and unburden myself of being black and just write about the situation in Northern Ireland. And I was devastated when he said that. John Edgar Wideman said to me, "You have to write about what you have to write about." But at another point some advice that Tate gave me was to just pour my heart out into the poems, and so by the time I was writing *Native Guard*, I was indeed pouring my heart out into the poems. But I was also not abandoning the very things "I'd been given to write," to use Phil Levine's phrase. I don't know what I would have written if I hadn't written about those things that I have been grappling with my whole adult life.

McHaney: You have also said, "We must identify with the despised parts of ourselves."

Trethewey: I think writing some of the elegies and perhaps even thinking about my place in the South had a lot to do with approaching the anniversary of my mother's death. I was approaching the twentieth anniversary, at the same time approaching my fortieth birthday which was the last age my mother ever was, and so I think those things were heavy on my mind. And perhaps returning to the South after many years in the Northeast made me rethink Southern history, American history, and my place in it, because I can get really angry about my South. Though I love it, it has given me plenty of reason to hate it. And one of the things that I hate, not just about the South but the way Americans remember things, is that so much of that memory is based upon a kind of willed forgetting and there's a lot that gets left out—of the historical record, of textbooks, of public monuments. I wanted to tell a fuller version of what stories I have to add to the historical record.

McHaney: Even as you are speaking of filling in the record or correcting the record, you are still in a sense talking of that public record. And now with these personal elegies, you are, as you have said, writing yourself into history. Your stories—your personal and family stories, stories of your mother, the wonderful lovely things that she did, the sweet moments as well as the tragedies—are also now being told and are therefore part of the public story.

I'd like to ask about some of those personal pieces to fill out that record. In a poem in *Domestic Work*, "Early Evening, Frankfort, Kentucky," you de-

scribe yourself "not yet born, only/a fullness beneath the empire waist/of my mother's blue dress" and your parents "young and full of laughter,/the sounds in my mother's throat/rippling down into my blood." Are you, then, their love child, conceived before they had to leave the South to marry in Ohio as you describe in "Miscegenation"?
Trethewey: Yes, indeed. I'm saying that on record.

McHaney: Readers can figure it out, of course, but it is there to be discovered or to be wondered about or to recognize that there is love.
Trethewey: Yes.

McHaney: You've talked of the lie about your mother's grave, but I had interpreted that there was a stone, but no name, and you are telling me now that it is an even deeper lie: there is no stone. Are there other places that you tell a story other than what you know to be true? We expect you to use poetic license, but this is complicated in such autobiographical poems.
Trethewey: There is an expectation of a different kind of truth. And even in the poem ["Monument"] where I tried to reveal the lie I told, I actually had a line that read, "Forgive me that I lied when I said. . . ." That line gets edited out of the poem, and what is left is the image of an untended grave, not an unmarked one, but one that hasn't been tended to, so the metaphor is that I have not tended to her memory. Now the physical thing that I have not done is to put a grave stone up. I think that not tending to her memory is a larger idea that can encompass the literal even though I don't come out and say it.

McHaney: What about the date in "Glyph, Aberdeen, 1913"?
Trethewey: I tend to stick to the facts with those kinds of things. In "Scenes from a Documentary History" even the title suggests that I am obliged to use the actual dates. The photographer who took those pictures lived and worked in Aberdeen, Mississippi, and that was the date on the photograph. So those things I stick to, but again, if you ask me about "Incident" and the cross burning, yes, it happened.

McHaney: After your parents left Kentucky to marry in Ohio, you were born in Gulfport, Mississippi, your mother's hometown. And did your father join your mother there?
Trethewey: Yes, he did come. We all lived at my grandmother's house for a little while until my parents found an apartment not too far from my grandmother's house, and she helped him get a job unloading ships on the docks.

He did that for a while, and later on he got into the Ph.D. program at Tulane, so he got an apartment with a roommate over in New Orleans, and he would come home on the weekends.

McHaney: What about the year in Canada?
Trethewey: We went there probably when I was a year old. My father was still in the Canadian Navy. When he left college, he became an officer, so we moved there with him. He was assigned to a ship that sailed around the world for the Canadian Centennial in 1968. He has written about that. During the Vietnam War his ship stopped in places, and he interacted with American soldiers. My father has an interesting story about being in a bar somewhere when King was shot and some American soldiers cheering.

McHaney: Did you know your father's parents in Canada?
Trethewey: For a long time I had a letter writing relationship with my grandmother, my father's mother, who is dead now, And I went back, years later, and saw all the family again. We felt that we knew each other.

McHaney: Do you feel that writing the poems, dedicating the book to your mother, and erecting these monuments have been sufficient? Do you feel that you have memorialized her now? That a stone per se is not necessary?
Trethewey: To tell you the truth, I think a stone is still necessary, and I think I have to say her name: Gwendolyn Ann Turnbough, because even as people have said, "Yes, you have created this monument to her," what I've created a monument to is Natasha's mother. I haven't created a monument to Gwendolyn Ann Turnbough. That's another thing. It hit me about a week after the Pulitzer. That if what I wanted to do is reinscribe my mother onto the landscape of our memory, I need her name to do that. It seems silly that I could not figure out the right language for this. I didn't want to put her name the name she died with because it was still my stepfather's last name. I didn't want that on a marker, a permanent marker and her resting place. I didn't want my last name, my father's last name, because that wouldn't acknowledge my brother. And it just didn't occur to me that I could put on the marker her maiden name—the person she really was. Well, now I know that, and I can do it.

McHaney: We've talked a little bit about how your work evolved from the third person to the autobiographical observations to reveal the erasures and to memorialize both personal and public history. Yet, the Pulitzer Prize award has shifted attention away from those national and regional stories and toward your private stories as we've just been talking about. I'd like to return us to that public story that you started with, the Louisiana Native Guards. Can you tell us a bit about Francis E. Dumas and how you discovered and perhaps identified with him?

Trethewey: He was mentioned in James Hollandsworth's book, and the interesting story that Hollandsworth points out about Major Dumas is that as the son of a white plantation father and a mixed race mother, he inherited his father's slaves and plantation when his father died. Apparently he did not want slaves, didn't believe in slavery, but it was illegal to manumit his slaves in Louisiana at the time, so he had them. When the Union was enlisting men for the Native Guards and he joined, he freed his slaves and encouraged those men of age to join as well. And I found that that was a compelling story because it represented what was perhaps a very personal dilemma for him. He and several other free men of color had actually been part of the Native Guards first when it was a Confederate Regiment. I think Hollandsworth mentions that some of the men felt coerced to join, that they felt like they would lose their property if they did not support Louisiana as Confederate soldiers. Perhaps there were some of them that were so into protecting their own and seeing themselves as so distant from the blacks and the slaves that they didn't care, but Dumas was one who did feel differently about slavery and so became a member again when it was resurrected as a Union Regiment.

McHaney: How do you see these ambiguities of Dumas's and of the other Native Guards that had been slaves but now were not slaves and who found themselves guarding the white Confederates, dying at the guns of their fellow Union soldiers?

Trethewey: I think that what Dumas represents, being of mixed blood, is the larger metaphor of the collection that the cover suggests, and that is the intersections of white and black, north and south, slave and free. I was taken by that idea when I found that Colonel Daniels had confiscated a diary from the home of a Confederate and cross wrote in it because there was a shortage of paper. That intersection was a gift. *Native Guard* is a book about intersections. Those very intersections are in me, in my very blood, they're in the country, they're in the very nature of history.

McHaney: Tell us about the metaphorical meanings of your title, *Native Guard*.

Trethewey: The literal is obvious: it is after the Louisiana Native Guards. But, I started thinking about what it means to be a native guardian, of not only personal memory but also of collective memory—and that is certainly what poets are often charged with doing, representing the collective memory of a people. And as a native daughter, a native guardian, that is my charge. To my mother and her memory, preservation.

McHaney: The first *O.E.D.* definition of "guard," that is said now to be obsolete, is . . .
Trethewey: . . . "to take care." I knew immediately that the title was going to be *Native Guard*, and I thought it was such a gift that these soldiers were actually named that.

McHaney: What is the relationship between a photograph and a poem? You've pointed out elsewhere that you were the first poet at the Duke University Center for Documentary Studies that usually brings historians and documentary filmmakers and photographers together. You said that the director, Tom Rankin, "believes that poetry can do the work of documentary and history." You studied photography and theory of photography at the University of Massachusetts at Amherst. How do you see those two things coming together?
Trethewey: I think again that it is a necessary intersection. I had two quotations. Lewis Hine said, "If I could tell the story in words, I wouldn't lug a camera." But Susan Sontag reminds us that "Nevertheless, the camera's rendering of reality must always hide more than it discloses." What this suggests to me is the need for both photograph and story to work together. What has always interested me about a photograph is that even though it seems to capture and elegize a particular moment, there are all the things that swirl around it, things that are cropped out of the frame, that which was just behind it that we don't see. And there is always a fuller version of the story that needs to be told. I believe the photographic image is a way to focus our attention, and it can be the starting point for a larger exploration of what else is there. As much as a photograph is about seeing what is there, it is equally about seeing what has been left out as it points in some way to what we might know if we are willing to imagine or to think about. What's been cropped out or what's not there—words are like that too.

McHaney: That reminds me how important narrative is within your lyric poems. What do you find that poetry can do when you want to tell a story? Why poetry then, and why not fiction?

Trethewey: Because of those elegant envelopes of form that poems are. Because of the music and lyricism and density and compression, poems can be memorable in a way that a long piece of fiction isn't. Not that the language of the novel or story isn't memorable, but the ease with which we might memorize a poem and carry it with us in our heads is appealing to me. The way a poem has a smaller space to fit into, and because that density and compression of a poem crystallizes and intensifies image, emotion, idea, sound.

McHaney: You have said that writing in form helps to avoid sentimentality, that refrain and repetition allow emotional restraint from excess or provide emphasis. Can you speak of your use of form, the ghazal "Miscegenation," the pantoum "Incident," the villanelle "Scenes from a Documentary History of Mississippi, 1. King Cotton, 1907"?

Trethewey: I had been reading the late Shahid Ali's anthology *Ravishing Disunities: Real Ghazals in English*. The introductory essay is so illuminating about what a ghazal is, the qualities of the ghazal. The particular one is the idea of disunity, the idea that these are closed stanzas that don't necessarily support or aim to support narrative or even linear movement, that they are separate, that in the juxtaposition of one stanza to the next is some sort of tension, and excitement can happen. And movement. And also that it is a form that is a kind of call and response—if the form is done traditionally, audiences know, based on where the rhyme appears, when the refrain comes and they say it with the poet. That is an interesting collective thing happening. Also, that the poet is supposed to invoke her own name in the final stanza is the thing that made that poem get written for me. I was thinking about all these disunified things. They were all connected but they were things that I didn't think I could write about in a straight narrative—my Jesus year or my parents breaking laws in Mississippi. These things are part of the same story, but I couldn't imagine a kind of linear narrative poem being able to put all of it together. So it was the idea of "ravishing disunity" that allowed me to do it.

McHaney: I reread the poem looking at each stanza to have it be its own separate unit as you said, and it does; it works perfectly. What about the pantoum, "Incident"?

Trethewey: Oh, I loved figuring out that that poem should be a pantoum and that it was suggesting itself to me. At first, it was an extremely different poem. I showed it to my students at Chapel Hill because I was talking to them about revision. I brought in a copy of two poems. One of them was "Incident," and the other was called "Target," one of its horrible pedestrian titles. I was trying to write about the cross burning, and I was writing bad poems about it because I was focusing on the narrative of it, the story of it, trying to tell the story and then figure out what the story meant. Ultimately I knew that poem wasn't working, and I mined it for what seemed to work of the narrative. In doing so, I got the first four lines:

[*Trethewey reads first stanza of "Incident"*]

In those first four lines, I get the scene of us peering from the windows while this cross is being burned, but also the lasting effect that it had on us, that need to retell the story, to keep the memory of this event alive. What is exciting about the pantoum or the villanelle, some of those forms, is the kind of mathematical way that they work. They allow you to see other possibilities. That was exciting. I knew I had to pull out those two lines and place them in the next stanza and then to write around them. It freed me from what can be the trap of linear narrative and it allows the poem to circle back on itself. A lot of the poems in *Native Guard* circle back on themselves. My impulse is to tell a story; it was form that made me do something different with storytelling.

McHaney: What is that trap of linear narrative?

Trethewey: When it is not working well, then that story just goes to an end and that end isn't really anywhere.

McHaney: Just a teleological impulse which is to get to the end, whereas your impulse is to circle back because you get a different view from every edge of the circle?

Trethewey: Yes, and to transform the meaning by circling back.

McHaney: I also read that in a pantoum the poet tells two stories, lines two and four become lines one and three in the subsequent stanza and the first two lines of each stanza build one story or theme and lines three and four another theme. In "Incident" the first two lines are the story, the cross itself, what was seen, and the other story is light, and shedding light and looking for understanding of what that was. So the pantoum was successful in form and in meaning both. What of your villanelle, "Scenes from a Documentary History of Mississippi, 1. King Cotton, 1907"?

Trethewey: When I am using a photograph, I begin describing literally what I can see before I move toward any interpretation. And in that first poem in "Scenes," "1. King Cotton, 1907," I saw the flags and the archway made of

bales of cotton; I saw clearly those two things in contrast to each other. And I saw how symbolic this was of that historical moment:
  [*Trethewey reads first stanza of "Scenes"*]

McHaney: You have been writing sonnets and blues poems since your first book; has your use of those forms changed over time?
Trethewey: I admire the sonnet form, little envelopes of small space, ten syllables in fourteen lines. You are forced to get rid of the unnecessary, the things that might try to trick you. There's no room for anything extra. You have to select, and what you select you must infuse with meaning. What is kept has energy, offers the right amount of story. Sonnets are traditionally written in iambic pentameter, the equivalent of the natural English voice, and in rhyme. Somehow, I didn't want to impose such a voice or such rhyme onto the speaker in "Native Guard." I am thinking also about the poems of Agi Mishol and Elizabeth Alexander who write about historical erasures in their cultural experiences. Mishol's poem "Woman Martyr" tells the story of the suicide bomber Andaleeb Takatka, but Mishol says it is not about Takatka, that poetry is always about language.

Rita Dove referred to a "syncopated attitude of the blues" in the poems of *Domestic Work*. I thought that sounded really wonderful and then I realized the real insight of Rita's comment. "Syncopate," in its simplest definition, means to shorten, usually by omitting something, like I described leaving out the unnecessary. But when you talk about syncopation in music, it is putting the stress on the typically unaccented note, putting the accent in an unexpected place, and in poetry, infusing the poems with a syncopated rhythm would be putting emphasis where one would not only not expect it, but would not want it—on the historical erasures, the biraciality, the circumstances of the Louisiana Native Guards who could read and write better than their white prisoners.

McHaney: And what are you working on now, Natasha?
Trethewey: I always pose for myself a question, often a historical question that I set out to research and try to answer. In *Native Guard*, I am talking about the Civil War and the legacy of the Civil War. Now I am researching casta paintings from eighteenth-century colonial Mexico. The casta paintings depict the mixed blood unions and the children of such unions in the colony. I'm fascinated by the language and iconography of empire, hybridity, and colonial history. The paintings are full of taxonomies to name the mixed

blood identities that are represented. For this project, I am looking at legal documents, the casta paintings, as I said, and looking at "found language."

McHaney: Circling back to *Native Guard*—when did you write the prefatory poem, "Theories of Time and Space"?
Trethewey: That was the very first poem I wrote for this book. I wrote that poem after going with my husband and my brother to Ship Island. I hadn't been in a while; Brett had never gone, and I wanted to show him the island. It's pretty, you can take a picnic, so we loaded up with beer and food and we took the boat out there. I saw again that on the tour they do not mention the black soldiers. So, I wrote that poem about being taken out to the island and being awakened to something, to trying to return home and nothing being like it was, primarily because of the way we are transformed and changed. It is odd to me that it is the first poem I wrote for the book, all very figurative at the time. Later Katrina hit and much of the imagery became literal in terms of my trying to return home.

McHaney: I think it is very daring to begin a book of poems of any sort with something called "Theories of Time and Space." It is so abstract. There's nothing concrete there.
Trethewey: Which is so unlike me.

McHaney: Yet all of the tropes that you are going to use are there: journeys, and "going home," "dead end," the "loose stitches," "man made," "random blank pages," "tome of memory," the "waiting," the "return." Every line, it seems, has something that carries us forward and alerts us to the histories that you are unveiling.
Trethewey: Yes.

McHaney: Tell us about the notes at the end.
Trethewey: My editor, Michael Collier, suggested the notes. I think it was a great idea. It acknowledges that this is a history. My father suggested notes early on and I misunderstood his suggestion. I thought he meant that this was a history that was not going to be readily familiar to people. I was thinking to myself, "Oh, he's a Canadian and that's why he's saying that. This is the Civil War, it's ingrained in all Americans."

McHaney: Your poem "Southern History," the notes, and *Native Guard* itself show that this history is not in school books. What about the corona sonnet, "Native Guard"? When did you get the idea to make it a corona sonnet, that the last line be the first line, showing the ambiguity and the polyvalence of language?

Trethewey: I think it had something to do, first, that I was coming off the heels of *Bellocq's Ophelia* where I had fallen in love with the possibilities of the nonce sonnet form—those fourteen lines, poems in a sequence to tell a larger narrative. I knew it was right for me to use it again, but I also knew it had to be different in some ways. This was a different voice. It was a different project. There was a different focus. My obsession keeps deepening, becoming more refined each time. I was reading about the soldiers, and I came across the passage describing when the Native Guards were shot down by their own Union soldiers as they retreated from Pascagoula to return to the ship. They were fired on and Colonel Nathan Daniels, in his diary, writes a bit about the incident. He records the speech that he gave to those men to honor the dead, and in that speech he says, "Their names shall deck the page of history." I was thinking about how I wanted to shift what he said to tell what really happened, that only some names decked the page of history. That's a grand thing that he says, but for so many it isn't true. Using a form allowed me to say essentially the same line, then to modify it subtly, to say something else—which had been influencing me in using some of the other forms in the book that have repeating lines—to say again and to transform what is being said.

I also wanted to circle back to those words, "Truth be told," to end with them and have them mean something different. At the end of the poem, it is a command, "Truth be told," whereas, the expression of it at the beginning is as if to say, "Well, honestly."

McHaney: You said that you "write what you would discover" as Yusef Komunyakaa says. What did you discover in writing the three sections of *Native Guard*, the elegies to your mother, the historic erasures of the Louisiana Native Guards, and the blending of the personal and public histories in the third section?

Trethewey: Some of that goes back to what we talked about before—why all these things went into the same book. I discovered something of what Mark Doty says: "Our metaphors go on ahead of us," that all of the research I was doing outside of myself, looking at history and looking at the Native Guards was leading me toward what I was really deeply concerned with, a monument for my mother. I started out saying, I want to create a monument for these lesser known soldiers and I ended up finding out that who I really wanted to create a monument for was my mother: Gwendolyn Ann Turnbough.

To an extent, the book is also about the canon of Southern poetry. Some time ago Memye Curtis Tucker asked me for some poems, and I sent her "Elegy for the Native Guards" and "Blond." I had misspelled the word "cannons" as "canons" and she wrote to ask me if I meant to say this, because she could see that what I was doing was interacting with the canon. That's one of the things that the third section is about, which is why I begin it with "Pastoral" in which I dream myself into a photograph with the Fugitives. Throughout the collection I am trying to assert the part of my work which is Southern. The book contains many mentions of Southern or other American writers: Robert Penn Warren, Faulkner, Allen Tate, E. O. Wilson. The epigraphs are from Whitman, the traditional folksong "Poor Wayfaring Stranger," and Charles Wright. I am very much asking, after Eric Foner's *Who Owns History?*, "Who owns southern history or southern poetry?" History belongs to all of us and our one charge is to present it well with all the complexity and humanity that peoples' lives deserve and that art requires.

Interview with Natasha Trethewey

Remica L. Bingham / 2007

From *PMS poemmemoirstory* (University of Alabama at Birmingham), number 8 (2008), 1–20. The interview was conducted 31 August 2007 in Atlanta. Reprinted by permission.

The day is a whirlwind. Professor Trethewey enters apologizing for her tardiness and explains that this has been another morning filled with unexpected demands. Even so, after appearances on *The NewsHour* with Jim Lehrer and *Fresh Air* with Terry Gross, most tasks are just footnotes on her path following the Pulitzer Prize. In April, after the prizes were announced and she was informed that she had won for her book *Native Guard*, everything changed.

Natasha Trethewey was born in Gulfport, Mississippi, in 1966. She attended the University of Georgia, Hollins University, and the University of Massachusetts before winning the inaugural Cave Canem Book Prize for her first book, *Domestic Work* (2000). Trethewey's work has appeared in many magazines and journals, including *Callaloo*, the *New England Review* and the *Southern Review*. In addition to *Domestic Work*, she has published two other books of poetry, *Bellocq's Ophelia* (2002) and *Native Guard* (2006). Her awards and accolades beyond the Pulitzer Prize include the Grolier Prize, two Lillian Smith Book Awards, a grant from the National Endowment for the Arts, and a Guggenheim fellowship. Currently, she teaches creative writing at Emory University.

After our interview is complete, Professor Trethewey and I are able to decompress. She elaborates on how she found out she'd won the Pulitzer—"They don't even call you," she says, "I was in class when it was announced. Someone had to come and tell me what was going on"—and how her life has been turned upside down since. By the end of the day, we have dined with friends and toasted the wondrous year, though Professor Trethewey does not dwell much on how things have changed; she covets history in her work much more than in her everyday life. Today, she is concerned with the here and now, fully present, and grateful, in the maelstrom that has become her everyday life.

Bingham: Do you remember your first encounter with poetry?
Trethewey: Well, my father used to recite parts of *Beowulf* to me as a bedtime story. It was terrifying [*laughing*]. He would recite the part about Grendel at the mess hall door. I think I was charmed by my father's performance of it; he had a big, booming voice and he could do part of it in Old English, so that was pure sound. Then, the translation was the story, which was gripping. After all that, he'd turn off the lights and I'd have to go to sleep [*laughing*].

Bingham: Did you go on to start reading poetry when you were young? Obviously, you were very young then and, of course, your father's a poet, so you had that influence as well. When did you start discovering poetry for yourself?
Trethewey: I don't have memories of the poems I read as a child. I have memories of being really taken by imagery in short fiction that I was reading. I remember encountering a story—and I've looked for it ever since—that was so vivid to me. It was about a man who was lost somewhere; it seemed like a frozen wasteland of a place. I remember thinking it was in some foreign country that was remote and snowy. He's lost out there and a Saint Bernard comes to save him. The Saint Bernard has a barrel under his chin and the man opens the barrel. Inside of it is a bar of chocolate and some brandy, and the writer describes the taste of the chocolate and the smell and warmth of the brandy in such vivid detail that I thought I could taste it. That was the first time I thought, wow, words could create an image that's so strong in its sensory detail that I could feel like I was experiencing it. Of course, there must have been the children's poetry that I encountered in various books, and the knowledge that my father was a poet, which must be why, in the third grade, I wrote a book of poems.

Bingham: In the third grade? Do you remember the title?
Trethewey: I don't, but I know that there were a lot of praise poems and odes to African American figures. I was writing to Dr. Martin Luther King Jr. and folks like that. The school librarian bound the little edition of poems that I made and put it in the library very ceremoniously. It felt like a big deal and it may still be at Venetian Hills Elementary School. I think I started

reading my father's poems for the first time, maybe, when I was in the seventh grade.

Bingham: So, you didn't come to his work until you were a teenager. Then you decided to pursue poetry or English when you went off to the University of Georgia?
Trethewey: Right. I think I was always an English major. In high school and in college, what I loved was diagramming sentences. I loved syntax; it was so thrilling to me. I really felt like a nerd because everybody else in the class would be miserable while we were doing all that, but I was just riveted by it. I think what led me to being an English major was the suppleness of syntax and, of course, the stories. I liked stories.

Bingham: Can you name three books of poetry or poets that changed your life?
Trethewey: When I went to graduate school, I got in as a fiction writer, so I thought I was going to write fiction. Within a couple of months into the semester, all that changed and I started writing poetry. My father gave me a copy of *Thomas and Beulah* by Rita Dove. I read it and thought, so you can write poems about this, your family history? I immediately started carrying it around with me everywhere I went. I began emulating it and learning from it, so I really think that it was life-changing in that way. It's the book that gave me direction or at least showed me into a beginning of what it was that I was interested in doing. Another book that was so important to me is the *Collected Poems of James Wright*. Also, Yusef Komunyakaa's *Magic City*.

Bingham: Had you written poems, other than those in the third grade, while you were at the university before reading *Thomas and Beulah*?
Trethewey: When my mother was killed, in my freshman year, one of the first things I did was write some poems about it. I think that's what people do, right? After 9/11, everybody wrote poems and a lot of them—probably most of them—were bad, as were mine. Mine were emotion ridden, in a sentimental way, and they were full of clichés. I never had the courage to show them to any teachers, fortunately. I remember asking one of my teachers if she would look at them and she said she would, but I never took the little sheaf of poems by her office. I remember, finally, showing them to my father and my stepmother. (They've gotten used to me telling this story now because they understand what I'm trying to illustrate about it.) The poem

was horrible. There was this image in it that said something about how I felt like I was sinking into an ocean of despair and the word "sinking" was going down the page diagonally. Well, they really ripped it to shreds and I remember leaving the dining room, crying, running up to my room and saying, "I'll never write another poem." When I was in my room, I sat there and thought about it. What I realized was that they were taking me seriously, believing in the possibility that I could write a poem, and so they gave me serious criticism. They didn't just say, "Oh, honey, that's good. You really got your emotions on the page."

Bingham: The Dark Room Collective was founded by Thomas Sayers Ellis and Sharan Strange in 1989 to help foster a community of emerging black writers. How did you become involved with the group and are you surprised by how significant it and its writers have become over the last few decades?
Trethewey: A friend of mine in the MFA program with me at UMass gave me a newspaper article from the *Boston Globe* about the Dark Room. There was a photograph of them and an article, so I read it with great interest and then filed it away with my things. Not long after that, my stepmother told me that *Agni Magazine* was doing a special issue on emerging writers and she suggested that I submit. It turned out that Thomas Sayers Ellis was one of the editors for that issue. I sent the poems "Drapery Factory, Gulfport, Mississippi, 1956" and "Naola Beauty Academy, New Orleans, 1945." Tom accepted both of these poems and then he wrote to me to tell me about the Dark Room Collective. We had a conversation about that and I came down to Boston to a reading where I met all the other members of the Dark Room. Apparently, they voted on me and said that I could join. So that's how it happened.

Bingham: What did you all do as the Collective; were you still doing a reading series, workshopping together . . . ?
Trethewey: They had been doing that, prior to my becoming a member. By the time I joined, they had already gotten so much publicity—they were already hosting a reading series at the Institute of Contemporary Art in Boston, before moving to the Boston Playwrights Theater. By the time I got there, it was really just these big road trips we would do, going and giving readings here and there, all over. We were young and excited just to be out there giving these readings. We were still finding younger writers who would serve as interns or sound people, doing whatever was needed, making flyers. It is kind of an amazing thing that happened. In some ways, it's both surpris-

ing and not surprising that the Dark Room gained the kind of attention and prominence that it did, because the young writers who were part of it early on were all very serious. They were all very devoted to craft, not any kind of foolishness, but the seriousness of reading, writing, and thinking about your work. I don't even think a lot of people realize it, but Carl Phillips was a member back in the day. A lot of people have gone through the Dark Room. Some were already in graduate school, but later Tom went on to Brown and Sharan went to Sarah Lawrence. Everyone was working really hard at the craft.

Bingham: You won the inaugural Cave Canem Poetry Prize for your first book, *Domestic Work*. In the book, you often deal with issues of race and how they have informed your life, and your family's life. One poem, in particular, "Flounder" reads in part:
[*Bingham reads from "Flounder"*]
This poem is especially interesting because you employ formal verse. How does a poem's subject matter or tone influence the form you choose to write it in?
Trethewey: Well, the impetus for even writing "Flounder" was my father giving me some of Theodore Roethke's poems. "My Papa's Waltz" was one that influenced me. I started thinking about rhyme and ballads after reading Roethke.

Maybe I can answer the question with a specific example, particularly from my recent writing. There's a poem in *Native Guard* that's a pantoum called "Incident." When I first started writing "Incident" it had another title and it was a poem very much about the particular incident of the cross-burning. Because I am a poet who is so rooted in story, because there's always one foot for me firmly grounded in the narrative in a poem, I was trying to write that poem as the narrative of what happened that night and it just wasn't working. I think two things were wrong: the form was wrong, but also the poem's direction was wrong. It was too focused on the story.

Bingham: Was it originally a free verse poem?
Trethewey: It was a free verse poem. I just knew that it was pedestrian; it didn't go anywhere. It seemed to have a kind of easy epiphany or resolution at the end and I wasn't interested in that kind of thing: I kept looking at the draft. I had to try to figure out what was key in what I had already written, and I realized that it wasn't what happened. The thing that was important was the necessity of remembering, of rescuing things from historical amne-

sia. It occurred to me that I should begin with the nature of trying to tell the story. The poem itself was trying to tell the story and that wasn't working, so I decided to think about the fact that we try to tell the story. That's why it begins, "We tell the story every year—" I think I wrote those first four lines very quickly. At that point, it was the first four lines of what happened, you know: "How we peered from the windows, shades drawn—/though nothing really happened,/ the charred grass now green again." Then I had those four lines and I thought, wait a minute. It was at that moment that it occurred to me: what was necessary was the retelling. Because the poem was about the necessity of remembering, of retelling, I knew that the repetition of the lines in a pantoum would be a way of enacting that very thing.

Bingham: At least in this instance, you were thinking about reinforcing the subject matter and the theme and historical erasure before you even chose the form. So, you chose a repeating form because you wanted to emphasize those things?

Trethewey: I think it came at the same time somehow. It just made sense. I had only written one other pantoum, one that, to me, was a kind of first try at a form. It wasn't a bad poem; it was very strictly following the rhyme scheme of a pantoum which "Incident" does not. I think because I had done that exercise for myself, I knew the way that these returning lines helped to pin down the thing that needs remembering. Which is probably why, once I got to "We tell the story every year . . . ," I knew that it was a pantoum.

Bingham: You've used sonnets, ghazals, blues poems, any number of rhyming forms, tercets, quatrains, pantoums, and other forms in your work. When I participated in your workshop at the *Callaloo* Creative Writing Workshops in 2004, I'm paraphrasing, but the gist of what you told us was that formal verse would often allow us to tell a story we'd been unable to tell in free verse. Does this hold true for you as well?

Trethewey: Yeah, I think so. Because I have such a strong impulse towards narrative, the danger for me is that I have a strong impulse towards telling a linear narrative that's going to be often really pedestrian. I want to not give up the content, not give up the fact that I believe some stories are worth telling, but to find a new way to make those stories sing and to make them go somewhere different than the simple linear progression of this happened, then this happened, and then we get to the end. I became more interested in, not a linear narrative, but a circular one. One that, I think, suggests that there is not a beginning or an end. I became very aware of that while I was working on *Bellocq's Ophelia*, which is why it seems linear but then the story starts and tells over again, circling back on itself. I wanted to embed that kind of motion into the narrative.

There is also the ghazal that's in *Native Guard*, "Miscegenation." I wrote it after hearing this wonderful ghazal that Michael Collier read one year at the Bread Loaf Writers' Conference and then reading (Agha) Shahid Ali's introduction to *Ravishing Disunities*. I was thinking about his discussion of disunity in the stanzas and that you could build upon these things that were seemingly disunified. I realized that there was still a thread that would make it a narrative poem, even as it's not supposed to work in that way.

Bingham: William Faulkner once said, "You must always know the past, for there is no real Was, there is only Is." You often express your interest in historical erasure or amnesia, and it's clear in all three of your books. How do you think artists can help prevent this type of erasure?

Trethewey: I think we help prevent it, in particular, when we begin to record the stories that we're losing. Early on, when I was writing *Domestic Work*, I was going down to talk to my grandmother to collect more of her stories. Listening to her, I realized that there were people in that neighborhood—next door neighbors—who were dying and taking with them their stories. They weren't necessarily the kind of people for whom the stories were being recorded. I remember thinking, oh my goodness, we're losing North Gulfport, Mississippi. So, I wanted to write all of that down. From there, I went on to think about what isn't written in terms of our larger public history and all the gaps in the stories we're told about our history. The work that a writer—someone who's doing imaginative literature—can do is to fill in those spaces. Even though we might "make up things" sometimes, we're filling in and telling a bigger story, aggregating those stories with the larger written and documented history.

Bingham: Photography has played a major role in much of your work. Can you tell me about what cultivated your interest in photography and explain the term *punctum*?

Trethewey: I think I was interested in photography because of what is elegiac about it. As a child, I found myself always staring at photographs and being acutely aware of the loss they represented, not only of the particular moment that they were made, but I think what was most poignant for me then was that they were often of people who had died. I would look at them and there would be someone who was gone, so photographs represented that kind of loss to me. Also, at the same time, they were objects that helped hold onto something, the way language can. Both represent loss. As Robert Hass has written in "Meditation at Lagunitas," a word is elegy for the thing it signifies. Such is a photograph.

I think I also used them because I had—what I imagined as a child as—a very photographic memory. I tended to create everything in my head as if it were a picture. I could remember everything in my grandmother's house like that: every single thing and where it was placed. I could go on the school bus, when I returned to school in the fall, and tell my friends about it. They seemed, somehow, interested in me telling them what my grandmother's living room looked like. Maybe it was just the vividness of the detail.

So, photographs were a starting block or an impetus to expand the moment of the photograph to see what else is happening just beyond it or behind it or before it. That's sort of what Roland Barthes was talking about when he coined the phrase punctum. It is that thing in a photograph that draws your attention to it and makes you think about what has gone on outside of the frame. It's the thing that carries you away from that still moment.

The photograph that made me write "Gesture of a Woman-in-Process" was stunning to me because it was just this photograph of two women standing there. One of the women, though, had moved her hand in such a way that it caught her apron and it looked like her apron was swirling in the middle of the photograph. That said to me that this is the way people from the past refuse to remain in the past. They are still moving through us now and moving into our contemporary consciousness, to go back to what Faulkner said.

Bingham: In your second book, *Bellocq's Ophelia*, the imagined woman who narrates the book finds work in a brothel and writes home. An excerpt from the poem "Letters from Storyville—October 1911" reads:

[*Bingham reads from "Letters from Storyville—October 1911"*]

Why was it important for you to illuminate the women captured in E. J. Bellocq's photographs and how did you come across them?

Trethewey: I wanted to illuminate the lives of the women captured in the photographs because they were very much relegated to the margins of history. It's Bellocq's name that we know, not the names of the women who were the models, who participated in the making of those photographs. I also wanted to tell their stories because a lot of them living in the mixed-race brothels would have been these white-skinned black women whose stories would have gone unrecorded, but whose lives are bound up in the fabric of American culture.

I found them in graduate school. I was in a class called Materials for the Study of American Culture. The professor, Judith Davidov, is an expert in photography as material culture. The first day of class she showed all these photographs from Cindy Sherman to Bellocq to FSA (Farm Security Administration) photographers to (Alfred) Stieglitz and Lewis Hine. I remember seeing one of Bellocq's photographs and being taken with it because it reminded me of the cover of my ninth-grade *Hamlet* text. It looked very much to me like Ophelia at the brook. I left class, ran through the snow to the library and found a book of his photographs. Then I found that image and sat right down there in the stacks and started writing the title poem of *Bellocq's Ophelia*. I didn't know, yet, anything else about why I was drawn to it and that became my research project for the semester. Of course, in doing that research, I learned that a good number of those photographs had been taken in the mixed-race brothels. So, these women who looked very white in the photographs—to our contemporary gaze—probably were not. At that time, I was looking for a way to write about my own experience growing up biracial in the Deep South and being told by professors to let it go.

Bingham: Specifically?
Trethewey: I was actually told, specifically, in graduate school that I should unburden myself of the death of my mother, unburden myself of being black, and write about the situation in Northern Ireland.

Bingham: Right, because Northern Ireland had everything to do with who you were as a person...
Trethewey: It was James Tate, and I think that there was a valid reason that he was telling me that, that his advice was not horrible advice. I needed to move away from myself a little bit, before I could find a way to successfully do it. Maybe if I focused on something else, something historical, something outside of myself—this is what I like to think when I think he was saying something useful—then I would find a better way in. And so I did. I wrote *Bellocq's Ophelia* because she was a character removed almost a hundred years...

Bingham: So you turned to persona because you were instructed to...
Trethewey: Exactly, but I kept it close to home.

Bingham: You've erected a double entendre in your third book's title, *Native Guard*; not only does it refer to the black Union soldiers, but also you've called yourself the "native guardian" of your mother's memory and the lesser-known histories of your Mississippi. The poet Stephen Mallarme said, "It is the job of poetry to clean up our word-clogged reality by creating silences around things." One perfect example of this is the poem "Genus Narcissus" in *Native Guard*. It reads in part:

[*Bingham reads from "Genus Narcissus"*]

How do you create silences, around the history or the past just beyond the poem, to make the poem work?

Trethewey: That's such a great question. I don't call it that myself when I think about it, but I should think of it like that . . .

Bingham: What do you call it?

Trethewey: Well, I think of it as restraint, but being restrained means withholding something and creating that silence that you're talking about. Phil Levine says, "I write what I've been given to write." I think of the things that I've been given to write (this is a thing that also comes out of my graduate school experience) and I remember turning in a poem when I was, early on, trying to grapple with my mother's death in poems. Someone in the class said, "This just seems so sensational. It seems like something that came out of a newspaper," and I was just sitting there thinking, for some people, these things are real life. The question is how do we write about things that are possibly sensational that happen in real life, but also have a kind of restraint so that the thing—or the occurrence—isn't what guides the poem, but, that the means of the telling does? The incident stands as the thing that makes me have to tell that story, but I want to let the means of the telling be the engine that drives the poem. I think I learned that what I had to tell, what I had to say may not be something somebody wanted to be told or to hear. So, the telling had to be restrained, and it had to be the engine.

Thinking about your initial question then, about the silence and then the necessary forgetting—what is withheld—*Native Guard* for me is the book that was so emotionally raw that, in order to write it, I had to really restrain myself. I think if I didn't—if I didn't use formal constraints, if I didn't allow for silences around certain things in the book—the pages would be dripping wet, soaked with my tears when a reader picked them up. When I think about "Genus Narcissus," "Graveyard Blues," "Myth," those three in particular—and my work to create certain silences around the details of the story or even my own feelings about it—what I realize is the way that a poem reveals something and should reveal, as we know, something new to the writer. It wasn't until after I finished this book that I learned that I had been living with a feeling of guilt for being the survivor all these years. I didn't know it until I wrote those poems. It comes out for me in the lines in "Myth": "Again and again, this constant forsaking."

Bingham: There is a thread of shared culpability . . .
Trethewey: Yes, I feel culpable in "Genus Narcissus" for giving her these flowers and not paying attention to what they represented.

Bingham: In an interview with the *New York Times*, you said, "For the sake of sanity there is a lot of necessary forgetting." What kinds of things are you trying to forget in your work?
Trethewey: Well, let me say something about that interview. I had to go back and forth with Deborah Solomon, the interviewer, about that quote because my whole thing about *Native Guard* is the necessity of remembering and the sheer danger of forgetting. She and I were going back and forth about this, and I think she wanted me to say that forgetting was also necessary. So, by the time I say the line that you just read, I'm conceding to her. What I was conceding to her was that, whereas I think it would be extremely dangerous for us to forget aspects of our public history such as the Holocaust, for example, it might be necessary to forget certain traumatic events from one's childhood.

Bingham: In *Native Guard*, you chose to employ very formal verse and diction. Some say that these aren't the "authentic" voices of the soldiers; they would have been young men, many former slaves, without education or much worldly experience, I think people were expecting to see dialect . . .
Trethewey: Well, they're not getting it from me . . .

Bingham: Why did you choose to use such formal techniques to create their voices?
Trethewey: This is a thing I've been dealing with since *Bellocq's Ophelia* because it's a similar issue in that book. There is a way that I try to answer that a little bit in *Native Guard* as well. One of the men who was stationed at Ship Island, Major Dumas, was a free person of color, the son of a quadroon mother and a white father. He inherited slaves when his father died, as many of his class would in Louisiana. Because it was illegal to manumit slaves at this time, he had to keep them, but he was not someone who liked having

slaves. Nor did he believe in slavery. So he freed his slaves, when he joined the Union, and encouraged them to enlist as well. The character that I've imagined as the speaker in "Native Guard," the one who's writing the letters for others, is the literate manservant to Dumas. Free people of color like him would have been educated in Europe, would have taken slaves with them, might have enabled their education. That's one of the things I paid attention to; to me, there was the possibility of a character who could have been educated. Let's not forget that I use an epigraph from self-educated Frederick Douglass. If that's not the one thing that says, here is what is possible . . .

Bingham: These people existed, too, and denying that is another part of historical erasure.
Trethewey: It sure is. That's exactly the point. Certainly there were people who—because of sheer desire and will and opportunity—could find the means to become educated, could read, could practice their diction, could become great orators. We have evidence they existed. And I'm more interested in human beings and their possibility and also the interior lives of those people than easy assumptions about their limitations. Certainly, if he's sitting around the campfire maybe he's spewing a few epithets with the other soldiers, but when he retreats into his interior life, is there no core of dignity and intelligence and seriousness of thought? Philosophical thinking even? Is that not possible? A person's humanity is not limited to her external circumstances . . .

Bingham: Or what we imagine their circumstances to be.
Trethewey: Just as much as someone might want to imagine this character as being uneducated and raunchy or whatever, I'm more interested in the fact that he's the literate, black, former slave writing letters for illiterate, white, Confederate soldiers. To understand the voices of soldiers I went to the Library of Congress and read their letters and diaries. There is a kind of nineteenth-century diction that is a little bit more poetic than ours. There's a formality to the written word that is different. It's different for all of us; I don't necessarily speak the way that I write.

Bingham: I ask everyone to read me one poem. I'd like you to read the fourth section in the crown of sonnets that make up the poem "Native Guard." Would you read it for me please?
Trethewey: Sure.
   [*Trethewey reads "Native Guard" sonnet "Today, dawn red as warning"*]

Bingham: In reading *Native Guard*, especially sections like that, I'm reminded of a poem by Bruce Weigl that ends, "Say it clearly and you make it beautiful, no matter what." How do you make such "terrible beauty"—to borrow Yeats's phrase—out of the ugliness in our history or even your own life?

Trethewey: That's another fabulous question. Claudia Emerson and I were just discussing that yesterday. She was saying that she believes, as I do, that a poem ought to make sense and it ought to be beautiful. She said that even when you're writing about harrowing things, they can be beautiful. And making them beautiful doesn't detract from the horror of what the thing was.

Looking at the poem that we just read, it seems to me, again, an issue of restraint. What I'm noticing as I listen to your question is that the poem is reporting what the former slave with the cross-hatched lines on his back is reporting to everyone else. There he is, standing with the image of his own back torn up and healed over, gesturing to another image of the ropes and the wild dance. That juxtaposition of the images—the torn up back, the horror of the ropes and the wild freedom of the tent—there's so much that's not said. It's hinted at and implied by an image with inanimate objects rather than the human body next to them upon which the horror would have fallen.

Bingham: You do that often—use inanimate objects to try to illustrate what's going on in the world around them. Immediately, I flashed back to "Cameo," a poem in *Domestic Work*, while you were talking. That's another poem that uses the technique, getting outside of the human to illuminate it.

Trethewey: I'm thinking of Terrance Hayes's poem "Postcard from Okemah." It's a poem about a lynching, but there's a way he describes objects and likens the people to certain objects. Then there's this amazing moment where he focuses on the flower pattern on the lynched woman's dress and that is just the high point of the horror to me. We are focusing on this delicately beautiful thing that stands in for all the horror that is behind it.

Bingham: You currently reside in Georgia, but you and your family are originally from the Gulf Coast. Subsequently, you all were hit hard by Hurricane Katrina. What was your first visit home like after the storm?

Trethewey: Right after the storm, I didn't make it all the way home. I went as far as Mobile, Alabama, because my brother had a quarter of a tank of gas, which was enough to get them out of Gulfport.

Bingham: This was before the storm?
Trethewey: No, this was after.

Bingham: They rode the storm out?
Trethewey: Yes, they went to a shelter and rode it out there. There were several days before I heard from them and then my brother finally found somewhere where he could get cell phone service. We arranged for me and Brett to drive down and fill up all these gas cans to go get them. Brett and I were in North Carolina at the time; it was that year that I was at Duke and UNC Chapel Hill. So, we were fourteen hours away, but we drove and got them.

I didn't actually go back to Gulfport for the first time until I went back with *The NewsHour* to do the Occasional Poetry Series feature. We took the boat out to Ship Island and walked around. It was . . . eerie for me. I had begun to feel this way before I saw it because the first poem in *Native Guard*, "Theories of Time and Space," is actually the first poem I wrote for this book. I wrote it years ago because I was contemplating the idea that we're transformed moment to moment, and that also when we leave a place, we can never return to that same place we thought we left behind. We're nostalgic, but the thing that we're nostalgic for never really existed. Time has changed it or it didn't exist in the way we recalled it or idealized it in memory anyway. When I wrote the poem it was all very figurative. But in a way, throughout *Native Guard*, I was elegizing my home.

Months after I turned the book in to my publisher the storm hit and the next day I thought, oh my God, what have I done? I wrote an elegy for my hometown, but it was like writing an elegy for a living parent. You never imagine what could happen. Then I went down there and I did exactly what the poem says; I drove down that road and when you get there it's a dead end. Now, all of a sudden, nothing of what used to be there is there, not the public library where I first started doing research for *Native Guard*, not the countless buildings and other landmarks on the coast that would tell me always where I was. There was no point of reference to know where—on that long road, along that beach—I was.

Bingham: Many would say there are already some issues of erasure taking place as far as Hurricane Katrina is concerned. Are you attempting to breach any of the political/social significance of the storm and the events surrounding it in your work?
Trethewey: Well, not in poems. I am writing a short memoir of the Mississippi Gulf Coast for the Page-Barbour Lectures at the University of Virginia.

It's a meditation on my hometown, cultural memory, erasure, and the legacy of Katrina. I think this is the right time for me to write something in prose about that. It will allow me to take on a lot of the issues in *Native Guard* that deal with historical erasure because there's so much that can't get into poems. For example, I had written a little bit about the meaning of region and place for the National Humanities Conference a few years ago. The main thing that I was talking about with historical memory or historical erasure was that in Gulfport, and along the Gulf Coast which has twenty-six miles of man-made beach, what they did in the first half of the twentieth century was bulldoze all the natural landscape, the man-made swamps that were there, to make them a different kind of beach. Because they did that—got rid of one layer of the past and covered it over with this more artificial thing—they created the situation that left the coast even more vulnerable to the storm. It's that erasure that actually allowed this hurricane to hit so hard—because the natural barrier was gone. That part, to me, is a sort of metaphor for these ideas about historical erasure and remembrance. We're now faced with a moment of heightened activity around rebuilding and remembering. The road down there was named the Jefferson Davis Highway. The naming of bridges and roads and the building of monuments inscribes a particular narrative onto the landscape and erases another. Here, the landscape is erased yet again and there's another chance to write another narrative onto it, but should it be the narrative of the Redneck Riviera or the high-rise condos that the people who are from there can't necessarily afford? How will we memorialize not only what happened, but also what was there before that and what was there before that?

Bingham: In April, you won the Pulitzer Prize for *Native Guard*. The Pulitzer is one of the most esteemed prizes in writing. Only three African American women, including you, have ever won the prize in poetry. How did it make you feel to be added to such a short, prestigious list?
Trethewey: There was that moment where it was like a line was drawn and I crossed over it. It's like knowing that, somehow, you're a part of history. Even saying that sounds like I'm promoting myself and I don't mean it like that at all, but I feel the weight of history. It's like the saying, with great privilege comes great responsibility. It meant so much to me because it was the book to honor my mother's memory and I wanted to create a monument to her. I never could have imagined that it would be a monument that was more than just this small thing I did, but that other people would know about it and because of the publicity of the prize, would know about her.

So, it was a deeply emotional and deeply personal book for me. For it to be recognized in this way is just tremendous.

Bingham: It must be serious validation . . .
Trethewey: Well, you know, in graduate school I was told to unburden myself of being black and of my dead mother. I think that's the funny thing about it. Rather than abandoning my subject, I wrote about it. Those stories are deeply American stories and, like all our stories, very much need to be told.

Bingham: There's a cyclical nature in your relationship with Rita Dove, another Pulitzer prize–winning African American poet. She chose your book as the winner of the inaugural Cave Canem First Book Prize. She edited the 2000 edition of *Best American Poetry* and included your work. She was awarded a Guggenheim; you were awarded a Guggenheim. She won the Pulitzer Prize for her third book of poetry; you won the Pulitzer Prize for your third book of poetry. The list of connections goes on. How do you think Rita Dove has served as inspiration for or informed your life as a poet?
Trethewey: Her work showed me a way into my own—particularly *Thomas and Beulah*. Once I read that I had to go back and read the earlier books. Seeing how she dealt with different things, ekphrasis—writing about paintings—and also writing about history in some of those other books was very important for me.

Bingham: The editor of *PMS*, Linda Frost, writes in her mission for the journal, "My hope is that *PMS* will add a very different tone to the chorus of writing by women in this new century, one with an edge appropriate for our millennium." What do you think the job of women writers is, especially writers of color, as artists in this millennium?
Trethewey: I can't remember who said that poets are charged with the collective memory of a people, but I think that we are. The duty is to create work that values the human spirit and dignifies humanity, in that it is willing to speak to and for, as much as possible, all of us. I think our duty is to learn to reckon with the human experience across time and space. We should create language that churns up that connection, language that looks at our relationship to other human beings within the web of history.

Natasha Trethewey Interview

Jonathan Fink / 2007

From *Panhandler* (University of West Florida) issue 2 (2008), 19–25. The interview was conducted in Fall 2007. The journal reprinted Trethewey's *Native Guard* poem "Myth" at the end of the interview. *Panhandler* is also an open-source emagazine, accessible at http://uwf.edu/panhandler/. Reprinted by permission.

Jonathan Fink: Welcome. This is Jon Fink. I am here representing *Panhandler* and the University of West Florida. We are thrilled today to have Natasha Trethewey to talk with. I guess we should start with telling you congratulations on the Pulitzer Prize.
Natasha Trethewey: Thank you very much.

JF: You read at UWF last spring and we all take probably undue pride in the fact that you won right after you visited us.
NT: That was one of the best readings because the audience there was just a terrific and warm audience. I felt really good, so thank you for that too.

JF: I was thinking of ways to start [the interview] and I was reading Michael Ondaatje's new novel *Diversidero* and in the start of it he has a Nietzsche quote I had never heard before. One of the characters says the quote, which is, "We have art so that we will not be destroyed by the truth," which I thought was a really interesting quote that I thought resonated in the work that you do, this idea of the nature of art. I was wondering if you could talk a little bit about if you see that as a connection in some ways to the artistic process?
NT: I hadn't heard that either and it is just a lovely way of putting it. I think about another quote—Phil Levine who said, "I write what I've been given to write" and I feel like some of the things I've been given to write in terms of their truth are very difficult things and it is only the art that in some ways frees me from the difficulty of those truths that I have to live with and carry

with me. But there is another writer who has said something wonderful that I think applies to this as well and that is Shelley who said that poems are "records of the best and happiest times and the best and happiest minds," and so for me what that means is that even when I am writing about very traumatic or difficult truths, the act of writing them, of making the art itself is the best and happiest time and so I definitely think that art is the thing that makes truth bearable as well as sort of carries it to us in the most elegant ways.

JF: What were some of the first works that you remember reading when you were younger that served as that sort of buffer to the world or entrance to the world?
NT: I think the most significant book that I read early on—this is just what I remember from fourth or fifth grade—was *The Diary of Anne Frank*, and that shook me deeply because I felt that there was this little girl who was my age or so (or maybe she was a little bit older) but her voice coming across time and space articulated something that I felt I had begun to understand as a child growing up in the Deep South between Mississippi and Georgia. Her experience spoke to me and I think it was reading that that I first felt what it means to have empathy for someone else who is different yet very much the same.

JF: I have always felt that as teachers of creative writing that what we are fundamentally teaching is empathy: how to conceive the world and understand the world not only from someone else's point of view but even your own point of view.
NT: I absolutely think so. I had an interaction with someone who will go unnamed who said that he found the idea offensive that I thought that either the goal or result of art should be empathy. He found that idea offensive.

JF: How come? What was his argument?
NT: I think he felt that art was somehow purer than that and above basic things like human empathy. And I thought, "Well then, why am I even talking to you?" [*laughing*] I felt sympathy.

JF: Tolstoy used to say that you want to "infect the reader with emotion" and I think that really comes across with the fullness of experience that's conveyed in your work, and that's experience not just in the circumstance of what's taking place, but the experience of the tone, the language, the

rhythms, the form, the structure. I think that all of that is an embodiment of empathy.
NT: I am deeply interested in the experience of other human beings, no matter how small or seemingly trivial it is.

JF: I was thinking about this a little bit when I was reading all the books together and appreciating seeing the different types of forms and structures develop and resonate in the different books. One of the things I was interested in was the letter form—the epistle form—because it creates such an interesting scaffolding for the poem because in one sense a letter itself already has an intended and specific audience to it and [a letter] is very different than like a monologue where someone is speaking generally to the air. In the poems the persona has a specific audience and then laid on top of that you as writer have a secondary audience that's the reader. How do you work with the pleasures of those layers?
NT: I love documentary evidence. I love the things that we might find in a strong box, in the bottom of a closet, like letters for example. So if we find letters written from this one person to another person for an intended audience but then we open it and read it ourselves. We're overhearing and participating in a way by overhearing that conversation and so I enjoy thinking about the formal elements of making an epistle like that because you have that intended audience to whom the persona writes that conversation and [the conversation] has to have the genuineness of the utterance to it. It has to really seem like something this person would say to that person. But at the same time it has to also be the kind of thing as utterance that is meant for a reader to encounter, that it includes so much more than that. I think the trick is coming up with how to give the information that the outsider, the reader, needs, while at the same time not creating a false document between persona and intended reader.

JF: I know this is a hard question to answer, but how practically do you do that? How do you anticipate what it is a reader will need to feel drawn into the poem?
NT: Well, I think the imagery, the things we always use in a poem. In writing letters you could certainly write shorthand and say, "Well you remember what happened there," but instead you can say, "I recall the color of the leaves that day," and the person to whom you might be writing a letter, even though they know the thing you're talking about, they have the image created for them too. I think that people wrote letters like that—that the letters

were vivid and full of imagery, and so the letter poem is doing that not only for the intended recipient of the letter but for the reader of the poem as well.

JF: What I have always appreciated about the imagery in your books is when the images contain a sort of tension in opposites, and that's something I see resonating in both the individual poems and collectively. Specifically, I think of the poem "Flounder" in the first book where you have the image of a flounder flipping back and forth and it's clear that the image itself contains the tension of opposites. And then something like "Genus Narcissus" in your most recent book—I love the development of the daffodils, which is a singular image, but has very different interpretations for the persona and her mother. What is the pleasure of that tension in opposites?
NT: Sometimes you find that the image is always—I suppose it was Pound who said, "The image is always the apt symbol."

JF: Yes, "The natural object is always the adequate symbol."
NT: And I find that so true because I can't imagine inventing something better than the actual flounder, for example, to represent my own tension as a mixed-race person—a person of a black parent and a white parent which my great-aunt Sugar was trying to help me understand and in her subtle ways which she talked about things. A flounder that is black on one side and white on the other has other characteristics that are interesting about it. A flounder has what, a single eye that goes straight through its head or its eyes are on one side of its head?

JF: Yes, it has one on each side I think.
NT: I could certainly have used that image instead, but that's not the one that was necessary for that opposition that you're talking about. I get excited (I assume like most folks) reading the OED. When I was working on "Genus Narcissus," the poem began for me just in a recollection of picking daffodils. Who knows where you go from there and how we get there and I don't know I can necessarily demystify the journey of how I get from one place to the other. But I did know that day something was missing for me from the poem and I went and I looked in the *OED* because I felt like if I did some research (which is always the place that I turn to), that if I knew something else, maybe it would help the poem go in an [unanticipated] direction. And I looked it up and that's when I found that daffodils were genus narcissus—that they were a narcissus flower, which I had not known. I did not know either that, even as I was aware when daffodils appear in the landscape, I didn't know

that part of their lifespan was to bloom early and to die young and so when I read that in the dictionary, I thought, "Well, here's why perhaps I was drawn to the symbol of daffodils." Not only did I literally pick them for my mother, but also there was another resonance they had that spoke to the very nature of her life, her short life.

JF: It's a beautiful poem. I know many times when we are teaching, a lot of what we are trying to do is demystify the writing process, right?
NT: Yes.

JF: Because you read something that seems so perfectly controlled and polished and finished and then students will read that and say, "Well, clearly the writer knew this to begin with."
NT: Right. Well, you can tell your students I did not. I believe it echoed in the poem because there's a moment for me where the poem just changes and it's that moment where I say, "childish vanity." Just the two-word sentence there. Before I got there, I was like, "Where is this going?" I looked in the dictionary and I thought, "Here is where this has been about all along."

JF: What are some of the other avenues for research that you use or see?
NT: Well, beyond the dictionary—I think the dictionary is the best one, I love staying in there and reading all the definitions and the usages of the word because it opens so many doors for figurative language that I may not have ever opened—also, I always do historical research. I always figure that there is always something more to know, even about things I think I know a lot about, and so, again, the dictionary is the easiest place to go to that first, but [I also go to] other histories [like] primary documents including paintings and photographs. I think of those things as places to go to do research because you are trying to do this thing in your head, but then you think, "Well, let me go and look at this again." Research can be looking at the primary document of the photograph.

JF: What was the story (I remember you telling me about this) where you first came to understand your subject matter? You were looking at the paintings at Virginia maybe? Someone was with you and said, "This is your subject matter"?
NT: Oh, right. This was when I was still at Massachusetts, and it was photographs. My teacher was Margaret Gibson. I was at UMass working on my MFA thesis. A lot of poems from my MFA thesis are, of course, poems that

made it into *Domestic Work*, particularly the title sequence of "Domestic Work." She and I went to a gallery on campus that had an exhibition of photos up that were depicting the great migration of African Americans in the early twentieth century from the cotton fields of the Deep South to places like Chicago. So they were on one side of the room. On the other side of the room there were these photographs of blacks in New England around the turn of the century that were taken by a photographer who traveled around a lot and his name is Clifton Johnson. Clifton Johnson did a lot of travel narratives and to places like "The South" and he would go and write the narrative and take a lot of photographs. So these were his photographs up on the wall as well and she looked at me and she said, "Look at this. Look really closely at this because these are the people you're talking about," and until that moment I hadn't thought that, as I was writing my grandmother's story, that I was writing a larger narrative of a people, that her story (that seemed so personal and so family) was also a story that spoke to the larger condition of people in the Jim Crow South.

JF: You mention in your most recent book the theme of psychological exile—the E. O. Wilson quote. What's the quote exactly?
NT: "Homo Sapiens is the only species to suffer psychological exile."

JF: How do you interpret that, both literally as a quotation and aesthetically in your own work?
NT: Quite literally that I could live in the Deep South—so I am not physically removed from my home, my South, the place that made me—and yet I am not fully a part of it either, and the fact that my parents' marriage was illegal when I was born in Mississippi, that the very fabric of government and custom and law in my home state wanted to do things to prevent me from existing. I can't image how you would get a greater sense of exile from the very beginning of your life as soon as you know that. I think poets are people who are like this; for whatever reason you feel psychological exile because you're always an outsider to something, no matter how "inside" you are. As a southerner, as a native Mississippian, I feel like I am always on the outside trying very hard to stake my claim in a state, in a region, in a country that renders me sort of less than a full participant. But language is like that too. Our relationship to language is also a great sense of exile. As Robert Hass says, "A word is elegy to the thing it signifies." So there is already that distance and that remove. But we have to live in it in order to try to make sense of what we have, and so there is always that disconnect.

JF: I think that a poem that illustrates that well—one of the poems that I absolutely love in your most recent book—is "Myth," how the language itself sort of circles and turns back, and the representation of the language itself becomes a way of conveying meaning, right? Could you talk a little about that form and structure and how it repeats?

NT: I didn't know this when I was working on the poem, but there is a form called a palindrome. Of course I know what a palindrome is, "Ah, Satan sees Natasha," "A man, a plan, a canal, Panama." [*laughing*]

JF: "Able was I ere I saw Elba."

NT: It never occurred to me that a poem could read line by line one way and then to reverse it all and go the other way. When I was working on "Myth" I just was trying to create the feeling of going into sleep and into a space where we often dream alive those people we've lost and that there is often that moment of waking up where for a couple of seconds the person is still alive, or at least you think, and then you readjust and realize they're not. And to me that really seemed just like Orpheus descending into the underworld to try to bring Eurydice back and when he turns and looks at her she vanishes again just like that moment of opening your eyes after waking—that fleeting, instant disappearance of this person who has been there with you in a dream. So I had gotten to the end of the first section of the poem and thought, "Is this where it ends?" and I don't know what (again this is the thing about demystifying) led me to look at the poem backwards. I wasn't going there when I started it, but I got to what I thought was the end, but it was not the end, it was a hinge instead and I did not know what the other side of the hinge was, that it was actually a mirror image. There are also some tricks that people do, like how you read your language to check it for some internal integrity of sound, and I think I was doing that. Perhaps I was remembering the late Shahid Ali. While he was at UMass he used to make students read their poems backwards just as a way to sort of find the weak spots. I think that is a way of finding a hinge too, because if you read it backwards maybe what you thought was the crux of the poem isn't really it and it appears somewhere else. So I think I must have done that and seen with my eyes really big that the poem can indeed enact exactly what I was trying to convey. So not simply that the words would suggest it, but that the movement could enact that movement of descending and then returning. It almost seems like a happy accident. Sometimes the best things are.

JF: Carver used to say that a writer is someone who is willing to sit and

stare at something longer than anyone else. What you are saying specifically, which I think really resonates, is how that inversion was fitting to that specific poem and that content, that it wasn't an arbitrary decision, but it was one that grew organically out of the process and subject matter itself. That universal awareness of forgetting you have lost someone and then remembering them—what is so heartbreaking about that is that you have that dual sensation of for an instant they are alive again, but then you have to re-experience, even if in a smaller way, their loss secondarily, so that sense of loss is continual rather than singular.
NT: That's right. It happens over and over again.

JF: Would you read it for us?
NT: I'd be happy to. [*reads poem*]

JF: Thank you. I am also interested in sequences and series of poems, and structurally what that allows you to do both narratively and imagistically. What do you feel are the generative elements of a sequence?
NT: I like the way that a sequence can build upon certain images that of course become motifs throughout a sequence of poems and build a kind of tension. I love how a sequence allows me ([although] I think I am someone who tends more towards a linear narrative) to do sequences that circle back on themselves. I am really interested in how I can tell a story that is obviously a linear story that has a beginning, middle, and end, and yet by circling back through the sequence it doesn't have simply that straight line through it. I mentioned those images and how they become motifs and how they are repeated or echoed throughout a sequence. I find that I like very much very subtle repetition and the way that certain sounds as well as certain images echo throughout a sequence. I think *Native Guard* is made up of individual sequences. There is the "Native Guard" poem. There is a four-part poem called "Scenes from a Documentary History of Mississippi." I think the elegiac poems for my mother can be read as a sequence, and yet *Native Guard*, the whole book, is also a sequence, although people will read it in whatever order possible, which is also fine because it is a sequence which is not exactly linear. [*laughing*] You can start and go around and around. I think I answer questions like that too. I start out with an answer and then I go over here and then I circle back to it.

JF: In "Southern History" it ends with the persona feeling complicit. The persona says [referring to the teacher's presentation of the past], it was "a lie/ my teacher guarded. Silent, so did I." The persona feels implicated in perpetuating the lies of history through her silence (and I'll let you answer the question instead of answering it [*laughing*]). But how do you see that resonating throughout your books or as an artistic directive?

NT: I think it is my artistic directive. I was contemplating this recently because I just came back from doing the Page-Barbour Lectures at the University of Virginia, and I was lecturing on (I was "meditating" I should say) the Mississippi Gulf Coast. The title was, "Beyond Katrina: A Meditation on the Mississippi Gulf Coast, Present, Past and Future." And after *Native Guard* came out and I started giving readings, and even more so after the prize, and I talked to people, I often got the question, "Are you going to write about the Gulf Coast now, after all of this that has happened? After the storm and the rebuilding?" and I kept thinking, at first, "Well, no. *Native Guard* was my elegy to the Gulf Coast." I thought that I was done and then Ted Genoways asked me if I would do this and I took it on foolishly, I think. I'm happy now because I've come to think that I would have abandoned my own directive had I not, and that my silence right now as the native daughter I have tried so hard to position myself as, the silence of that native daughter at this moment, would have been that kind of complicit silence that relegates some history to the margins. And so—I am going around in a circle again—but I absolutely see my role as a poet in some way is to try to recollect the collective and historical memory of a people through the very individual people because I have always been deeply concerned with erasure: those things that are left out of the larger story. To me, the only way we can tell a fuller version of history is to try to reclaim and to get as many of those erased stories back into the larger narrative.

JF: What has been your recent impression about how things are going on the Gulf Coast after the hurricane?

NT: There is all the rebuilding stuff, all the problems that are germane to the idea of what will be rebuilt and for whom and how. But in my own way I am also thinking for the future in how the actual rebuilding, the construction of the buildings and economy that we need, is connected to the kinds of monuments and memory making that are being built right now too. The memory of the coast is being rebuilt brick by brick but also word by word in terms of the recollections. The people I talked to on the coast are worried that they will be forgotten, that the man-made tragedy and travesty of New Orleans—while it gets, rightfully so, the attention that it gets—in some ways is playing a role in subjugating the story of the natural disaster that happened to the citizens on the Mississippi Gulf Coast. So that is a story that needs to be told and remembered and we need to erect the kind of markers of collective memory in the nation that let us keep that story too.

JF: What are you working on now? Can you talk about it?
NT: Oh, well I had begun working on a new book of poems before I found out about the prize which has made me very busy the last few months.

JF: We feel so sorry for you. [*laughing*] There, there. There, there.
NT: All I will say is that toward the end of working on *Native Guard* I was hanging out in front of my *OED* just reading some definitions and I looked again at the word "native" because I just kept thinking—I continue to think—about what it means to be native to a place and I was really surprised to find that the first definition, the primary definition of the word, was not at all what I expected. I was imagining something like the way that a plant is native to a region, or I might say, "I am a native of Mississippi." But the definition that came up was, "Someone born into the condition of servitude, a thrall." And, of course, "thrall" means "slave." So I was thinking about what is it to be enthralled to anything, to language, to memory, to nostalgia?

JF: Well, we will look forward to it. Thank you, Natasha; it was a real pleasure.
NT: Thank you, Jon.

An Interview with Natasha Trethewey

Wendy Anderson / 2008

From *Bookslut* (February 2008). The website for the online journal is http://www.bookslut.com/; Anderson's interview is archived at http://www.bookslut.com/features/2008_02_o 12353.php. The interview was conducted 21 January 2008. Reprinted by permission.

Poet Natasha Trethewey spoke about her 2007 Pulitzer Prize–winning book, *Native Guard*, on Martin Luther King Day—perhaps fitting for someone who chronicles growing up biracial in the South with a black mom and white dad who were not allowed to get married in their own state. A portion of the book is in the voice of one of the Native Guards of the Civil War, part of a black Union regiment sent to watch Confederate prisoners at Fort Massachusetts on Ship Island off Gulfport, Mississippi. Trethewey often visited the island with her grandmother without ever knowing this history, untold in official park narratives. Yet another portion is Trethewey's poignant homage to her mother, a social worker who was abused by her second husband, Trethewey's stepfather, and finally killed by him after they divorced, when he shot her in the head at close range. Trethewey was nineteen and away at college; her half-brother was waiting outside their home for the school bus. Each of these sections by itself is solid and haunting; together, the parts connect and complement to form a mighty collection of tremendous loss, tinged with continuation and hope.

WA: Did you write the poems about your mom's death all at once, or was that a dam that burst over time?

NT: I think it became more like a dam that burst. I tried to write the first one when I wasn't even thinking of myself as on the path toward becoming a poet. I wrote them not long after she died, in the summer of my freshman year at college and my sophomore year. They were horrible—trite and abstract. I didn't write any more of them for a while. Then I wrote one in James

Tate's workshop my freshman year of graduate school . . . I tried to write about these plants of hers that I inherited after her death and had been carrying around. With each move that I made over the years, they got beaten up more and more, to where I could no longer keep them alive. It felt like a moment where part of whatever else I had held onto of her had finally died.

That poem had a memory of her twenty-sixth birthday. I could remember this birthday because my grandmother and I baked a cake for her in the shape of a watermelon cut open. We decorated the cake with twenty-six black seeds, and that's the first awareness I had of my mother's age. There were always these anniversaries. In graduate school during that MFA program, I reached twenty-six. It was stunning to me to reach that age where I was first conscious of my mother's age.

For a time, Trethewey believed she could not make art of her mother's death. Someone in her workshop remarked that the story was almost too sensational, like something from a newspaper, which indeed it was. The writing began to flow a bit more when Trethewey was on a fellowship at Radcliffe when she was thirty-three. When discussing the various things recipients did with their fellowships, the program director said that one woman spent her time grieving for her dead father. Trethewey was struck by that and began writing poems she put in drawers, considering them private and of little interest to readers.

And then I got a job at Emory University—the actual geography of my childhood, my mother, her murder. [*Her mother had moved to Atlanta after she and Trethewey's dad divorced, when Trethewey was six.*] I never planned to come back here, but a job's a job. I literally moved down the street from the courthouse [*where her stepfather's sentencing was held*]. I think it was impossible for me not to return. I not only was approaching the anniversary of her death, but also my own fortieth birthday. She died just shy of her forty-first birthday. And I reached the midpoint where I'd crossed over, where I had lived more of my years without her than with her. All of that converged, and I started writing.

WA: This book is in three parts: your mom, the Native Guards, the South and your biracialness. Did you see these three things as connected when you wrote them?

NT: It was very much later. For a long time I thought the main thing was the Native Guard. When I took my grandmother to a restaurant on the beach on Ship Island, someone heard our conversation and told me this history that I hadn't learned my whole life. It occurred to me that there was all kinds of historical erasure like that—things that get left out of the record and are equally important in the history of us as Americans. I started doing research about the guards, and that was what I wanted to write about.

My more personal poems, about me and my place in the South, started to enter into this book. I saw that connection. I started thinking about my place as a southerner, and as biracial, and as a black southerner and what gets left out of history and who's responsible for remembering, recording, those things that are left out—the native duty of many of us.

I was jogging in the graveyard near my house one day, and there's an old part where a lot of Confederate soldiers are buried. I'm one of those people who can't not read every tombstone—they scream at me for their names to be heard. I was thinking about that when I came home and planned to write about that. When I sat down to write "Graveyard Blues," what I recalled was burying my mother. That was when I came to understand what was going on in my subconscious. I wrote the poem "Graveyard Blues," and the final couplet has an image of me laying my head down on her stone. When I finished the poem, I thought the couplet made sense for what the poem was trying to get at.

[*Trethewey reads from "Graveyard Blues"*]

That image is real because my mother does not have any kind of stone on her grave. That sort of hit me, the history that had not been properly memorialized, remembered, tended by someone native to her—it was my mother's history. She was just like those black soldiers. No monument existed, and in that way she was erased from the landscape.

WA: Have you put a headstone on there?

NT: My brother and I have talked about it and plan to do it. All those years I didn't think I could put a gravestone on my mother's grave because I thought I'd have to name her with the name she had when she died, my stepfather's name. I didn't want to see that. And I didn't want my father's name because of my brother. It never occurred to me I could put her [maiden] name: Gwendolyn Ann Turnbough.

When Trethewey researched the Native Guards, she learned that many times the African American soldiers were abused, and even killed, by their fellow white soldiers. She was struck that their achievements, indeed their existence, were buried with their bones.

WA: What intrigued you enough to write the Native Guard series?
NT: That it was buried history, historical erasure. When I began to read about the Native Guards, what really got me was that their colonel had confiscated a diary from a Confederate in Louisiana and took it for his own and began to cross-write over what was there. That hit me as a perfect metaphor for what I was trying to say about our history of the South and of Americans; this cross-hatching a perfect intersection of north and south, black and white, that you can't separate.

They also were about me, being a Southerner, wanting to write myself into history, wanting to be a recorder of another period.

Down here I drive around all the time with this sense of exile because everything is named for Confederate heroes; you'd think the South won the war. During the flag controversy [*a movement in Georgia and elsewhere to ban the Confederate flag from government buildings*], there was a letter to the editor saying all true Southerners love that flag. It was his way of saying all true Southerners are white Southerners. It was important for me to say: This is my South; I love it and I hate it, too, but it's mine.

Trethewey employs forms in many of her poems, from sonnets to pantoums. The poem "Incident," for example, repeats lines from verse to verse, to different effect, as it describes a cross burning on her grandmother's lawn when Trethewey was a baby with her family, inside the house. [Anderson quotes from "Incident."]

WA: You use a lot of forms in your poems. Many writers find them constricting, but they can help you pare what you say. Why do you use them?
NT: As a tool of restraint. I'm writing about experiences that are pretty difficult for me. I tried writing "Incident" for a long time with a straight narrative lyric, but it kept getting bogged down by the incident, reduced to a little incident about the cross burning. It wasn't until I turned to that other envelope of form and repetition that I even understood what the poem was about—[not centered on the incident but] how we remember the incident.

WA: When did you first discover the power of words? Did you write as a child?
NT: I did. I did a collection of poems around Martin Luther King Jr. I went to an all-black elementary school from first through third grade. Black history was important. My third grade librarian bound them and put them in the school library.

WA: Do you think a lot of people today live lives bereft of poetry?
NT: I try to inculcate in my students a love for poetry, so that when they leave the class they think they like it.

One of the most wonderful things happened to me. I had a reading in Charleston, South Carolina [*after she won the Pulitzer*], and my husband went with me—it was my birthday. We needed maintenance on the air conditioner of our hotel. A man came and fixed it, and waited with us for ten to fifteen minutes to see if it would kick in. We had a bottle of champagne a friend had sent, and this man asked about it. My husband told him, and he was very impressed. He opened my book to my poem "Incident." He looked at it and read it out loud. Then he put it down and folded his hands in front of him, and recited Countee Cullen's "Incident" [*a short, powerful poem from 1925 that still resonates, about an African American boy remembering only of his visit to Baltimore that a white boy he smiled at called him a derogatory name*]. I found that stunning. This guy carried around in his memory that poem. I like to think lots of people carry around poetry.

Trethewey clearly carries around poetry. She uses words from various sources to mark sections of her book. The passage that begins the book and sets the tone for what is to follow is by poet Charles Wright. [Anderson quotes the epigraph on memory as a cemetery.]

WA: How did you choose the Wright quote?
NT: I must have come upon that and thought it was perfect for the way I was thinking about the buried history we overlook. Really so much of it is literally beneath us—the real bones of the people who are beneath us.

I think I'm someone who has a constant awareness of things that are invisible . . . I think it in some ways comes from growing up in New Orleans. My father was for so many years a graduate student there. [*Her father obtained his doctorate at Tulane. He is a poet and teacher at Hollins University in Virginia; her stepmother, too, is a poet and teacher.*] Of New Orleans, people either love it or they hate it. People who hate it think it's seedy. I always think that seediness is just the presence of this history. There are ghosts everywhere around you.

Conversation between Natasha Trethewey and Alan Fox in New York City, January 31st, 2008

Alan Fox/ 2008

From *Rattle: Poetry for the 21st Century* 14.2 (Winter 2008), 179–90. Reprinted by permission.

Fox: We're in New York City on January 31st, 2008, with Natasha Trethewey. For a young poet, you've won a lot of prizes. How has that affected you?
TRETHEWEY: The most recent prize of course is the one that I never could have dreamed of in a million years. But at some point while writing *Native Guard*, I began thinking about trying to create a monument in words to my mother, and it was really important for me that the book come out on my fortieth birthday, or while I was forty, I should say, because that's the last age my mother ever was; she died just shy of her forty-first birthday. And so, it was one of those symbolic things—I was getting to that last age she was, and I was also approaching the twentieth anniversary of her death. All of that was coming together at the same time, so the book meant a lot to me because I wanted it to be a monument to her. I couldn't have imagined that it would become such a public monument, and that makes me very happy.

Fox: Why do you think that happened; why do you think it became so public?
TRETHEWEY: Well, in the most basic sense, because of the sort of publicity that the book got because of the Pulitzer. People who had known my mother—maybe they saw me on TV or they read about it in the newspaper or they heard an interview I did with Terry Gross on NPR—realized that I must have been her daughter. I started getting calls and letters from people who were so happy to see that her daughter had remembered her this way;

I think they were relieved to see that there could be a happy outcome after a tragic, tragic death.

Fox: What influence did your mother have on your life?
TRETHEWEY: I don't know. I think it's immeasurable, really. It's a lot easier when people ask me what influence my father had on my life—it's easier because I can point to specific things; I can say, "My father's a poet." Of course, his influence is immeasurable too. But my mother's influence goes beyond the specific, and then losing her influences my life in countless ways.

Fox: What do you like best about being a poet?
TRETHEWEY: Oh, finding the words to say it. Being able to find the words to say, sometimes, what seems unsayable. And finding that there are other people who are interested in hearing those things—that kind of connection across time and space that links a poet to other human beings, along the thread of empathy.

Fox: Reading your work, the word "empathy" came to my mind, because you took photographs that empathize. Could you talk a little bit about that?
TRETHEWEY: This is one of the things that I would say I remember about my father, to go back to that earlier question a little bit. My father had a great influence on how I became someone who could empathize. I can remember being a little girl, probably four years old, going to pick flowers for my mother and seeing—this is going to sound so trite, in a way, but seeing a dead turtle; I used to cry at the deaths of all sorts of animals, and my father was constantly having to make sense of death and explain these things to me. And I think his poems are also poems that keep empathy at the center of how they look at the world and other human beings. It reminds me of something Phil Levine said once about how he wanted the words in his poems to become almost invisible—this is probably a bad paraphrase—so that they became more like a window through which you could look and see clearly the people. I think my approach to writing about photographs is a way of trying to see into the lives of people.

Fox: Do you feel that you express or expose a part of yourself in reading into the photo?
TRETHEWEY: Certainly, certainly. But that's what we have to do to empathize, right? [*laughs*] I mean, to see in other people ourselves, our own suffering, our own joy. When I wrote the poems in *Domestic Work*, my first

book, about my grandmother, so much of me imagining her life was me imagining how I would feel in her life and connecting to that. I remember when she first read the poems. She knew I had been writing something for so many years, because I kept asking her questions; I'd listened to her stories all my life but then there was a time when there were some other things I wanted to know, and so I started asking the questions, and so later when I finally gave the book to her she read it and said, "That's just how it happened." The poems required a great deal of imagination, not simply reporting—and it took a good deal of empathy to get everything about her life right in a way that convinced her of the emotional truth I had created.

Fox: That's high praise indeed.
TRETHEWEY: Yeah, that was sort of the big prize, from my grandmother.

Fox: How, in your family—how has life changed from your grandmother's day to today?
TRETHEWEY: You mean, in our family life, or . . .

Fox: Or general. Just forty, fifty, sixty years ago. Do you think times are very different?
TRETHEWEY: Oh, certainly. I do things that my grandmother couldn't have dreamed of being able to do, as a black woman born in Mississippi in 1916. And my mother also who was born in 1944, how different that was. Mississippi is a place now that, even as the vestiges of my grandmother's time and my mother's time hang on, much change has occurred. For example, I'm going to go back to Mississippi next week to receive the Mississippi Governor's Award and the state legislature is going to make a joint resolution on the floor. I was joking with my father, "Are they going to apologize for the anti-miscegenation laws? Probably not." [*all laugh*] But for me to go back to be honored that way as a native daughter of a state in which the circumstances of birth rendered me illegitimate or illegal because my parents' marriage was still illegal (I'm not even sure if Mississippi has repealed or removed the law from the books) suggests a tremendous amount of change. The state of Alabama just removed the anti-miscegenation laws from their books. They put it to a vote and 40-some percent of the population still wanted to keep the law even though it can't be enforced. It's a symbolic thing, so that it could still be on record, in the language of law, that parents like mine couldn't be legally married and people like me born legally in the state. I mean, think of that!—your question "have things changed?" The an-

swer is yes, but still 40-some percent of the population of that state—and you never know who they are—would rather not see my parents be able to be married.

Fox: I was probably in my twenties when I found out about those kinds of laws. I didn't understand it. I mean, why do that? But, that's . . .
TRETHEWEY: Well, and now here we are with a biracial man campaigning for the Democratic nomination.

Fox: Absolutely.
TRETHEWEY: Things have changed, and yet the vestiges hang on.

Fox: Yes, absolutely. When did you start writing poetry?
TRETHEWEY: Well, there are two answers to that. I wrote poetry as a little kid, like a lot of people do, and I can remember some of my third grade poems and the librarian who bound this little book of them and stuck it in my library at Venetian Hills Elementary School. But I didn't start writing poems the second time until I was in my first semester of graduate school. I'd gone to Hollins thinking that I wanted to tell stories and so write fiction. And then about a month or so in, all that changed.

Fox: An event happened, or . . . ?
TRETHEWEY: Yeah. I think, for one, I was a terrible fiction writer (my professor at the time was Marianne Gingher). A friend of mine in the program, a poet, challenged me to write a poem, and I'd said I'd do it just to prove that I couldn't. And so I did it and it wasn't that bad. He told me that I lost the bet. But anyway, I gave it to Marianne, (I put it in her mailbox) and the next time I saw her she came running down the hall and said, "Oh, Tasha, you're a poet!" That also meant she got to get rid of me and my horrible stories [*laughs*] and send me over to one of the poetry professors.

Fox: What was your father's reaction; was he supportive?
TRETHEWEY: Oh, yeah. I think he, being a poet himself, hoped I might have become a fiction writer in order to have the chance of making money as a writer. [*laughs*] But he wasn't disappointed; he was encouraging. And he was one of my teachers, so once I switched from fiction to writing poetry, I took a class with him and I also took a workshop with my stepmother, to whom he was married at the time, Katherine Soniat.

Fox: What can be taught in terms of writing poetry? How much is learning and how much is ability; what's the interplay?

TRETHEWEY: I was just having this conversation with my students the other day, on the first day of class, and we were just talking about how elements of craft, the things that poets have in that toolbox, are things that can be taught. People can learn about using imagery rather than abstraction; they can be taught to think about lineation and to be concerned with the music of the line, and the heightened sense of sound; and to recognize those things not only in their own work but in the work of others. So often the students that come are very intuitive—intuitive of course in that way that is the result of prolonged tuition. But they don't know that they know these things, and so I think a class can help them identify what they know intuitively. And so, they can consciously make decisions when writing their poems, rather than simply letting their intuition guide them.

Fox: Is it possible to generalize about where the best students come from, or who they are, or what kind of people they are?

TRETHEWEY: I don't know about that, and I think that probably different people would say different things. I think people would probably disagree on what best quality a student might have. Obviously, it has to be someone who has some facility with language as well as a passion for it, but when I was growing up my father used to tell me that he thought I needed to be a writer because I had a story to tell. In that way, it seems if the story was there but had I not been able to develop a facility with language, a way to say it, then having all the story in the world wouldn't have made a difference. I think there are some people who begin with having a story to tell, and the hope is that they also have the ability to tell it, that they find the elegant language. There are other people who begin with a heightened ability with language and then they have to find their stories, find what they must say.

Fox: How much does that have to do with being able to go deep; in other words, being truthful to what I think of as the truest truth, truths that are deep, not just "I ate pancakes for breakfast"—that's true, but it's not too important.

TRETHEWEY: Well, I would say that I'd like to believe that the best poets are also ones who are deeply self-reflective, but I imagine that not everybody has the same depth of self-reflection. I think there are probably still some fine poets who have some truths that they still can't touch.

Fox: Do you think it's valuable for a poet to have an MFA, for example?
TRETHEWEY: I think it's valuable for writers to go to a place where they have time to immerse themselves in their craft and in concentrated study. I don't know that you necessarily have to go to an MFA program for that, but they do make that space a little bit easier.

Fox: You say "immerse themselves"—how do you go about teaching; what do you do with the class?
TRETHEWEY: Well, we read lots of poems, in anthologies and in a couple of full-length collections. I think what I like best about teaching is that it's a conversation in the best sense, with people who are also interested. That's how I like it to be; it's not always that because our classes meet a writing requirement so sometimes I just have students who are there because they figure writing a poem, because it's short, has got to be easier than writing essays in another class. And that can often change the dynamic. But in a class like that I'm hoping to make more lovers of poetry and readers of poetry. I like it if I can surprise them; they come to the class for one thing, but if I can get them hooked on poetry, they'll leave with something else.

Fox: You say you have a story to tell. Do you ever censor yourself, not wanting to talk about someone or family things or anything like that?
TRETHEWEY: You know, I haven't had that issue, though that's another one that I talk about with students, because sometimes people are reluctant to write poems that reveal things about family members. And my father and I are not as burdened by that fear. We seem to be able to reveal all sorts of stuff. And it even became a shtick in our family; at one point, my father was giving a reading from a new book and his mother came down from Canada and was in the audience, I don't know if she'd ever heard him read, and he read this beautiful poem called "Rescue" about his younger brother who—during the time the poem describes—was getting into trouble at school. In the poem my grandmother sends this younger brother down to be with his older brother who is getting a PhD at the time, thinking that this would help straighten him out. And my father describes the brother standing in the parking lot and he describes how his jeans are kind of worn with some holes at the knees or something and my grandmother at that moment, from the back of the room says, "No way I would have sent him to the United States with holey jeans!" [*Fox laughs*] I mean, just in the middle of the reading. Everybody laughed, and then she did it almost every other time; it became

this little call-and-response that she would do in the middle of it. So that's to say that my father has been writing poems about his family, about me. And when I was becoming a poet, I knew that he was both happy and excited anticipating it, but also that he was dreading the stories that I was going to tell—which I consider to be setting the record straight. There's his version and then there's *the* version, which is mine. [*laughs*] So, we often read together now and we've sort of made a good conversation out of our own poems. We just stand there together and go back and forth, and our poems speak to each other. I think together they reveal even more than if you read them or encountered them separately. That's a long answer to your question about things that I censor in terms of family—I mean, I'm sure there are plenty of things that I'm censoring but they're so censored that I probably don't even realize it.

Fox: I kind of like that. What do you enjoy about readings?
TRETHEWEY: Oh, I think what I enjoy most about a reading is always the time afterwards, having the occasion to meet and talk to people. I always love it when there are young people in the audience who have just attended their first poetry reading and tell me that they're going to come back—you know they were forced to go by their creative writing teacher and probably never would have wandered in on their own, and now they'll come back.

Fox: I always think it's somewhat like a Shakespearean play, which you can get a lot out of it by reading it, but when it's performed, I get more out of it because the actors have studied and bring more to it.
TRETHEWEY: Yeah, you know, when I answered that, I think I thought your question was about what I like about it when I have to give a reading, not if I'm an audience member at a reading, which of course is really being able to sit there and listen to the music of someone's language and be transported.

Fox: How has your writing evolved over the years?
TRETHEWEY: Oh, I think—well, I hope—that I'm a bit more conscious about the possibilities of language than I was before, but I think that the biggest change for me with finishing my most recent book, and even the poems that I'm working on now, is that I'm less afraid to say certain things. I feel like I'm maybe a little bit more daring. I think I've always had a kind of restraint that maybe in earlier work bordered on perhaps what some people

might see as a distance from the emotional material of the poem. I think that in *Native Guard*, there's not a lot of distance between me, or the voice in the poem, and the emotional level of the poem. I gave a reading once and Ellen Voigt came up to me afterwards and said—and I loved when she told me this—that she could just hear the anger seething beneath the surface of those poems. I think it is particularly evident when I start talking about Mississippi. I wouldn't have allowed myself to be angry in a poem a couple books ago.

Fox: How do you write? Do you write every day, or when inspiration visits?
TRETHEWEY: In the summer or when I'm on leave, I like to have a nice schedule like that where I write every day. When I'm teaching and doing committee meetings and traveling, I have maybe a day or two that I can set aside to write during the week, where I don't have to go in and meet students or I don't have to go to a meeting or something like that. So, it's not every day when it's during the semester.

Fox: When you're writing a poem, how do you know a poem is finished?
TRETHEWEY: Well, I don't know that I know that it's finished, but I know that I am, [*all laugh*] that there's probably nothing else that I can do, at least for a long time. When I can get to that stopping point, whether that means it's really finished or not, I can put it away for a while. The poet Ron Padgett came to Emory last year and talked about this in a way that was useful for me to consider. He had just published a collection called *Poems I Guess I Wrote*, made up of poems that he had set aside in a drawer for twenty years because he hadn't been able to finish them. But as he began taking them out of the drawer all those years later he could see what each poem needed that he hadn't seen before. I have poems like that, that it's taken me years to "finish."

Fox: It reminds me of the line from Shakespeare, "Ripeness is all." When it's ready, it comes; when it's not ready, it doesn't. When you're ninety years old and looking back on your career, what do you want to be able to look back on with pleasure?
TRETHEWEY: Well, that I continue to learn and grow as a poet and that I will have written better poems than the poems that I have right now. If they keep getting better, and I'm still writing them at ninety—if I can write a better poem at ninety than I ever did—I think I'd be happy.

Fox: That's always the challenge, isn't it, to try and do it better today than yesterday?
TRETHEWEY: Yeah, right. I think that would be the best thing to be able to say when you look back on your writing life.

Fox: Who are some of your favorite poets?
TRETHEWEY: Oh, I have so many. Of course, Phil Levine is one of them. I like to think about the contemporary poets, these living word poets that I love. I love Ellen's work, too. Yusef Komunyakaa. Rita Dove's work, of course, meant so much to me early on because in her *Thomas and Beulah* I learned that you can tell stories about ordinary black people.

Fox: She wrote a very nice introduction to your book.
TRETHEWEY: She did!

Fox: Do you feel there's a generational difference in poets, like the younger poets as opposed to the old-timers?
TRETHEWEY: I feel kind of old-timey myself. I feel like I probably cleave more toward a kind of poetics that seems to have been more in fashion at another historical moment than some of the younger poets who are writing today. Does that make sense?

Fox: That makes sense. What causes you to think of yourself as a more old-timey poet?
TRETHEWEY: Well, I've been called that, for one. [*laughs*] Yeah, I have. Claudia Emerson says she thinks a poem ought to be beautiful and it ought to make sense. And I agree with that, and I think that's old-timey. But I also think it's a value judgment that never goes out of style.

Fox: When you write, do you share with anybody else before you consider the poem finished; do you get feedback or just do it yourself?
TRETHEWEY: I used to send my poems to my father a lot and he would send his. These days, I read them mostly to my husband, and he's a historian, and not someone who feels that he knows anything about poetry. But he knows what expectations I have of my poems and so he is a good reader for me.

Fox: When you're teaching, do you find that students are open to discus-

sion, suggestions—I won't say criticism—or are some open and some opposed to that?
TRETHEWEY: Oh, yeah, I think there are varying degrees of openness. I think some students, like any of us might be, are a little bit nervous about the whole process of having their work talked about by this group of people. And I try very hard to make sure that the discussion is thoughtful, that people have spent a good deal of time reading the person's work, that we try to remove our personal evaluations from it and talk about the poems on the level of craft, how they're doing whatever it is they're trying to do. And I think when we do that, people feel more open and they feel safer knowing that the criticism is really thoughtful.

Fox: So is it important to create a safe environment for students?
TRETHEWEY: I think so.

Fox: Do you ever find that some students are extremely critical of other students' work and you have to kind of buffer that?
TRETHEWEY: I have not had that experience very much and I think it's probably because of the way I set the terms for discussion early on.

Fox: How do you do that?
TRETHEWEY: Well, to give credit where credit is due, because these are certainly not things that I came up with on my own, but one of my first teachers, and an important teacher for me, was Margaret Gibson, and she created a list of questions to ask of a poem, things like, "What's the balance of image to statement?" or "Does the language name things properly in the world of the poem?" They're really useful questions that allow a kind of entryway for anyone into a poem.

And then I was at Bread Loaf as a fellow a few years ago and Ellen Voigt was my teacher—she is an amazing teacher—and she talked about the difference between descriptive and evaluative criticism. She always began a workshop with people describing the means of the poem; I mean, simple things, like whether the poem is in a traditional meter, or if it is a free verse poem. All kinds of descriptive things about elements of craft instead of evaluative judgments about a poem.

And so, from having learned from these two teachers, I devised a set of categories that help my workshop participants describe what's going on in a poem in terms of a poem's geography, its constitutive elements such as linguistic geography, sonic geography, the architectural geography, aesthetic or intellectual geography, etc. I think that those things are for the most part present in successful poems, sometimes in varying degrees. So that when we talk about a poem's linguistic geography, for example, say it's a poem about a farm or work on a farm, there's a whole linguistic geography that'll go with that, the objects, the naming of things, and if the proper naming of things is absent from the poem, then that's probably a reason a poem like that might fail. So, it's easy in a workshop to talk about the geographies that we see most prominently at work and what seems to be missing. The writer gets to hear a discussion that's descriptive about those categories, and I think can figure it out from what's missing from the discussion what is missing from the poem.

I don't like a kind of workshop that is about editing—I don't want to sit there and be an editor. I don't want to tell someone how to "fix" a poem. I don't like line editing and fixing and all that. I'd rather have a larger discussion about the poem and how it is doing what it's doing, so that the writer can hear that and go back and make her own decisions.

Fox: And how do you work with an editor, for your books, for example? Does an editor have much input, or do you make changes, or pretty much as submitted?
TRETHEWEY: Pretty close to as submitted.

Fox: Do you respond differently to poems you've written a few years ago than you did at the time?
TRETHEWEY: Well, I have now gone back and looked at poems in *Domestic Work* and made some changes on the poems. I used to see my father all the time when he'd go up to give a reading and he'd have the book there, but he will have made some changes, and so now I've gotten to that point. I can look at certain things in terms of syntax or punctuation and I can see how I would do it differently now.

Fox: Do you ever surprise yourself when you write something and say, Ooh, I didn't know I knew that?
TRETHEWEY: I had an experience of a big surprise like that when I wrote the last poem in *Native Guard*, "South." There's a line that reads, "State that made a crime of me." I was taken aback that I would say that. The censor in me wanted to take it out because it just seemed like it was stating it too

plainly, and I thought, "How can I just say that?" But I think it ultimately was necessary that I say it.

Fox: What is your view on the state of poetry in the United States? And I say that in the sense that many other countries seem to appreciate poetry and poets more than we do in the U.S.
TRETHEWEY: I have experienced that firsthand. I went to Ireland a few years ago and I was riding on a boat and somebody started talking to me and my husband and asked us both what we did. And when I said I was a poet the response was great—as opposed to when you're on a plane and get that sideways glance, like you're kind of odd or something. But I'm pretty optimistic; I think that things have happened recently that are making the American public feel a little bit differently about poetry. Every time I see Ted Kooser's "American Life in Poetry" column, or Pinsky's Favorite Poem Project, or the *NewsHour*'s "Occasional Poetry" series—I feel that more and more poetry is becoming part of the fabric of American life.

Right after I won the Pulitzer, I had to go to Charleston to give a reading, and my husband went with me because it was also my birthday. Some friends of ours found out where we were staying, and they sent us a bottle of champagne to celebrate. Well, the air conditioning in the room was still set to heat, and we had to call down for maintenance. When the man came up to fix it, he saw the champagne and asked us what we were celebrating. Brett told him, and he asked to see the book. As he flipped through it he must have seen a poem called "Incident." Then he closed the book and folded his hands in front of him, very formally, and proceeded to recite Countee Cullen's "Incident." And I just thought people *do* carry poems with them, more than we might think. There he was in our room to fix the air conditioner, standing there reciting a poem. I think I'll never forget that.

Fox: That's wonderful.
TRETHEWEY: Yeah.

Fox: My father wrote a book of poems that he had printed, and it was delivered to him, and the UPS guy said, "You know I happened to read your book, and I'd like to buy a couple of copies," which is very encouraging.
TRETHEWEY: Yeah, yeah. We just moved not too long ago and one of the guys who was on the moving crew, a young kid who was probably a senior in high school, had a notebook he was carrying around and writing poems in and showing them to me while they were moving furniture.

Fox: That's terrific.
TRETHEWEY: That's why I'm optimistic, because I think it's popping up in places that we might not expect.

Fox: Well, this is kind of the age of the "sound bite" and poetry is certainly a very succinct way of communicating important stuff.
TRETHEWEY: I've never heard that comparison, but I like that very much, that if we think about, you know, not those kind of sound bites, but a poem as a compact way of saying . . .

Fox: When I go to readings, if I hear a novel that's read, after two minutes I'm bored and I know I'm going to be bored for forty-five minutes. With poetry I know, another—
TRETHEWEY:—another one's coming shortly, right! So you can think about your grocery list for a moment, and then come back at the next poem. [*laughs*]

Fox: Okay, well, Tim and Daveen, do you have any questions?
GREEN: You mentioned that your husband is a historian, and *Native Guard* is such a book based on history, and I'm wondering two things about that: First, if you had a preconceived notion before you started writing the book that you were going to focus on this subject, and also, how much research—what was the role of research in the book?
TRETHEWEY: When I first set out to write it, I thought that it was only going to be about the Native Guards, because that's the thing that struck me, that this was a lesser known history that doesn't get mentioned when you go out to Ship Island, that you wouldn't know anything about because there's no monument out there or anything that tells you this part of the story. And so, historical erasure and historical memory are things that I think probably undergird just about everything I write; I mean, I can't imagine ever turning away from that as one of my obsessions. And so, this became a good way to investigate that again but specifically with the Native Guards.

But Mark Doty says that our metaphors go out ahead of us, and what I didn't find out until much later on, was that the book was very much also about my mother, and that what my mother had in common with the Native Guards was that she has no monument on her grave, that I had not yet properly done the work of memorialization that is my responsibility as daughter, as native guardian of her memory. That's the point at which I realized that all this belonged in the same book, rather than the elegies for her being put away in a drawer and me thinking, "That's for another thing."

And the role of research is really important for me. I always do a lot of research for books of poems. It's something I love. The book is footnoted with the various histories that I read and the primary documents I used such as the letters of the colonel who was stationed on the island.

Fox: Sometimes the most powerful writing is stories that are important and not known. It's just shocking that things happen that we don't know about that are important.
TRETHEWEY: Right. And it's easy to forget so much of what has shaped our thinking about the past—those things that become "buried history." And we often have different understandings of these things because of the way different regions remember the events of the past.

Fox: Yeah, it is very different. Daveen and I traveled—we have a friend who has developed "Sojourn to the Past," and he does civil rights; he takes high school students to the South, to Mississippi—
DAVEEN:—to retrace the civil rights movement; it's a ten-day trip.
TRETHEWEY: That's all? [*all laugh*]

DAVEEN: It's incredible.
TRETHEWEY: I bet it is. You know, it is so generational. I'm thinking about another thing that Phil Levine said, "I write what is given me to write." I was born a hundred years to the day that Mississippi first celebrated Confederate Memorial Day—the daughter of miscegenation. I know I was given that to write.

Because of Blood: Natasha Trethewey's Historical Memory

Lisa DeVries / 2008

The interviewer provided a copy of her original transcript for this Conversations volume, including dialogue that was omitted from the original publication in *TCR: The Common Reader: newsletter of the ECU department of English* (East Carolina University) 26.6 (May 2008). The newsletter website is http://english.ecu.edu/tcr/?page_id=2. The interview, conducted in April 2008, is archived at http://www.ecu.edu/english/tcr/26-6/trethewayinterview.html. The transcript is reprinted by permission of Lisa DeVries.

She reads with a clear cadence and soothing tone, occasionally glancing at the page for formality's sake, as if she has the poem memorized. Here is a little secret; she does. "I tend to be a real foot-tapper," states Natasha Trethewey, the third African American woman after Gwendolyn Brooks and Rita Dove to win the Pulitzer Prize. She visited East Carolina University April 2 for a public reading and book signing. Her upcoming work, *Thrall*, deals with telling the untold stories of history, identity politics, racism, and miscegenation. She claims that she writes only what she is given, "a violent history, and the terrible beauty of my South—my Mississippi."

Lisa DeVries: The Pulitzer Prize has a history of honoring what is in the moment, celebrating what is happening now. Why do you think this is *the* moment for *Native Guard*?
Natasha Trethewey: On the one hand, I think my story is the quintessential American story; this miscegenation is America, this history across the color line intersected is America. It is a truly American story that we have been waiting for someone to tell. A Civil War history is bringing to light those stories that get subsumed and erased. This book seeks to tell a fuller story of our history as Americans. Not "this" side, or "that" side, because there are no sides. We are not two trains running on separate tracks in America;

it is all intertwined, and here is a book that says so, such as when the black soldier is writing letters home for the illiterate white soldier, and their voices become mingled, one, as he writes for the other. The story mingles in my own blood; it is that voice that has to tell the story.

LD: One of your new, unpublished poems from the reading, "The Book of Castas," seems to deal with a kind of blood consciousness, some kind of historical pre-knowing identified with the body. Do you believe there is an unconscious connection between the history inside the blood and writing poetry?
NT: I think I merely write what I have been given to write. August Wilson believed that his subject matter came to him through some memory in his very body, the history of African Americans, the Middle Passage, slavery, Jim Crow. He felt that it came through a kind of blood memory. I do not believe that in relation to my own work. I like thinking about it for August Wilson, though, because he is such a terrific playwright. The danger, however, is that it begins to sound a little essentialist, about how we inherit what it is we have. I think what I have inherited to write is in my blood, in as much as my blood in the state of Mississippi was a problem, but that is a thing outside of me, not inside. That was law and custom, history and society. It is my place in the world and along the continuum of history that I have been given, the thing I am drawn to make sense out of.

LD: "Castas" also seems to deal with the historical amnesia that usually accompanies colonial societies. With your next work, are you trying to explore more the similarities between the colonialism of America and the colonialism of Mexico?
NT: I am. My obsessions stay the same—historical memory and historical erasure. I am particularly interested in the Americas and a history that is rooted in colonialism, the language and iconography of empire, disenfranchisement, the enslavement of peoples, and the way that people were sectioned off because of blood.

I am moving away from the American South, and moving away from the twentieth and nineteenth centuries, but in terms of the research I always do, that has stayed the same. I am interested in the eighteenth-century natural philosophy, science, particularly botany, the study of hybridity in plants and animals, which, of course, then allows me to consider the hybridity of language.

Thrall, which is the name of the new book, arises out of finishing the research on *Native Guard*. I always go to the *Oxford English Dictionary* and look up every single word that I think I already know. I looked up the word "native" again, and I was thinking of native in so many ways. You cannot say it and not think of *Native Son* or *Notes of a Native Son*, or Native Americans. There are all kinds of ways that one must think of that word, and when I looked it up, my expectation was that the first definition would be something that referred to native plants, or someone that is native to a place, like Mississippi. But the first definition is "someone born into the condition of servitude, of thrall." All of a sudden, the new title came to me. Why do we have this word "native?" When we claim land, the people who are there are the "natives"; it is about colonialism, it is about empire, and the word "thrall" is right there. I began to think, "Okay, so a thrall is a slave, and yet we are enthralled to all sorts of things." We are enthralled to the language that seeks to name us; thus "mulatto," "quadroon," "octoroon," "sambo," "albino." Then, when you think about travel narratives and captivity narratives, it was language that they were using to shape the understanding of a place and its inhabitants. When you look at those colonial maps that have drawings of the people there, it is the iconography, as well as the taxonomies of who they were that they were enthralled to. *Thrall* is just another digging in to that same obsession I have always had.

LD: Your mother pervades several poems in *Native Guard*. Are you trying to keep her from becoming one of these "untold stories" of history?
NT: Absolutely. I didn't know that when I started writing *Native Guard*; all I knew was that I wanted to write about the untold stories of those black soldiers. I think about Mark Doty saying, "Our metaphors go on ahead of us." And so there I was, chasing down this story from the past with all of the historical research it entailed, looking outward from myself, and that outward looking into the past and into history led me back inward to the thing that was really driving me—a desire to create a monument to my mother, because like those black soldiers, there is no marker, no monument, that inscribes her former presence on the American landscape.

LD: If she were alive today, would she still be a subject of so many of your poems?
NT: I can't even imagine that. I've written a couple of poems about my father, but I think that those poems are poems that are particularly rooted in what our lives have been—having separated as a family when I was young, and then both of us losing my mother. I think that a defining moment in my life was her

death, and it has shaped everything I've done. If I think about the things that have defined who I am as a poet, and what I feel it is my duty to write, such as being born of mixed race in 1960s Mississippi, it was losing my mother.

LD: When did you know you wanted to be a poet?
NT: I have to answer that in a couple different ways. My father and my stepmother are both poets, so growing up I had them encourage me to write poems. Just the other day he showed me a poem that my mother had sent to him that I had written probably when I was in the third grade. I also remember that my third grade teacher found several of my little odes and other poems to famous African American historical figures and the librarian put them in my school library, but I do not remember thinking as a child that I wanted to be a poet. I wrote a great deal.

Once I ran into a friend of mine from high school, and she said, "You told me when we first became friends in the eighth grade that you were going to be a poet," and I had to believe her that it was true, but I do not remember saying that. It might have been a secret ambition that I would not have said to anybody because those secret ambitions are often the ones we do not think can really ever happen. I think, in some unguarded moment as a child with my best friend, I revealed the truth.

When I went to college, I did not write at all. I did not take any undergraduate creative writing classes; I regret that very much now, but that was sort of a time of turmoil for me. My mother had been killed at the end of my first year. I was not a very good student after that; it took me until the end of my senior year to scramble enough of a GPA together to graduate. My father still really believed that I could be a writer, and I have often wondered if that was simply because he recognized some genuine talent, or that it was his father's pride in a daughter that could write. He talked me into applying to graduate school, and I applied in fiction. For a while, I was a would-be shortstory writer and within the first month or two realized that I was a poet. I did not quite realize it like that, but a friend of mine in the program who was a poet dared me to write a poem, and I took on the dare because I thought I was a really bad poet. I remember when I was nineteen, after my mother died, trying to write poems about it because often we turn to poetry in difficult times. I remember trying to record my grief in language and writing a line that said something like "sinking into an ocean of despair," and sinking went down the page; it was extremely trite, one big cliché. Later, I showed it to my father and stepmother at dinner one day, and they proceeded to just rip it to shreds. I ran crying up to my bedroom, saying I will never write a poem again. When this friend of mine in graduate school said, "I dare you to write a poem," I took on the dare because I was going to prove to him that I could not. And I wrote a very decent, not-so-bad poem. I put it in my fiction teacher's mailbox, and the next time I saw her she came running down the hall saying, "Oh Tasha, you're a poet." She might just have been saying that to get me out of her fiction class (*laughs*), but I went with it.

LD: The poem "Pilgrimage" ends with the line "the ghost of history lies down beside me, / rolls over, pins me beneath a heavy arm." Do you find that historical memory and historical erasure is a heavy burden to bear, or is it more like feeding your pen?
NT: It's both. People do talk about the burden of history, and for me the sort of tongue-and-cheek thing about those lines is that I have come to believe that the burden of history is a burden that I willingly take on, and that willingness is an intimate thing. It means you might have to lie down with it. History is intimate; you sleep with it.

Joel Brewer wrote in his essay "Cleo Rising" that the muse of history actually holds little influence on contemporary American poets, that there is a tendency to always gaze inward, a kind of navel gazing. He goes on to say that contemporary poets merely claim, "I am here," instead of looking outward to claim, "They were there." My entire life my father has said to me, "You have a story; yours is an important one to tell," and yet at the same time, I am resistant to a complete navel gazing. I am nervous about being self-indulgent with my own interior life and my own stories, and so I turn to the external, which is history, as a way of looking outward. However, it is also a way to place my own stories in a larger historical context. A poem I write is not just about me; it is about national identity, not just regional but national, the history of people in relation to other people. I reach for these outward stories to make sense of my own life, and how my story intersects with a larger public history.

LD: *Native Guard*, and your upcoming book of poetry, *Thrall*, must require a great deal of research. Do you write or research first?
NT: It goes back and forth. Sometimes if there is some historical question that I have asked myself I will begin writing from what it is I think I already know. Then I conduct research, and at some point try to set it all aside and write from what I have come to know, so that it seems intuitive. There are moments when I become nervous because it seems so organic; once it happens, I sometimes think I must be misrepresenting the facts. Then I have to

go back and read again to fact-check. I am always excited to find out that I have made notes or scribbled in the margins things to remind me of "this is where I found it," that this is indeed something that is rooted in historical fact.

LD: What do you think makes poetry a significant endeavor in today's world?
NT: Poetry requires our single attention, and that is getting harder and harder. Yet I think there are still people who want those moments of singular attention, to be able to make sense of that crazy frenetic pace that we live in most of the time. Ted Kooser's "American Life in Poetry" publishes short poems once a week in the newspaper, always on some aspect of American life, usually ordinariness, like an old couple sitting in a restaurant together and the husband is delicately cutting the sandwich for her. It does not seem like it would quite rise to the occasion of poetry, but it does. There are all of these little ordinary, everyday experiences that speak to our human condition, and that is the kind of thing that lay audiences are probably delighted to see. After modernism and poets who were writing poems that were almost indecipherable to anyone but them, you can see why ordinary folks would turn away from it. What did it have to offer to invite them in? There are poets who still want to invite people in, to communicate, and be that one voice talking to someone out there who wants to listen. That is the thing that will continue to make poetry relevant.

LD: Do you view poetry as a performance?
NT: My father is also a poet, and on several occasions we have given readings together. We stand at the podium and read back and forth together, poems that create a conversation with each other. I once tried to talk him into not choosing the poems beforehand. I wanted him to just go up there with me and read a poem, and then I would respond with a poem, and on and on like that. I thought there would be something exciting about that kind of call and response, or improvisation that would happen, responding to another person in much in the way I think about responding to an audience, or to what I am feeling at a given moment when I am standing in front of an audience.

I often have an idea of what I might read, but I change my mind when I am onstage. I do not like to have it so rigidly planned that I do not leave room for echoes that might arise and thus point to a different poem that I should be reading instead.

In terms of the idea of the performance of it, the thing I think about most is voice. I am someone who cannot sing, but I am very conscious of wanting to be able to modulate my voice in such a way that works with the particular microphone I have been given, or the acoustics of a room. I am also concerned with cadence. I tend to recite my poems when I am driving down the road or walking around so usually I have them memorized, but I am holding the book and looking at it like I am reading it.

LD: Do you ever see yourself writing about the present moment?
NT: There are things that I think people are a lot more open to acknowledging if they happened a hundred years ago. If I say, "This is what is happening now," there are people who would immediately draw a shade down and not listen. I can mention that just eleven years ago the state of Alabama voted to get rid of the anti-miscegenation laws, but the poem is about my parents and my childhood. People always want to be on the right side of history; it is a lot easier to say, "What an atrocity that was" than it is to say, "What an atrocity this is."

Years ago I read some of the poems from *Native Guard* and Ellen Bryant Voigt was in the audience, someone I admire tremendously. After the reading she said, "I can just hear the anger seething beneath the surface of these poems." There is anger, a tremendous amount of grief, restraint, and moral outrage. Even when I say the lines, "state that made a crime of me," I have to keep my lips from baring my teeth, which is why *Native Guard* was a departure from my other two books. One reviewer said that there is a certain cold-bloodedness that I am doing in *Native Guard*, because I think it is the angriest book I have ever written. It scared me to write it because I have been so restrained in the past. I have always wanted to be even, and hope that the image I give is enough to evoke in the reader's mind the thing I am trying to do. It took everything I had to push what was rising to the surface in *Native Guard* down. I would not have said one, or even two books ago, "state that made a crime of me." For me, the book communicates white hot emotion and rage, but maybe that surface level of restraint, that form mediates. It should I suppose, because if I came off like that you probably would not want to listen to me at all. I would be didactic, like Barack Obama's minister, "Goddamn America." But, am I not saying that? Why else would I use Nina Simone's epigraph? "Everybody knows about Mississippi." Do you know what song that comes from? "Mississippi Goddamn," and I am just implying that you remember that when I use the line.

An Interview with Natasha Trethewey

Christian Teresi / 2009

From *The Writer's Chronicle* 44.3 (December 2011), 42–55. The interview was conducted in November 2009, with updates between that time and publication in *The Writer's Chronicle*, the journal of the Association of Writers and Writing Programs. Following the interview, *TWC* reprinted Trethewey's poem "Knowledge," later included in *Thrall*. Reprinted by permission.

Christian Teresi: Each of your books has an increased formal element. How much of your maturation as a writer played into your ability to progress formally?

Natasha Trethewey: I did not write, at first, in traditional forms as much as I do now—even though one of my first published poems, "Flounder," is a ballad. Early on, my father—who was one of my first teachers—would challenge me to write in certain forms. He'd pull out a copy of Roethke's "My Papa's Waltz," for example, and say, "Can you write a poem like this?" I think my answer was to write "Flounder." I remember also being moved by the poems of Gwendolyn Brooks that I was reading in a graduate seminar, and her modification of form—how she would take certain traditional forms and revise them for her own purposes. That was really exciting to me, and it was the first kind of formal experimentation I did. There are poems in *Domestic Work* that were my attempt to do what I thought Brooks was doing.

Teresi: How much of it is a conscious decision? Particularly with the second and third book, which seem to have a more pronounced sort of formality.

Trethewey: I thought about formality a lot with *Native Guard*, especially moving from *Bellocq's Ophelia* in which I had written a sequence of unrhymed sonnets. I think the rhythm of those were in my head when I started writing *Native Guard*. The first thing I started writing for *Native Guard* was the long title sequence, the crown of unrhymed sonnets. I was a little worried that because it was coming straight out of my experience of writing

Bellocq's Ophelia, I was doing a similar formal thing, and that's one of the reasons I decided to make it a crown—to add another challenge within the poem that would perhaps push it in a different direction. Once I did that, it occurred to me that the repetition involved in a crown, and the repetition involved in many of the other forms I use in *Native Guard*, was an important technique for addressing historical erasure. The use of repetition was a formal decision I made early on in the writing because what I was trying to do was to reinscribe what had been erased, what was lost or forgotten—it was not necessary just to say a thing, but also to say it again.

Teresi: As someone who uses familial and communal photographs to explore various themes, what do you see as the dangers and benefits of writing ekphrastically in your work?
Trethewey: The benefit for me, and I think a benefit for others who would do it, is the given image, something that is concrete from which to start. So, for me, rather than starting with abstractions, I can begin with something that is already there to look at, and think that is a good way to enter into whatever one's subject matter might be.

Teresi: Are there dangers?
Trethewey: Certainly there must be. Well, I write about photographs, but when you first said the word ekphrastic, I was immediately thinking about my work writing about paintings, and mainly that's because I'm writing a lot more about paintings now. *Bellocq's Ophelia* was about a series of photographs, but it starts with the painting *Ophelia* by John Everett Millais. I would think that a danger might be in misreading the work, which might cause a kind of historical anachronism I am trying to avoid. But I can also imagine that for some writers this would not be a danger at all: perhaps misreading an image would allow exciting things to happen; it could make the poem take off in a different direction. But because I am interested in history, I'm trying to avoid making interpretive mistakes. I'm trying not to impose my experience in the contemporary moment on a moment in history. A misreading of a painting or photograph could lead to that.

Teresi: The question for me comes from seeing all these books of poetry produced about visual art. I think a lot of people do take liberties, and either purposefully misrepresent or misrepresent because they aren't being careful.
Trethewey: I know what you're talking about. I've been trying to write about Renaissance paintings and ones with a lot of religious imagery. After I

finished the MFA program at UMass, I was in a PhD program in American studies, where of course one learns to read material culturally for what it reveals about a time and place and the people in it—just as in the study of art one has to learn the iconography. I could totally have fun and misread religious iconography in paintings, and that would be one way to make a poem, but I'm interested in learning the iconography so I can understand what those images meant to the people of the time when they encountered them in paintings or as altarpieces in churches.

Teresi: I think there are poets and academics so beholden to certain ideologies that, as a consequence, their aesthetic standards suffer. You deal with a lot of sensitive issues in your own work, and it made me wonder how much you think about trying to make those issues resonate beyond your own personal beliefs?
Trethewey: I've been trying to do that since I was first learning to be a poet in graduate school. One of my professors was not very interested in experience. He was only interested in the imagination and thought that if something happened to you it probably wasn't worthy of being a poem. At the same time, I also knew that there were people out there who believed—and perhaps he believed it and didn't even know he believed it—that other people's experiences are of less interest to us. I felt like I was always being told, "No one wants to hear that anymore. No one wants to hear about those kinds of experiences." I had to try and find ways to make sense of the things I've been given to write about in such a way that it's bigger than me. I hope that's what I'm doing, which is why I turn to history over and over. The sensitive things I write about don't just belong to me. They belong to history, which means they belong to all of us. If I can remind people that what I'm writing about is a shared history, not merely a personal history, that my personal stake in it can resonate and connect across time and space to other people and their personal stakes in history, then I think I'm able to avoid the trap of my own personal ideology.

Teresi: Who do you think about when you think about audience?
Trethewey: I think about the world.

Teresi: That's funny because of what your professor said to you, and how much backlash there is against the lyric narrative. Yet all of the most recognizable poets in contemporary American literature have significant contributions to the lyric narrative.

Trethewey: I know. Isn't it strange? This same professor said to me, "Unburden yourself of being black. Unburden yourself of the death of your mother. Write about the situation in Northern Ireland." I tried to take that advice, but of course, what it did was make me read many more Irish poets and eventually write *Native Guard*—which is all about the very things I had been told to let go. Reading poets like Heaney and Boland and seeing the way that they claim Irish history and their places in it—their relationship to homeland and to ideas of exile showed me a way into my own material, not in Northern Ireland, but in Mississippi, in the Deep South. Reading Heaney's *North* helped me to understand my relationship to my South.

Teresi: You have that line in *Native Guard* from "Pilgrimage," "The living come to mingle with the dead." Do you see the primary importance of a poet is to keep a record of the past and to not be working purely in an imaginative state?

Trethewey: I do, and I feel that at least one of the duties I want to take on is the work of recording and remembrance. My mind keeps to things poets have said about this. Like Keats's, "To sharpen one's vision into the heart and nature of man." For me, doing that means understanding something about the historical moment in which we live. As Faulkner says, "The past isn't dead, it isn't even past." It's always here. The dead are always here with us.

Teresi: So how important do you see keeping an accurate record of history is with regards to your own efforts? Do you actually see your work as a redressing of inaccuracies, not only within history, but also in your own community, background, and the culture around you?

Trethewey: Absolutely, and when you say it like that, I remember an essay Robert Hayden wrote that was very much about redressing the mistakes or the errors in history about African Americans. Growing up in the Deep South, I had a profound sense of exile. That exile came because of what I saw as historical erasure on the landscape, in the history books, in the erecting of monuments—all those places that are there to remind and tell us about the past, and about who we are. But of course, these monuments and things are never simply about the past. They are about who we are now, and what we think about ourselves right now. All I could see was what we thought about ourselves in the South then did not necessarily include stories about African Americans—particularly in the Civil War. I grew up—I think a lot of people grew up—having no idea that nearly 200,000 African Americans fought in the Civil War. It was accessible in the records, yet when some people wrote the history books, when they inscribed the landscapes with monuments and named roads and buildings and bridges, they told only part of the story. I wanted to redress that. I wanted to fill in what I saw as gaps everywhere.

Teresi: What makes people so willing to believe in an inaccurate history?
Trethewey: Well, it has to do with the narratives we need to tell ourselves about ourselves. Even sitting here and doing this interview, I'm very concerned about the story that I'm creating and that we'll create together about me or about this moment. I think we all want stories that present us in a better light. That's why memory is so flawed. The more you repeat memories to yourself, the more you might edit them or change them so that you might come off appearing a little bit better than you actually were. I think a lot of the revisions or omissions in Southern history are about people not wanting to end up on the wrong side of history, because once everything changed, once we had the civil rights movement, it was clear that the events of the past were unjust. Who wants to be on the side of injustice when the world comes to acknowledge the horrors of it?

A good example of the inaccuracies of history is in the flag debate in the state of Georgia. The flag with the Confederate symbol on it that was changed in 2001 was not the original Confederate flag of the state of Georgia. It was the flag adopted in 1956 as a reaction to the *Brown v. Board of Education* decision, in protest of desegregation. Back then, ironically, the Daughters of the Confederacy were against the change because the flag that was already in place was proposed by their organization and adopted after the Civil War to represent the Confederacy. So all the people who are running around saying these issues are about heritage, not hate, are misrepresenting the history as evidenced by the historical documents. This is not unlike the people who want to insist the war was not about slavery—just states' rights. But states' rights to do what? Among other things, to determine whether or not its citizens can own slaves.

Teresi: How did you come to write *Beyond Katrina*? It made me think about erasure with regards to the books of poetry about Katrina. Inevitably, even in absolute earnestness, I think those books have to take one viewpoint over another. They never get at the totality of what they're talking about. I wonder if you think there is a way to go about a discussion of Katrina, or tragedy in general, that makes poems more responsible.
Trethewey: *Beyond Katrina* began as lectures I gave at the University of

Virginia. The book's greatest influence and literary ancestor is Robert Penn Warren's *Segregation*, which is a very lovely, thin book, and, in a way, a travel narrative. *Segregation* represents a kind of reporting and interviewing, based on Warren's journey back to the South after the Brown decision to rethink his earlier position on the South from *I'll Take My Stand*. And I love that about him—that he undertook this project to reexamine his feelings. That's what I was trying to do when I went back to my home to consider what this storm meant and what was happening.

The people on the Gulf Coast already feel like their story has been subjugated beneath the story of Katrina in New Orleans. Katrina in New Orleans is a travesty, and it's clear why that story became the story in so many ways. It was about the horrors of the aftermath when the levees broke. But the storm made landfall on the Mississippi Gulf Coast where I'm from, and completely devastated many towns whose names people can't recall—Pass Christian, Waveland, and Bay St. Louis to name a few. I've found that when I travel around the country and ask people what they think of when I say Hurricane Katrina, it's always New Orleans.

Teresi: There is that moment *in Beyond Katrina* where a woman in Gulfport says to you, "There's a difference between a natural disaster and the man-made disaster of New Orleans. Don't forget about us."

Trethewey: Right. She just wanted people to remember. Like a lot of people, I sat there and cried watching what was happening to New Orleans, because I love that place too. But I wonder (and maybe this answers your question about responsible ways of dealing with tragedies that happen), how can we leave the ideology behind? Certain reprehensible ideological positions make some people feel that the suffering of one group of people is more deserving of our sympathy than the suffering of another. Buried under that is an idea about race and class that often goes unspoken, unacknowledged.

Even that narrative about Mississippi is a contentious one. There are some Mississippians who would like to tell you we fixed everything, but we didn't fix everything—not for the poorest citizens in the state. They are still suffering. They are still struggling. They have not seen their fair share of money because it has gone to businesses and wealthier citizens . . . I don't know. There is a responsible way to write about it. I just keep going back to the idea of trying to tell a fuller version of the story. I don't know how any one of us does that. I mean, I understand my own limitations when I'm trying to tell a fuller version of any story, and yet I think that by acknowledging my own limitations, I help to make room for another story rather than suggesting that the story I am telling is the only one. In writing *Native Guard*, I wanted to correct the misapprehensions in the narrative. I never wanted simply to erase or subjugate the narratives of the Confederacy that people hold dear to their hearts, but I would like to put them side by side with another story so that there are not two separate histories—two trains running on separate tracks—but stories intertwined in the way that our shared histories always are.

In writing *Beyond Katrina*, I wanted to make sure that the story of the Mississippi Gulf Coast wasn't completely forgotten, subjugated beneath the story of New Orleans. Early on, an editor asked me if I could make the book more about New Orleans. He said, "I think the problem is that people are going to see this title, *Beyond Katrina*, and think it's about New Orleans, and buy it, and then they'll return it when they see it's not." But that was the whole point I'd been trying to make. Mississippi had a story too—and it needed to be told.

Teresi: What was it like to go back there, to write that story?
Trethewey: The first thing I did was get out my *Let Us Now Praise Famous Men* to reread and rethink what it means to try to document the lives of struggling people. I also read George Orwell's *Road to Wigan Pier*. This time, reading those things, I was profoundly uncomfortable with the lens through which each writer was looking at the people, even if the people were made noble in many ways as they are in *Let Us Now Praise Famous Men*.

When I went to Gulfport with the NPR producer who accompanied me, the first thing that occurred to me was the feeling that I was no longer an insider. This was the place and the people I had always felt part of, but when I came back, I was the documentarian with a lens I was turning on them, and that made me really uncomfortable. That's why the poems I wrote for the book, unlike the beautiful poems in *VQR* by Susan Somers-Willett about Troy, New York, ended up being as much about me as they are about the place. I could not help but interrogate the very project I was sent there to do and my position in it, which is why there's a poem about being a prodigal daughter. I felt like a prodigal going back there.

Teresi: Why did *Road to Wigan Pier* and *Let Us Now Praise Famous Men* make you uncomfortable?
Trethewey: It was particularly the Orwell book. You know Walker Evans and James Agee and Orwell went and stayed with the people they were writing about. They stayed with the sharecroppers, and Orwell stayed in a

boarding house, a kind of flophouse place where these men who worked in the mines stayed. They inhabited these spaces, but even so they inhabited them as outsiders. When I went home in the past, I would go to my grandmother's house and write from in there. When I go back now, because her house was so damaged in Katrina, I stay in a hotel. So I wasn't even staying "in" in the same way Agee and Orwell were. What made me uncomfortable about Orwell was the ways he couldn't help—even in his generosity, with all his empathy—looking at them as other. There's a way that the people were so different from him that they were rendered other. An interviewer in South Korea once asked me: "Because there are problems people associate with writing about the marginalized or oppressed, how do you feel comfortable doing that?" I said, "I'm not writing about someone I'm not. These are the people from whom I have come." But then, when I finally went back to Mississippi to do this work, I realized I wasn't the insider I had been anymore.

Teresi: Was that part of the problem—that you felt uncomfortable by Agee and Orwell and thought you were going to do something different, but it felt like the same thing? How do you rectify that situation?
Trethewey: Well, I kept trying to turn the lens on myself, and not to navel gaze, but to indict. I was thinking about W. B. Yeats: "Of the quarrel with others we make rhetoric. Of the quarrel with ourselves, poetry." I have to make the argument ultimately with myself, or all I'm going to be doing is finger pointing. That goes back to your earlier question about how to make these things I write about resonate beyond my own personal beliefs. The quarrel must be with myself—even if I have a bone to pick, or something to redress in history, or with the historians who have erased or been irresponsible about recording history—and I must understand my own complicity with such aspects of erasure that as human beings we can't help but be involved in.

Teresi: I wanted to ask you about your mother and the poems in *Domestic Work* about her that sort of hint, create mystery, and give glimpses about the tragic circumstances surrounding her death without ever fully disclosing the details of what happened. In the poems about her in *Native Guard*, you give more details, but again you never fully disclose, certainly not in the way you have in interviews. This made me wonder what it was about those details that were unnecessary in the poems, particularly when so much of your work is concerned with bringing to light forgotten history.
Trethewey: I think I have a natural reticence in poetry that I would call restraint. I'm not necessarily reticent about what happened. I'm quite will-

ing to talk about it. I was going to say pleased, but that seems strange. There was a time in my life that being able to talk about my mother's murder was so necessary—that I could tell someone this, this thing that was weighing on my heart so much. I don't mind talking about it. I even think talking about it in interviews has been good, difficult, and bad at the same time. Good in that many women in domestic violence shelters and people all over the country heard it and, I think, were moved by it. People who might not have paid attention to the way poetry can address certain subjects were moved to pick up the book and write to me. At the same time, there would be these times when I would go to give a reading and someone—well-meaning, no doubt—would introduce me and say, "This book *Native Guard* is about three things: her relationship to the South, the forgotten history of black Civil War soldiers, and her mother's murder." Well, *Native Guard* is in no way about my mother's murder. The book is an elegy for forgotten people and lost places. The murder is the backstory in my own life. That's how she got to be dead, to say it plainly. I never meant to intentionally be cagey or tightlipped about it. I do remember writing a poem in graduate school that dealt actually with her murder, and the response I got in workshop was so odd. The assumption was I had written this sensational poem because I had read something in the newspaper. I was being accused of just creating this sensational thing. They had no idea, because I guess I don't wear it on my sleeve, that this was actually my experience.

From then on I said, "Well, hands off. No one wants to hear these sensational things that happened to you even if they did happen." I'm not interested in confessing. I don't think of my poems as confessional in that vein. I don't mean there is anything wrong with confessional poems. I just don't think that's the mode I'm writing in. I think that the details of how my mother died weren't important for the particular poems thus far. The poems in *Native Guard*, for example, are dealing with erasure—not how she died, but that she was gone and wasn't being properly remembered. Like those soldiers without a monument—nothing on the landscape inscribed her memory.

I started writing the poems about my mother at the same time I started writing about the Civil War, and I did not think of them as belonging in the same book. The poems about my mother were poems I had to write, to make sense of the grief I had been grappling with for years. They were bearing down on me because I was approaching my fortieth birthday, which was the last age my mother ever was. I had also lived as many years without her as I had with her. I had reached that midpoint anniversary. I was approaching the twentieth anniversary of her death. I had moved back to Atlanta, the physical location of her death—a place I thought I would never go back to—because I had a job at Emory. All of those things, the confluence of those things, made me start writing the poems, but I thought they were deeply personal. They were about my own grief, and I was putting them away in a drawer and working on this Civil War history that was the thing I thought I was really interested in.

Then one day, as I was jogging through the Confederate section of the graveyard near my house, I thought about writing a poem about this graveyard and the way that all the names on the tombstones seemed to be calling out to me to be spoken aloud and remembered in some way. When I got home, what I started writing, however, was about the day we buried my mother, which turned out to be a poem called "Graveyard Blues" in *Native Guard*. The final couplet of that poem reads, "I wander now among the names of the dead:/My mother's name, stone pillow for my head." And it seemed an emotional truth to me in the poem to utter those lines, because I was thinking of the kind of cold comfort one might get by lying down on the tombstone, putting your head on it, and yet it was in that moment that I told a great lie in the poem.

I realized what this whole Civil War stuff had been about the whole time. Like those black soldiers, my mother doesn't have a stone on her grave so the erasure was that, and it was my doing. She had been in this place and on this land, and then she was gone, and there was no marker to remember that, nothing to inscribe her onto the landscape. The one whose duty was to remember her—her daughter—hadn't done it. That's the argument with myself. You'd think the argument was with the South, or my country for not remembering those black soldiers, but it was a bigger argument with myself for not doing the work of memory that I alone was charged with doing. And when I published *Native Guard*, I did it again, and it didn't occur to me until after all the attention the book got because of the prize, that I had created this monument to Natasha Trethewey's mother because of the dedication in the book "To My Mother"—and not Gwendolyn Ann Turnbough. So the same problem that had plagued me with the erasure on the landscape was stupidly enough that I didn't think I had language to name her on the landscape, because even though she was divorced, she died with my stepfather's last name, which was my brother's last name. I didn't want to put that on her stone. I couldn't put my father's name because that would not acknowledge my brother. It never occurred to me to put her maiden name, Gwendolyn Ann Turnbough, the name she was given when she entered the world, and so I had erased her, and then I erased her again in my own book. That's the erasure I'm concerned with in *Native Guard*, and that's why the details of her death, which are sensational, are not part of the poems. I don't know if I would know at this point how to deal with them. I do think people often have an empathetic interest, but then there's also prurient interest too. I think there are writers who can handle such material, but I don't know if I can tell that story, or what the value of it right now would be. What do the actual details of her murder mean that would make a poem do what I think a poem needs to do?

Teresi: What do the poems about your mother have to do?
Trethewey: I think they have to investigate loss. That is certainly a shared human emotion. When I read someone else's elegies, I read them because they show me back into my own heart. I hope my own might do that for someone else. I think poems are supposed to show us to each other, and in so doing show us ourselves.

Teresi: History seems to be the constant through the three books, but I wonder if you ever try to avoid discussions of history?
Trethewey: I don't think I try to actively avoid my obsession with history. I figure that's the only thing I know worth following. Sort of like the way George Orwell figures out it's the political purpose for him, that even though he has other impulses to write, he believes he knows which one is best for him to follow. I feel like that. I feel like the only way I'm going to write anything of consequence is if I follow my obsessions and allow them to guide me. What I try to avoid is approaching them in the same way. I have to try to find through form, or locale—the different locales I might investigate—a way of continuously pushing that investigation of history beyond where I left it the last time. I think the same obsessions undergird the poems always for me, but I hope to find something that makes the investigation different, that makes the poems sing a slightly different tune even though the baseline is the same.

I think if I weren't obsessed with history, I don't know what I would write about. I think if I didn't have this particular history, that I'd been given by birth, the fate of my geography, I don't know what I'd be doing. So that seems like the only thing worth sticking to, to see where it takes me.

Teresi: Do you know what your next book of poems is about?
Trethewey: It's about history—and, in many ways, my father. I'm a little

uncomfortable knowing this as early as I do, because that feels false to me in some ways. Like if I know already, then I don't really yet know; I only know what has revealed itself. It could be a barrier rather than a path.

Teresi: Do you feel like it's superficial?
Trethewey: That could be the problem. I always approach history in order to remove the impulse to simply navel gaze and write only about my own feelings or my own experience. History is a way of doing that for me, of contextualizing my own place in the world.

This new book that I'm working on begins in that same way, with that historical investigation of the language and iconography of eighteenth-century casta paintings in colonial Mexico that showed the mixed blood unions and the offspring of those unions in the colony—the taxonomies of the children inscribed right there on the paintings. I became obsessed with these families—mother, father, and child—and always the white father, the black mother, and the mulatto child. Of course, there was a reason I was fascinated by that. I thought it was just this language or iconography, but indeed it's about my own family, and so the difficult thing I've learned is that these poems are about my father, and the history of colonization, and who the colonialist is, and who the colonial bodies are.

That's why it's difficult, because my story is not just mine, but the way it's tied to the history of imperialism, colonization, power, and knowledge. Ways of knowing.

I think this is going to be difficult for my father.

Teresi: Your father must have some idea about how difficult some of this stuff is for you.
Trethewey: Yes. My father has this very lovely poem called "Her Swing" that he must have written when I was three or four years old. He wrote it, I think, to get at some of the difficulties he imagined I would face. Growing up, I heard my father read this poem a million times. Now, when we do readings together, standing side-by-side at the podium, and he gets to the line, "I study my crossbreed child," I feel like an exhibit in a museum of natural history. I've been living with that my whole life, and I never knew why something about the poem, as sweet as it is, never felt quite right to me. Now I think it's that he used the language of zoology, of animals, to describe his own child. No human being is a crossbreed. To be a crossbreed actually means to be born of different species. It's one thing to be named in the racial taxonomies of the Spanish casta paintings, in the language of census records

in New Orleans, in the constitution of the state of Mississippi, or the state of Virginia, or the state of wherever, and yet another thing to be named and categorized—even for the purposes of a poem—by one's own father.

Teresi: In the loosest way of referencing, your father's background comes from a different part of the history of western civilization.

Trethewey: Yes, my father is Canadian—another connection to the British Empire. Our story is emblematic of how even in families it's impossible to escape some of the things that are embedded in history and are still having an effect on our day-to-day lives. When I was finishing up *Native Guard*, I looked up the word native in the dictionary and was surprised to see the first definition of the word. I thought the meaning would be as we use it most, as in "I'm a native of Mississippi." Or, "That tree is native to Connecticut." But what comes up instead is, "Someone born into the condition of servitude; a thrall." So it has this history of imperialism built right in: when we go there to conquer that land, and colonize those people, they are the natives. So the new book is called *Thrall*, but thrall gives me a lot of other possibilities. Not just the idea of being in bondage or captivity, but also of being enthralled, as I think we are to language, especially language that seeks to name us and thus make us occupy certain positions in society, in history. That's particularly relevant to me because of a word like miscegenation that entered the American lexicon during the Civil War, and then was written into the law books of so many states. There is legal language meant to define me, and also render me illegal, or illegitimate. Antonio Nebrija, in his fifteenth-century Castilian grammar book wrote, "Language has always been the perfect tool of empire." I'm interested in those systems of knowledge. Enthralled by them.

Interview with Natasha Trethewey

Ana-Maurine Lara / 2009

> From *Torch: poetry, prose, and short stories by African American Women* (Fall/ Winter 2010). Four of the "Taxonomy" poems, later included in *Thrall*, were reprinted at the end of the interview. The website for the online journal is http://www.torchpoetry.org/TORCHJOURNAL.htm. Reprinted by permission.

This interview was conducted in December 2009, as Natasha Trethewey completed the James Weldon Johnson Fellowship in African American Studies at the Yale University Beinecke Rare Books and Manuscript Library. The interview came on the tails of a conversation between Elizabeth Alexander and Natasha Trethewey, sponsored by Endeavors: Perspectives on Black Life and Culture—a year-long graduate colloquium organized by the graduate students in African American studies, in which both poets discussed family, place, and poetry in the contemporary era. Natasha Trethewey is author of three poetry collections—*Domestic Work* (Graywolf, 2000), *Bellocq's Ophelia* (Graywolf, 2002) and *Native Guard* (Houghton Mifflin, 2006)—and a nonfiction piece, *Beyond Katrina: A Meditation on the Mississippi Gulf Coast* (University of Georgia Press, 2010). She is the recipient of numerous major awards, including the 2007 Pulitzer Prize for *Native Guard*, and the 2008 Mississippi Governor's Award for Excellence in the Arts for Poetry. In 2008 she was named Georgia Woman of the Year. Trethewey is a professor of English and the Phillis Wheatley Distinguished Chair in Poetry at Emory University in Atlanta, Georgia.

Ana: It's been so great to have you here at Yale. We're going to miss you. How was your time here?
Natasha: It's been lovely. I completed a ton of work, met a lot of people, and had great conversations. When I came here, I knew that I was interested in Mexican casta paintings because of their representations of mixed-blood people and the taxonomies that were assigned to these mixed-blood people.

Being a mixed-blood person myself, I'm really drawn to the iconography and how this identity is presented across time and space. I had written a sequence of poems about a set of those paintings and so I came here knowing that those images were driving me toward whatever investigation I was going to end up doing.

What I figured out during my time here is that what I'm working on is also about something very personal and something about family as well. In each of those paintings there are representations of families: father, mother, and child. In Mexican casta paintings, they always begin with the white father, quite literally. I have a white father and a black mother; I'm a mixed-race child.

One of the things that I discovered is my relationship to the language of my father's poems. My father is also a poet, and there's a lovely poem of his called "Her Swing." My father wrote this poem in the 1970s. I've been hearing this poem for as long as I can remember, and it is very sweet. It's a reflection on his daughter (me), but there was always something that bothered me about it. I just figured out what it was, and why it is now connected to those Mexican casta paintings and those taxonomies. There's a line in "Her Swing" that reads, "I study my cross-breed child." I figured out why it bothers me: "Cross-breed" is the language of zoology, not the terms I think we use for human beings, particularly not ones who are our own. It really sounded scientific, or even pseudo-scientific, of course, because I'm not a cross-breed. Cross-breed suggests a different species. That's what a mule is. A human being who has a black parent and a white parent is not a cross-breed. He wrote that thirty-five years ago, and maybe there wasn't access to other language, but I don't believe that. And even if that were true, he's had a lot of time to revise. That's what you can do with a poem; you can revise the words you chose until you find the best ones.

A: What I love about reading *Domestic Work*, *Bellocq's Ophelia*, and *Native Guard* side by side is not just reading them in relationship to each other, but also considering the narratives of your life. What is so amazing about all of these works together is how you reconstitute bodies as integral beings, how you reconstitute black female bodies in the landscape as integral to that landscape, to making that landscape possible. How do your own landscapes impact the creation of your poetry, impact the language that you use, and the frameworks that you use?
N: *Domestic Work* had a lot to do with the idea of the natural landscape versus the man-made landscape. Even as I say this I realize that this tension

is also there in *Native Guard*, and it's the thing that keeps coming into all the work: the intersections and the contentions between the natural and the man-made. The Mississippi Gulf Coast, where I'm from, has the longest man-made beach in the world. When they tried to make it into a resort area—like Florida—they did away with the natural coastline of mangrove swamps and all the natural flora and dumped white sand on top of all of what was there, for twenty-six miles. It's a layering of the natural with the man-made.

My grandmother's house sits right beside Highway 49, which is a legendary highway of blues music. When they sang about Highway 49 in the blues, they were singing about the old one, which is on the other side of her house. It was a small road that went through this area called Four Corners, but when they decided to expand it and connect I-10 to I-90, it cut right through the middle of the neighborhood, North Gulfport, one of the oldest African American communities on the Coast since after the Civil War. It divided my grandmother's house from where my great-uncle and my great uncle's son lived. What had been a pasture in my mother's childhood became a big highway. My grandmother agreed to allow Marine Life (it's like Sea World) to put a billboard half in her yard, because her house sits right next to the highway. Big eighteen-wheelers are passing by all the time, and all through the night. And there's this huge giant Marine Life sign shading my grandmother's house. My father once said to me, "Why don't you write a poem about nature?"

My father comes from rural Canada, and his relationship to nature and the rural landscape is very different from mine, and all I could think about was that for me, if nature was my grandmother's yard—where I used to track crawfish in the ditch and pick the fruit from the fig trees—nature always had a highway cutting through the middle of it, or a big billboard overshadowing it. That juxtaposition is central to my understanding of nature. So for me, in terms of landscape, there's always a duality and a contentiousness between what is there and what has been erected there. What story is being told by what's there, what's not being told by what's there.

A: Which is an apt metaphor for the mixed-race body, too. Can you speak to the physical connections you make between the personal and the public, the historical and the atemporal as we can see in poems like "History Lesson"? As you are going through memories, whether or not they're your own or fabricated, or informed by history, continuities and discontinuities, do you ever have that experience of discontinuities or atemporalities? When

you are writing in the here and now, but writing about memories you may or may not have witnessed, how do you experience that in your process?
N: You know the BBC production of Sherlock Holmes where they start off with a photograph from the 1800s and sometimes there are people in them? All of a sudden the scene that has been frozen in its historical moment comes to life, the people start moving, and that's how the movie transports us to that place. I sometimes feel like I'm in one of those photographs or one of those scenes. For me it's necessary to try to go to that place to create something that seems of that moment.

A: What are you looking for when you go there?
N: I'm trying to figure out something about what it was like to be in a different time and place. For example, I was in New Orleans not too long ago and decided to walk the length of Dumaine Street in the French Quarter, starting closer to the river and moving away from it. That was a street my grandmother had lived on when she lived in New Orleans, and it was the street where my mother was born. It looks very much like it must have looked in 1944 because the same architecture, the same little houses that were along that street are still there. Sure they've been fixed up or more rundown or whatever, but I just walked along there trying to imagine what my grandmother saw or heard or felt walking through that place.

A: That makes me think about memories and how our bodies carry memories.
N: Well, I knew that I had to create Ophelia as if I was remembering. As much as I used photographs in that project to bring what I was seeing to life, I spent a lot of time in New Orleans. I had spent a lot of time there growing up, so it felt like a landscape that was part of my development. But I went back to be in it in a different way, to take notice of things that I might not have taken note of with as much intent, and it was only that way that I could begin to imagine a persona: Ophelia. When I was working on Ophelia, I really began to think of her as existing at that moment, as co-existing. It wasn't simply that she had existed and I was writing about her; it was as if she's existing right now. This must be what fiction writers feel when they're working on their characters. I was thinking about what she was doing or what she was going to be doing, not always what she had done.

A: Does the fact of her (Ophelia) or of the domestic workers you speak of, does the fact of them change you and the way you move through the world?

N: I think that what they give to me is knowledge of the lives of other people. Even though Ophelia was invented, I fully believe that she existed as a possible human being, that there was someone who thought and felt and experienced the world as she did. I think that I write for that reason, in order to know something about the lives of other human beings across time and space. And that's why I think of poetry as a social practice, not just an aesthetic one.

A: I'm curious about labor. In *Domestic Work* you write about black women as laborers as domestic workers, as sex workers, as mothers, grandmothers, and aunts, as the cultural memory keepers. How do you see poetry, if you do, in that schema of labor?
N: I think that the work that I'm interested in taking on as a poet is the work of cultural memory, the preservation of a cultural memory of a people, of a time and place.

A: Would you say it's kind of like the creation of ruins?
N: Ruins is a perfect word to describe so much about me. I used, in this prose piece that I just finished, *Beyond Katrina*, I used the Hegel quote: "When we turn to look at the past the first thing we see is nothing but ruins." When I used that quote, I was literally looking at ruins and yet, even in something that isn't literally destroyed, as Gulfport was when I was looking at it, there are always ruins.

A: In what sense?
N: Another one of the writers whose quote I used in this book is Flannery O'Connor's. She says: "Where you came from is gone, where you're going to never was there, and where you are is no good unless you can get away from it."

I'm certainly a nostalgic person, and yet I also know that the very definition of nostalgia is this sort of longing for something that probably never really existed in the first place, at least not as you would have it. That's a ruin to me: something that was never, really. That place I came from has been gone; the moment after the moment I inhabited, it was gone. I try to get at that in the poem, "Theories of Time and Space," the first poem in *Native Guard*. I'm speaking literally because there's always a foothold in the literal from which I'm trying to extrapolate. But, literally you go on this boat to Ship Island, and there's a photographer there who takes your picture, and hours later when you come back, he's hung them all up. All the pictures are there waiting for you in hopes that you will then pay five dollars and buy this picture they took of you before you went out on the boat. It was in that moment that I realized what I came back to was a ruin because that picture of me and my husband and my brother, that's who we were hours before we took another route.

A: Before you were transformed by the experience?
N: Everything that is constantly transforming us. The past is breathing down our necks because it's always right there like our shadow. Those people, as they were in that moment, didn't exist anymore. For me, something is always gone. I started writing about photographs because it was the way that I could locate that feeling I had of constant loss: the loss of a moment that is gone from us.

A: What can a poem do that a photograph can't?
N: What I'm trying to do in poems is to create a momentary stay against the inevitability of loss. I'm thinking about Robert Hass when he says a word is an elegy to the thing it signifies. The thing is now gone from this moment of the poem, so we just have these words reminiscent of the thing that's gone and they bring it back to us. Perhaps photographs do this, too. They bring back to us that which is gone. Somebody had sent me a review that someone had written of *Native Guard* in *Poetry* magazine, and in the review the person seemed to understand my desire to memorialize or to erect monuments to things that had been forgotten or passed, but her take was that a statue is a static, dead thing so even if you write a poem to the thing, it also is a dead thing. I totally disagree with this because the point isn't for the statue to just be out there. A statue is a living thing. You can't tell me every time I see a Confederate statue that it doesn't matter. It lives!

A: You reference the connections between labor and exile in speaking about nostalgia; can you say more?
N: I think it's connected to the questions you ask about labor and the work of the poet. I'm not someone who confuses physical labor or that kind of work with the kind of work that I'm doing. I've written about people who are doing physical work. But I do think that the work of memory and forgetting is a kind of work as well.

I think that I have always lived with a sense of exile. Perhaps that is a condition that is shared by a great number of people, for whatever reason. My feelings of exile are rooted in the duality of the mixed-race body and are rooted in the laws of the state of Mississippi, in the laws of the U.S. that rendered a person like me illegitimate and rendered my parents as law breakers. To be born into a place that is the only geography that I have and in which I am rooted and tied to—and yet to be told that I am the illegal or illegitimate product of this place—created a sense of psychological exile. That same sense of psychological exile in the laws of Mississippi is also embedded in custom and in history.

Growing up in the Deep South, I was confronted constantly with the absence of narratives about who I was and the people that I felt closest to. We know the work that people did, and yet what got inscribed on the landscape through its monuments and the naming of roads and buildings was an entirely different story that was subjugating this other group of people, rendering them non-citizens or second-class citizens, as it has been called. I remember being so stunned that people who were so opposed to justice and equal rights would be given buildings named after them. Why are we going to erect a monument to a staunch segregationist who didn't believe in equal humanity of all people? That made no sense to me. There was this constant barrage of things constantly battering my psyche and making me feel like this is mine and yet it's not. I'm constantly being told that this does not belong to me, which is why I use the quote, "Homo sapiens is the only species to suffer psychological exile." I could be in Mississippi, in my grandmother's house, and still not feel home. So the only home that I have found is the one that I've made in language. *Native Guard* was my grand attempt to say, "This place is mine, and I'm going to inscribe it, and I'm going to change it so that it reflects more of the fact of me. This is mine, and it is us."

Labor and exile, side by side—it's what I knew. It's not simply that I just happen to know so much about my grandmother's work. She talked about her life in terms of work. When she narrated her history, it was a labor history. If you wanted to know anything about her past and you asked her, there was always labor connected to it.

A: It makes me think that given the second-class citizenship, or lack of citizenship for many people, required that people make themselves through their work.
N: I grew up with the idea that if you were black your class status was still black. In Mississippi black people were laborers. There were certainly people who managed to work their way out of being laborers, but the general understanding about who black people were and where they came from was always about physical labor. You could work the land, you could build the

buildings, you could do all that stuff and yet be rendered a non-citizen or psychologically exiled. It seemed to me that whatever work I could do to reclaim this place that I had been constantly exiled from was through language. Now the state of Mississippi can't get rid of me!

People have looked at the history of African Americans and of white Americans as two trains running on separate tracks; we've got to have Black History Month because black history isn't interwoven into the larger curriculum. So the common perception is, "Here's what everybody else was doing, and here's what the black folks were doing at the same time," not that it is an interwoven, absolutely dependent history. The cover of *Native Guard* shows the diary of a Confederate confiscated by a Union soldier. Because of the paper shortage the man who confiscated the diary had to cross-write over the diary that had already been written in. So you have the intersection between the narrative of the Confederate and the Union, and I gave that to my black soldier so that it becomes the intersection of North and South, of black and white, slave and free.

In its embrace of me, Mississippi has to also embrace the story I have told about us as Mississippians, black and white, and everything else. My father was there with me when I received the Governor's Award, and he was tearing up. He and I never would have imagined when I was born in Mississippi in 1966 and someone wrote on my birth certificate, race of mother "colored," race of father "Canadian," that I would ever be standing in front of the State House in front of the Senate and the House of Representatives.

A: What was that like for you?
N: I think I realized that I had wanted my home state to claim me my whole life. I had to force them to do it. But they have. And they had to do it reckoning with the history I was making them reckon with, too. It had to be done. I received a Governor's Award from a Republican governor.

A: It's powerful to stake a claim in the midst of exile.
N: It's an irony, a great irony but a perfect one. I was born a hundred years to the day that Mississippi first celebrated Confederate Memorial Day: April 26, 1966. On April 26, 1866, a year after the Civil War, they developed that holiday because they refused to celebrate the Fourth of July because that was American. And they kept it. That's the day I was born. Growing up and even as an adult, my birthday was a holiday. And I am born mixed race on Confederate Memorial Day, and we know that miscegenation was a huge hot button issue that entered the lexicon in 1863. There was a little pamphlet

written by a couple of reporters. It was a hoax, and they were trying to drum up a lot of anger against Lincoln because Lincoln was the president of amalgamation, so they were saying that if Lincoln was elected again we would have miscegenation run amok.

A: Because it did not already happen.
N: Right, it didn't happen before. But it was all of a sudden going to happen. I just think that it's crazy that this is what I was given. You can't make this up.

A: All of the ironies! We've come to my last question. In consideration of the power of claiming that space, what are the *creative* spaces that have given to you in your creative work?
N: I was a Bunting Fellow at Radcliffe in 2001. I went there ostensibly to work on *Bellocq's Ophelia*, and it was where I first started thinking about *Native Guard*. It was the first time that I've ever been given space like that, and it was constructed around giving women space to do this kind of work. That was really useful because I learned something about how I like to work and think.

I think that the most critical thing for me was figuring out that what was important to me was worthy of writing poems about. When I was in graduate school, my father had given me a copy of Rita Dove's *Thomas and Beulah*. That book opened my eyes. I remember looking at it saying to myself, "I could write like this. I could write a book that records the life of my grandmother and all the work she's done, and it could be of some value." If her book was a space that I entered, then that was the first critical creative moment.

The second moment was in my second year at U-Mass. Margaret Gibson came. Her book *Memories of the Future: The Daybooks of Tina Modotti* helped me figure out *Bellocq's Ophelia*, so if there's a direct ancestor for *Bellocq's Ophelia*, it's Gibson's book *The Daybooks of Tina Modotti*. When I first met her, she was really kind, and I think she took a liking to me, and I hadn't had that before with any other professors. She was the first one who really liked what I was doing and seemed interested in nurturing it. I remember one day there was this exhibit of Clifton Johnson's photographs. He had traveled in the South and had taken a lot of photographs of African Americans. A group of photographs from this exhibit became the sequence of poems titled "Three Photographs" in my first book. I remember walking around and stopping in front of one photograph, and Margaret was standing there beside me, and she was saying to me, "You see what's here, don't you?" It's like she was saying, "You know these people. You know them in a way that this photographer doesn't know them." I knew what she was telling me because in those photographs I saw the faces of my grandmother and my great-aunts, and I knew that I had something to add to the story that this photographer had inscribed in his work, and it was because of Margaret.

A Conversation with Natasha Trethewey

Marc McKee / 2010

First published in *TMR: The Missouri Review* 33.2 (Summer 2010), 144–59. Reprinted by permission of *The Missouri Review*.

This interview was conducted in March 2010 at the University of Missouri, where the poet participated in writing residencies with the graduate students of the creative writing program. The conversation took place, it should be noted, after a very pleasant lunch.

MARC McKEE: Natasha, I'd like to start by asking you where a poem begins. Often when I'm reading a poem I find fascinating or galvanizing, I wonder what kernel of energy allowed for the poem's genesis. Could you talk a little bit about that?
NATASHA TRETHEWEY: I do that too. I always try to read other poets' poems to find that moment in the poem where things seem to have begun. For me poems begin in a lot of different places. I can't say that there's any one place that I can always count on to be the germ of a poem, though. Often it is a phrase or a line or a few words that will come to me that I then memorize and repeat over and over until they become some kind of talisman that suggests a direction to go in. But because I do a lot of research, often ideas for poems or the germ of a poem come from finding the luminous details—you know, Pound's phrase—in some history text I'm reading, some image or detail that strikes me as so strange it's worth asking questions of. All my poems tend to begin in inquiry. There's always some question I'm asking myself. I want to know why this is a thing in history or what this has meant across time and space.

McKEE: Is that something that's remained constant over the arc of the three books that you've written—or has it undergone slight change from book to book?

TRETHEWEY: It must change. When I think about a lot of the poems I was writing in *Domestic Work*, mainly the sequence of poems in the "Domestic Work" section, those poems seemed to arise out of a memory of a particular instance, an image of something that was just stuck in my head—seeing a room a certain way and the people in it, and all of the other images of smell or touch that go along with it. And I wanted to describe that moment and expand it, go out from there to figure out what it means or why it has remained so long in my memory. I don't think I have proceeded exactly the same way throughout my other two collections, though that does continue to happen. The more I've gotten interested in writing about history and making sense of myself within the continuum of history, the more I've turned to paintings, to art. I look to the imagery of art to help me understand something about my own place in the world. By just beginning to contemplate a work of art, I find myself led toward some other understanding.

McKEE: All your books share a very scrupulous, fastidious attention to the way they're made. I'm thinking about what can sometimes be the chaos of the process of making the poem: How do you feel about going from a draft? What is a draft for you, and what does it take for you to get from a draft to a poem? What to go from a poem or a sequence of poems to a book?

TRETHEWEY: Now, that certainly feels different every time. Writing *Native Guard*, I didn't know I was working on a single book. I began writing that book because I was interested in the lesser-known history of these black soldiers stationed off the coast of my hometown. It was stunning to me that I hadn't known about this growing up, so I started doing research about black soldiers in the Civil War, trying to imagine the voice of this one soldier who might have things to say about then as well as now. But at the same time, I had begun writing elegies for my mother, and I was approaching the twentieth anniversary of her death. Those poems didn't seem to have anything to do with my interest in the buried history of these Civil War soldiers to whom no monuments had been erected. It was later on that I wrote a poem which hit me and made me realize these things belonged together. Once I knew they belonged together, I could begin fashioning an entire book from these sets of poems.

With *Bellocq's Ophelia* it was different because it was even more of a project than *Native Guard*. *Native Guard*—part of it—was a project. That was the Civil War part, but the rest of it wasn't. The entirety of *Bellocq's*

Ophelia was a project, and I was interested in doing research and looking at photographs and writing about them, imagining this woman Ophelia and what her life was like and the kinds of things she thought about. I began just by writing about the individual photographs to see how they gave way to a story of her life or emotional geography. There was a point where I could look at what I had and decide where there were gaps. And so I would begin to try to think of how I might write a poem that helped fill in some gap in her experience or her evolution as a self. At first, because I was at once writing the letters and writing her diary, I didn't know that they were going to be separate. I thought they were going to be interspersed because I was very interested in the difference between the public self we present to an audience, like the person to whom you're writing letters, and the private self who exists in a diary and the way the same information can be skewed so differently. I thought going back and forth would be an interesting way to see that. Then I realized that in terms of the shape the book would take, it might be interesting to show—to tell—the same story or at least the same time period for her year and a half in the brothel, side by side: the diary intact and the letters intact, so you could see the contradictions between the two stories.

I know that my tendency is to be linear, and I'm trying to find ways to subvert that. And so in *Bellocq's Ophelia* my device for subverting it was to tell the story and then to tell it again; it always circles back to this one moment, and it's not linear, but it's round in that way, and much of *Native Guard* is like that. So many of the formal decisions I made are about circling back, so the narrative circles back in on itself and can't simply proceed in a linear fashion.

McKEE: Since you do so often play with the voices, with inhabiting the voices of the other speakers, how do you feel about a reader's tendency to either see you in those other voices or to not see, perhaps to miss you in those other voices?
TRETHEWEY: You know, I think I would be completely happy if readers did not find me in those voices, if they found instead this probable or possible character, this human being who might have existed in a certain time and place, who might have thought and felt the things the poems reveal. At the same time, I'm not annoyed if a reader or someone in an audience I've just read to asks me questions about the links between the persona in my poems and my own experience. I've learned that my poems give way to those kinds of questions, so if it's a burden, I'll take it on. But I also think it's important to talk about how we make poems, how we create a persona from

tidbits of our own experience, our own interior life. I don't think I could create them if I did not give to them aspects of my own interior life. I remember reading Kundera's *The Unbearable Lightness of Being*. There's a part where I think he talks about how all his characters are sort of unrealized parts of himself—they get to be acted out in the language of his fiction. And so I give to my characters—I gave to Ophelia parts of my own interior life, the feelings I had about certain things—things I thought about—but I also gave her certain physical details of my life.

McKEE: For example?

TRETHEWEY: When I was a young girl, I would go to visit my father once my parents were divorced. I would go to New Orleans, and when I would see him the first thing that he did after we hugged each other, once we'd gotten into the car, he would grab my hand and turn it over and look at my fingernails. You know, it's a kind of thing all parents do, I suppose. He was just checking to see if my fingernails were clean. Maybe he'd check my ears. I understand that about it, but because I am my white father's black daughter and I know about things in history, I could never completely escape feeling that there was something problematic about that inspection. It bothered me, I think, because he didn't see me very much. We saw each other a few weeks or so in the summer, and he had this amount of time to figure out who I was, who I was becoming in his absence; all of these inspections were part of him figuring that out. It bothered me that these were all the things I had that were going to somehow reveal myself to him. And so that feeling I gave to Ophelia, but I place it within a context of chattel slavery, when people purchasing slaves in Louisiana would inspect them the way you inspect livestock. You look at their teeth, you stick your fingers in their mouths; there's an inspection that happens that objectifies the person who is on display. Display. I felt like that. I gave to Ophelia the feeling of being on display, so in that way she's made up of my interior life. Though the circumstances of hers are quite different.

McKEE: We were talking a little earlier about Ophelia and how within the sections of the book there seems to be a kind of arc, whereby she is subject at first . . . well, for example, when the madam is giving her instruction about how to be in the brothel for potential johns, and it's all about how she's supposed to imagine them looking at her and conform to that being looked at. And yet by the end she starts to take ownership of the ways of looking at the world. Do you see those as arcs that resurface in other parts of your books, where the speaker is involved in figuring out, and then in mastering, how things work?

TRETHEWEY: The first thing I was thinking, while listening to you describe it, is how Ophelia was complicit in her own objectification. That's a very interesting thing to me, and it's an important part of that book, but I think revealing complicity in one's own position is always a part of the work I do. And that is because I do believe Yeats's words, "Of the quarrel with others we make rhetoric, but of the quarrel with ourselves, poetry." The same thing goes on in *Native Guard*. Ultimately, though there is an argument I have with the nation and national memory, I'm guilty of the exact same thing. When I don't put a tombstone on my mother's grave, when I don't evoke her name and speak it, I've erased her. I haven't erected a monument; I have not tended to, as my own native duty, her memory. I keep coming back to the role of the self as complicit.

McKEE: I've seen elsewhere, when you were talking about *Native Guard*, the idea that the erasures of history require of us or of poetry in some way an accounting, a kind of monument. I'm wondering, if we understand language as being mutable, more mutable in our minds than a stone, for example, how is poetry going to fulfill the sense of the monumental there?

TRETHEWEY: Well, the poem is a living monument. I would argue that stone monuments have a life to them, too. But let me just say that a poem is a living monument—it lives and breathes each time it's spoken, read, heard. We can keep these things a long time, and they can continue to be part of our cultural memory the way songs become part of it, the way things live on in our memory and get shared with other people and passed down and passed around. But I don't want to diminish the power of physical monuments on the landscape, either. I saw a reviewer once writing that the problem with my attempt to create a monument is that monuments are these cold, dead things. But people are always talking about how the reader completes a poem. Well, the viewer completes a monument. If I go up and see it and look at it and respond to it, it's alive. And believe you me, there are a lot of Confederate monuments that got a second life when I was going around looking at them. They are not dead!

McKEE: One hopes they got a peculiar second life.

TRETHEWEY: We got to interact!

McKEE: If we can talk about *Native Guard* some more, in the initial section there are elegiac poems of address to your mother, followed by the Native Guard sequence and the poems that are in that section, and there's the poem that I'm thinking of specifically; there's the hilarious poem with the Fugitive Poets. It seems as though the space of the poem exists between the reader and the poet. And in the elegies it's very personal. We get to observe an address from the poet to the mother. Then we have these poems of the historical past and then poems of a kind of self-accounting. Is that similar to how you understand your own story? Do you have to speak to someone in your life first to help you understand history, and then you move to reflect on yourself? Or is there some other process?

TRETHEWEY: The problem with me seeing it like that is that even though there are in that first section poems addressed to my mother, there are also poems not directly addressed to her, and those are also reckoning with myself and my role in being complicit in a kind of erasure. This may not answer your question, but I want to tell you this and see if it's useful even for talking about the structure, because I think we're talking about how it's arranged in sections. There are divisions. At first, I had named section titles. I called the sections, in this order, "Monument," "Document," and "Testament" because the elegies were monuments to my mother, to her memory; they were monuments to my own grief, monuments to that sense of loss that I encountered. The second section, "Document," is called "Document" because it tries to create an imagined historical document, something we might discover in the archives somewhere or in somebody's attic. And the final section was my own testimony, my testament as native Southerner, as exile, as daughter, who perhaps had not done the work I should have done. When I took those section titles out, it was killing me that I felt like without them there was some piece that was going to be missing, or it would be somehow overlooked, and so I got around it by naming one of the very last poems in the book "Monument." If you really look at the collection, it might seem like it belongs in that first section because it is a poem about me looking at some ants and being reminded of having not erected a monument or tended to my mother's memory by tending to her grave site. It has all the markers of going in that first section. But it appears in the third section as testimony to anchor the whole thing. It's there that I make that final confession that I hadn't really done the work for her, and it doesn't come until the very end of the book. It's just after the poem called "Elegy for the Native Guards," where I'm accusing the nation of this forgetting, and then I put mine right beside it. That's why the poem appears there and not earlier, because I'm hoping that juxtaposition will complete this arc I'm going for.

McKEE: In September your new book is coming out, reflecting on the Mississippi Gulf Coast after Katrina, I'd like to talk about that, too, but I wonder if first we can talk a little about your history as a writer—when you made the decision that poetry was your calling? Or maybe the first poem you loved, that really took hold of you?

TRETHEWEY: A couple years ago, before *Native Guard* came out, I was at a restaurant in Atlanta, where I had grown up, even though I'm from Mississippi. I was sitting there with my husband, and there was a group of women at another table, but I hadn't looked at them, so I didn't recognize anyone sitting there. As they got up to leave, one of them came over, and she said, "Yeah, I thought that was you." It was a woman who had been my best friend in high school from eighth through twelfth grade. She said, "I read both your books, and I'm so happy for you. I remember you told me in eighth grade that you were going to be a poet." And I had no recollection of that. I couldn't imagine I had ever said such a thing: "I'm going to be a poet." But it means I liked poetry. I did; I liked writing. I was the president of the literary club, that kind of thing. I know that I wrote poems as early as the third grade. The librarian got them from my teacher, and they bound them in cardboard, and they put them in the school library, so I was becoming a poet in the third grade.

It's hard for me to say what the first poem I loved was, because even though I am the daughter of a poet and my stepmother is also a poet, I loved short fiction. When I first went to graduate school, I went thinking I was going to write short stories, and I quickly learned otherwise. I didn't think that there was a place for me in poetry, in entering the world of a poem, its language, its imagery, its story, any of that. Poems just somehow did not speak to me. And then, all of a sudden, they did. I can't remember what poem it was that said, "Welcome! Come on in!" I don't remember—I wish I could remember what it was that just so turned my head around like that. I know that happened more in graduate school than in undergrad. I remember trying to write poems when I was an undergrad. I was a freshman. My mother had just died, and I turned to the language of poetry to try to make sense of it and wrote really bad poems, horrible poems, and then I didn't touch that again.

McKEE: You took a break from poetry from the beginning of your undergraduate years to the beginning of your grad school years.

TRETHEWEY: I took a break from a lot of things. It was a really traumatic time for me. I made bad grades, I couldn't concentrate. It was during exam time when my mother was killed, at the end of my freshman year, and it took me years to even be the student I had been before that happened.

McKEE: When did you realize you could write poems about your mother? I've seen you describe it as being like a dam bursting.
TRETHEWEY: I think I always held it in the back of my mind as something I needed the language of poetry to make sense of, and yet I didn't feel capable of doing it. The first poem I wrote that I think of as a good poem—a successful poem about my mother's being gone, I should say—is the last poem in *Domestic Work*. It's a poem called "Limen," and it really is just about recalling seeing her, an image of her hanging wet sheets on the line. That's an image I had been carrying around for a long time, you know, this scene of my mother hanging up this wet curtain, and I'm on one side of it and she's on the other, so I see her as through this screen, which probably stuck with me because that's a haunting way of seeing someone, behind a barrier, this really liminal kind of thing. You only see them as a shadow, but moving behind it, which is sort of like what the loss of her is like: she is a shadow moving behind this screen that I can't get to the other side of.

When I wrote that poem I didn't know I was headed toward being able to write more of them. And if the phrase "dam-bursting" got used to describe this by either me or, I think, more likely the interviewer, it's probably because I talk about this convergence of things that were hitting me all at once. I was approaching the twentieth anniversary of her death. I had reached the point at which I had lived as many years without her as with her. I was approaching my own fortieth birthday, which was the last age she ever was, and I had moved back to the physical landscape of her death, to Atlanta, to take this job at Emory. All those things brought that loss to the forefront of my imagination. But even when I started writing poems about it, I still didn't think I was writing poems. I thought, "Well, I've got to put something down because it's right here, and if I don't get it out of my head, it's just going to stay here." I started writing these things and thinking, "Oh, you know, they're so deeply personal. This grief is such a personal thing. How would anyone be interested in reading such things?" I just put them away in the drawer, but I kept writing them and never imagined really taking them out of that drawer. You know when a poem is coming together, it's exciting, and you have a sense of whether or not the poem is working. I never had that feeling about those. They were mysterious to me. I couldn't tell one way or the other. They just seemed to have a kind of urgency.

McKEE: Who made you take those poems out of the drawer?
TRETHEWEY: I had relationships with certain editors at magazines who would occasionally solicit poems from me, and I write pretty slowly, so I wouldn't always have any poems ready, but I wouldn't want to not send anything, because I wanted to keep a cordial relationship. I wanted to suggest, "Well, this is all I have, I know it's probably not what you're interested in, but just have a look at it." And every time I did, they would take the poems. And it was weird because these poems would end up in the *Pushcart* or in *Best American*. I thought, "Huh. Okay." People must have liked them, I guess. People must have found something of value there.

McKEE: The precision of the emotion in poems like that, even if it is a mystery to you, really allows for a lot of empathy on the part of the reader.
TRETHEWEY: Well, that's why elegies work, right? I mean, that's why we've had them for a long time. In his new anthology *The Art of Losing*, Kevin Young writes about how elegies are for the living—the loss that the living feel is constant. It transcends class and time and space and culture.

McKEE: To change the subject, when you got dared in graduate school to write a poem—was it to write a poem? Or just to start writing poems?
TRETHEWEY: Yeah, just to write a poem. My friend Mark was a poet, and he thought I could write a poem. And I said, "Oh, no. You have not seen how bad I am at writing poems." And he said, "No, I don't believe it. And I dare you—I dare you to write a poem. I know it's not going to be that bad." I took the dare because I wanted to prove to him how bad it would be. And then it wasn't that bad. I gave it to my fiction professor, Marianne Gingher, and the next time I saw her she came running toward me saying, "Oh, Tasha, you're a poet!" I still think it was a way of her saying, "'Cause you're not a fiction writer—get out of my class." It might have been very self-serving on her part, but I am grateful. She was a very generous mentor to me.

McKEE: Do you ever take up fiction now?
TRETHEWEY: No. It was a grand effort to even take up nonfiction for this book I have coming up.

McKEE: Let's talk a little bit about that book.
TRETHEWEY: Well, it is not a memoir. It is creative nonfiction, and the book is interested in the past and the present as bookends to this moment in the middle, which is Hurricane Katrina. The first half of the book consid-

ers the history of my hometown and the rise of the gaming industry on the Gulf Coast, the kinds of decisions that were made in development that have affected the environment and the way those environmental factors like erosion and runoff left the coast much more vulnerable. For example, had the mangrove swamps that were native to the coast been intact, then the storm surge would not have been as bad as it was. It is about those issues and my family story woven into it, because my great-grandparents arrived on the coast around the same time that Gulfport was chartered as a city. The first half of the book leads right up to a few days before Hurricane Katrina hits, and it really turns on my brother's life because he was the one in my family who was still there and carrying on this family business, who then lost everything because of Katrina. It follows the aftermath in his life, which echoes ideas about recovery and rebuilding and historical memory that are taking place on the coast right now: his life as emblematic of what has happened to so many people.

McKEE: One of the concerns one heard a lot about in the wake of Katrina with regard to New Orleans was that when it was built back it would be rebuilt differently, that actual history would be covered over and made obsolete, actually. Was that the same risk you're kind of taking up in this series?
TRETHEWEY: Yes, particularly when I'm concerned with historical memory and erasure. Because the building of the coastline was one historical erasure. But what I realized in the writing of this is that that's been the history of the Gulf Coast the entire time. There's always a new inscription on it, and so this idea that I had that it was one way and then that all got wiped away is wrong. It had always been—

McKEE: Wiped away.
TRETHEWEY:—and being reinscribed, but I do think that there are certain landmarks, certain things, and certain ways of being that had been there a long enough time that people are worried about their absence and the way a corporate vision is now writing the new narrative of the coast because of the casinos and the condos.

One of the biggest things I encountered as a worry that people have on the Mississippi Gulf Coast is being forgotten; they're worried about the narrative of the Mississippi Gulf Coast being buried beneath the narrative of the travesty of New Orleans. They want to make sure people remember the difference between a natural disaster—the largest natural disaster in American history, which hit the Mississippi Gulf Coast—and the man-made disaster that hit New Orleans a day later when the levees broke. But what they realize is that so many people, when asked about Katrina, immediately think New Orleans. That's the story, that's the imagery that's stuck.

McKEE: Your work has a lot of power when it is addressing historical wrongs. Does it feel even more challenging to address them as these obstructions or deletions are happening?

TRETHEWEY: Mmm-hmm. I have two great examples of that. When I sat down with the first editor at the press that the book was supposed to be coming out with, he told me I needed to change the title. He said, "Can you make it more about New Orleans?" And then he said, "Well, I think you need to change the title because people are going to buy this book because they think it's about New Orleans, and then they're going to realize it's not, and they're going to return it." I was stunned, and I looked at him; I was, like, *that's exactly what I'm fighting against in this*. Here he was, supposedly going to be my editor, actually participating in that erasure, making it happen.

And with *Native Guard*—I love this—this was crazy—I don't know if you've ever thought about how you get the cataloging information on the inside of your book, but what happens is someone at the Library of Congress reads the book, and they come up with those ways to catalog it. So then they sent it back to the copy editor, and the copy editor gave it to me. When I got the galleys of my book from the copy editor, it said on the inside cover something like "Mothers: Poetry," "Interracial Marriage: Poetry," "Mississippi: Poetry," "Bi-racial People: Poetry," and then "Title." Nothing about the Civil War. Nothing about black soldiers or their participation in it. I called the press, and I spoke to the assistant to the editor, and she said, "Oh, no, no, no, don't worry about that, we're going to market the book that way; that's just fine." And I said, "No, you really don't understand what I'm talking about—I'm worried about the lone researcher who's interested in finding as much as they can about the black presence in the Civil War, who has never heard of the Native Guards—because a lot of people haven't—who's going to want to put into a search engine 'black soldiers,' 'Civil War,' 'Mississippi,' maybe. If my book isn't catalogued that way it's never going to come up, which would have been just yet another erasure." I'm thinking, if someone gets my book, someone who may not be interested in poetry will flip to the back and see all of the notes, the various historians whose work I consulted. Perhaps that will then lead them to find out more about what they're looking for. She thought I was being annoying and said something like, "Well, I think you're really making a big deal about this. I just don't know how this relationship is working out."

But in spite of that she went back to the copy editor, and he agreed with me, sent it back to the Library of Congress, and they redid it. We were fighting an erasure that was happening right in front of us, and it was happening to me. It was happening to my book—and to the Native Guards again.

McKEE: What informed the decision to write *Beyond Katrina*?
TRETHEWEY: After *Native Guard* I felt like I was done with the Mississippi Gulf Coast. It sounds horrible to say that now, but I felt like as imaginative terrain for me, I had been there. And so then the hurricane hit, and Ted Genoways, who is editor of *VQR*, contacted me in late August to ask me if I could fill in for another writer who was supposed to give the Page-Barbour Lectures at the University of Virginia but three months before the lectures had to back out. And so Ted said to me at Bread Loaf in August, "I need this big favor. I want you to write these three lectures and deliver them in November at UVA." And he said, "I've got it all worked out in my head for you. I know exactly what you're going to write about, and I know the structure." I said, "I'm listening." So he said, "I want you to go down to the Mississippi Gulf Coast, and I want you to look around and write about what you see there in the wake of Katrina. And I want you to structure it like this: present, past, and future, and that's the order that you'll deliver the lectures." And I said, "Okay!" Because I'm crazy. Ted Genoways can just ask me to do stuff, and I'll be like "Sure!" So I did it. That became the first half of the book.

I had begun to talk with an editor at the University of Georgia Press, and I was writing a proposal to explain how I was going to expand it a little bit, and the world got turned upside down. My brother's life just took a sharp turn, which then directed the book, the rest of it, where it went. There are a couple poems in it. The poems are there because, yet again, Ted Genoways called me up last summer to do a project called In Verse. It's a partnership with a producer at NPR and photographers; they send poets to certain locations to report. And the whole question was, what kind of news reporting would we get if we sent poets to do the reporting? This time he said, "I want you to go back to the Gulf Coast, and I want you to do this again, but this time I want it to be in poetry." I kept saying, how can you ask poets to do such a thing? How can you ask poets to write this thing on demand? How can you ask them to report? And, of course, my poems didn't become reports like that at all. And I kept feeling like I was really disappointing them, because what I wrote is not what they wanted. But I went, and something happened and I went with it.

McKEE: I'll have to check these out.
TRETHEWEY: Susan Somers-Willett was the other poet. She wrote about Troy, New York, and I think her poems are fabulous. They're wonderful. So look at those.

McKEE: All right. I was wondering if you'd talk a little bit about your feeling of contemporary poets who take up the questions and are making the poetry of social conscience that really lives now. Talk a bit about the people who are writing along with you.
TRETHEWEY: There are actually a lot of people, and it would be hard to even begin to list all of them. I think that Jake Adam York's project is worth mentioning. The history of the Civil Rights Movement and all the kinds of violence and injustice that led up to it and surrounded it and came after it is something that he's interested in. His poems tell us, in the elegant language of poetry, things we might otherwise overlook. The stuff that he talks about, we get in the news—for example when we read in the paper that they're bringing to trial someone who bombed a church a long time ago or who killed a civil rights leader a long time ago. But when we read those things in the newspaper, we go on. I think there's something about the poems that makes us not just read them and go on the way that we might when we read a news story—which is one of the ways poems create a space for us to empathize. Also Martha Collins. Her last collection, *Blue Front*, for example. She's working on a really interesting project that continues in some ways from *Blue Front* (in which she deals with a lynching, something her father witnessed, also the knowledge that her father had been in the Klan). She extends her consideration to the inheritance of that legacy, the inheritance of whiteness. I'm really excited to see how she approaches those subjects. They are two people immediately that come to mind.

Poetry's about empathy. When I am confronted with a voice—distant, different, compelling—I'm asked to engage with something outside myself that sends me back to myself, turns the mirror in such a way that I learn something else about me. That's an act of empathy, to understand yourself in another place, in the place of someone else, to be brought in through language to some other consciousness. When the consciousness that speaks to us is crying out to convey something about the past or the present, with all the injustices inherent in both of those positions, it's an opportunity for us to engage with things we might not have thought about. It asks that we do that. It welcomes us to do that, you know?

I was reading Charles Wright's introduction to *Best American Poetry 2008*. People are always talking about what poetry can and cannot do. In his essay he writes that poetry doesn't save lives, though it can save an individual life. And so poetry may not create social justice, but it might get someone to think differently than they might have because of that intimate interaction, through language, with another voice.

Outside the Frame:
An Interview with Natasha Trethewey

Regina Bennett, Harbour Winn, and Zoe Miles / 2010

From *Oklahoma HUMANITIES Magazine* (Fall 2010), 25–29. The interview was conducted in Oklahoma City in April 2010. Lance Gill and Arm Warren recorded and transcribed the conversation. The journal is also available online at http://www.okhumanities.org/magazine. Reprinted by permission of the Oklahoma Humanities Council, publisher, on behalf of Dr. Bennett, Dr. Winn, and English major Zoe Miles, all of Oklahoma City University.

Natasha Trethewey was the featured poet at Oklahoma City University's annual Thatcher Hoffman Smith Distinguished Writer Series, supported in part by a grant from OHC. Trethewey's poems explore cultural memory and ethnic identity, which reflect her own experience as the child of a black mother and white father and her fascination with lost histories. She won the 2007 Pulitzer Prize for poetry for *Native Guard* (Houghton Mifflin Harcourt, 2nd edition; 2006), a collection of poems about the Louisiana Native Guard, the Union army's first all-black regiment in the Civil War. Trethewey's other poetry collections include *Domestic Work* (Graywolf Press, 2000) and *Bellocq's Ophelia* (Graywolf Press, 2002) based on E. J. Bellocq's twentieth-century photographs of prostitutes in the Storyville District of New Orleans.

Regina Bennett: Tell us about your relationship to the discipline of history.
Natasha Trethewey: When I was a freshman at the University of Georgia, Charlie Wine, a wonderful professor, came in the first day of class and had us write our names and hometowns on a note card; I wrote Gulfport, Mississippi. This was in the days before Internet research. The next day, he introduced us to each other by talking about some aspect of history from our hometown. I was stunned. He connected me to a place and its history. This is what I would later do in *Native Guard*, talking about the idea of geography

as fate, of Henry James's words: "Be tethered to native pastures even if it reduces you to a backyard in New York." I couldn't have known it then, but I think Dr. Wine planted a seed for where I was headed in that engagement with history and place.

Harbour Winn: I am wondering about your sense of the value of arts integration. You use photography in *Domestic Work—*
NT:—and there's photography in *Native Guard*. *Bellocq's Ophelia* begins with what is both a photograph and a painting, and a play in the backdrop.
HW: How do you understand arts integration as a professor, as a poet? How do you use it?
NT: I'm a very visual person and I like the engagement of a given image. With photography, it was about imagining what was cropped out of the frame as you make a choice about the subject of the photograph—which of course was leading me to that idea of historical erasure, the things that get cropped out. [In *Bellocq's Ophelia*] I was interested in what might be behind an image, and Storyville was a great metaphor for that because there was a glittering façade of glamour and excess and music and champagne at the same time that there were silverfish crawling behind the walls. It's what's just beneath the surface, beneath the flocked velvet wallpaper, behind the hedges that separated backyards from alleyways. I was always interested in what had been pushed aside and left out of my view. That's why I approach photographs; that's what they do for me.

Paintings are another way to access history. I'm particularly interested right now in religious paintings of the Renaissance, the Mexican *casta* paintings that are, in many ways, ethnographic. It's as if these paintings have a documentary edge because of what they show us about the particular moment, the circumstances, and the people in them. Using them as material culture allows me to investigate the past through the given image. In writing a poem you're always in conversation with the poems that come before you. I think we're also in conversation with all these other art forms and those relationships get pushed against each other.

RB: I don't know if you've seen this news yet, but the *Washington Post* was reporting that Virginia's governor has reinstated April as Confederate History Month. You write a lot about historical markers of the Confederacy. Any comments about this governor's actions?
NT: I think that the problem is a kind of exclusive history. There are people who want to say, "Heritage, not hate," that it's just celebrating a kind of

culture. That "moonlight magnolia" culture forgets how many white people ended up going into the Civil War because they were paid by the sons of wealthy plantation owners to go. I don't think that's necessarily included in this notion of Confederate history—nor are the other citizens of the United States, many of them slaves. Confederate culture was built around keeping those slaves. I think it's a willful forgetting or a kind of willed blindness to ignore that part, to say that we can celebrate this without also recognizing what was terrible about it. Growing up in the Deep South was, for me, the root of this sense of psychological exile that I have.

HW: You've used the phrase "mixed race" to describe yourself. I think this is more than semantics. Why not "mixed ethnicity"? Aren't we just one race?
NT: I have also used "mixed-blood." I think what you're asking about, ideas about race and biology and racial formation, is the thing that I'm interested in. Yes, I'm aware of the recent science and the not-so-recent science.

HW: The person that might match my DNA most closely could be in Cambodia.
NT: Right. We certainly need to change the language that we use at some point, but until our perceptions and policies and our treatment of people catch up to the science, we still live in a very racialized society, and it's not going to change just because we stop saying that someone is mixed race or that people are of a different race. I'm a pragmatist when it comes to that. I live in a racialized world. I'm constantly being reminded of that by the world I live in.

Zoe Miles: Your father's a poet. Do you see your wordsmith abilities as innate or as something that you caught on to as you grew up?
NT: My father would probably want to claim responsibility for my wordsmithing abilities, and I certainly would give him some credit because he was one of my earliest teachers; but the other people that I spent a good deal of my life with were amazing at idiom and metaphor and the cadences of language and the richness of sound and figurative imagery. I had that at my grandmother's house when I listened to women from her church talking about the Bible, chanting hymns and psalms. I was surrounded by the lovely cadences of different human voices. So, while much might come from a natural talent that passed to me from my father, a great deal passed to me from my mother as well.

HW: The emphasis in gender criticism is that the dutiful daughter must defy the father, the patriarchal controller of language, to become self-defined. It's interesting because you mentioned you were going to be writing poems about your father.

NT: My father is very, very precise about grammar and I love that about him, and I've loved learning the language from him. But at the same time I have to remember moments when, if I spoke something in a very colloquial way that was rooted not just in Southern-ness but also in some of the syntax of black English, he would constantly correct me. I think he wanted to push it out of me. Even as a child, I knew I didn't want to get rid of it; I wanted to be able to code switch, to have access to that other language. There are other syntactical Englishes that are rich and really useful for poetry.

I remember when I first went to graduate school I would say something like, "I'm gonna run in 'right quick' and check my mailbox." The other graduate students would correct me and say, "Don't you mean 'quickly'?" and I said, "No, I mean 'right quick'!" They didn't understand that there was a difference between how I write and what I might say when I'm feeling comfortable and in a space of colloquial speech.

You asked this a few minutes ago, Harbour, and it's made me think of a poem I'd like to read "right quick," because I think it can answer a couple of these questions that we're talking about. My father has a lovely poem called "Her Swing" that he must have written when I was three years old. When my father and I give readings, we stand beside each other and "Her Swing" is one of the poems that he will read. Every time he would read it, I'd be standing there and I started to feel really strange and didn't know why. It wasn't until recently, when I wrote this poem, that I figured out what the problem had been for me. It's a problem of language and knowledge, ways of knowing, and how we use language to suggest that knowing.

[*Trethewey reads her poem "Knowledge," from* Thrall]

So you asked me about saying "mixed race." In this poem, I point out a line from my father's poem in which he uses the word "crossbreed." Now even if you want to forgive him and say that forty years ago that's the only language he had access to—which I still wouldn't agree with because we call animals crossbreed because they are different species—he's had a long time to change that. For me, there is this master language and then I have to constantly rewrite or revise some of that master language. That's why I like using his own words to dissect, as the poem does, what is happening both with the body and with the language. That woman on the table is very much the woman for inspection, the child that I was, being studied. To even use that language, "my crossbreed child," you have to ask the question, *If I'm a crossbreed, what's my mother, what species is she?* It's a really painful thing for me. It's one thing to be "othered" in your own country, in your own state, but when it happens at home . . . It's about imperialism and the colonial body. I think it does go back to that gender theory that you were asking about.

RB: I can't believe you can read it with such emotion and come back to Harbour's question as if it was nothing.
NT: It's a poem I really like, but it's also one I worry about how my father will feel about it. I don't think he's seen it—or he's pretended not to. If you read his poem, it's really loving, it's sweet. There's still an edge and a blindness.

ZM: I have a lot of hesitancy as a young poet. I feel that once my poems are out, they are no longer mine. How do you deal with that?
NT: I have gotten to a point where I trust my poems and I am willing to follow them where they lead me. It's as if I have been waiting my whole life to write those poems. I thought when I was writing *Native Guard* that my whole life had been going up to the moment when I would say the things about cultural memory, historical erasure, and amnesia, that my life was almost a metaphor. I've talked about *Native Guard* and how it led me to the poems I really needed to write about my mother. This book has started, at least the process has started, in the same way for me. I got interested in those Mexican *casta* paintings because they showed the mixed blood unions in the colony and the children of those unions as if you were mixing paint: if you put this and this together, you got this. They tended to make them in sets of sixteen and they always began with the white father and degraded from there with the different blood mixtures, everything else is a little bit less than that.

RB: So it does become a conversation with your dad.
NT: It started with those *casta* paintings. I didn't know that looking at that image and looking at all those paintings was about the father. They are also about, not my mother separately, but the ways those interracial unions are portrayed, the imagery of them even in colonial Mexico.

HW: When you write a poem, can you enter into the "otherness" of age or race or gender—that which is "other" from you?

NT: I think any of us can do that as long as we have a strong sense of empathy. Where do you find your connections to people who are very different? The first time it happened to me was when I read *The Diary of Anne Frank*. It was not hard for me to connect my own experience growing up in Mississippi and Georgia with that little girl in the attic writing her heart out in a diary. I think that we can do that, and we should, because it exercises the muscle of empathy.

RB: What's it like to be the Phillis Wheatley Distinguished Chair in Poetry at Emory, to live with that kind of legacy?
NT: It's a lovely title, but even when they created it for me, it was not without irony. Phillis Wheatley did require the signatures of all those learned white men to say that indeed she had written the poems. I take on that mantle with a good sense of irony about what it means.

Southern Crossings:
An Interview with Natasha Trethewey

Daniel Cross Turner / 2010

From *Waccamaw: a journal of contemporary literature* (Coastal Carolina University) number 6 (Fall 2010). The journal's website is http://www.waccamawjournal.com/. The interview is archived at http://www.waccamawjourna1.com/pages.php?x=324. Reprinted by permission.

This interview was conducted on April 23, 2010 in Loudonville, New York, where Trethewey served as the featured writer for Siena College's Greyfriar Living Literature Series.

Daniel Cross Turner: Looking back, do you see a sense of progression—or perhaps "direction" might be a better term—in your career as a poet, from *Domestic Work* to *Bellocq's Ophelia* to *Native Guard*?

Natasha Trethewey: Yes I do. I see in my volumes a deepening of my main concerns. In *Domestic Work*, I began with the historical impulse and the impetus to recover from the margins the stories of those people who often get left out of public histories. In that volume, I explored the life of my maternal grandmother, placing the narratives that she told me, the stories of her life, within larger historical contexts: American history, the history of the American South, the history of Jim Crow and the Civil Rights Movement. Her own history is firmly set in those broader cultural moments. Transitioning from there to *Bellocq's Ophelia*, we hear again a woman's story that is infused with a particular time and space. The character Ophelia represents that kind of person who would have been ignored in official public histories, who may not have left records for us to know her individual narrative. I continue to be attentive to matters of historical memory and historical erasure, questions that are central to *Native Guard*. I can see now that this interest began in simply trying to relate a story about my grandmother's life.

DCT: Your poems often have strong narrative lines, like a series of vignettes that accumulate value and momentum as we move through them altogether. Why not fiction? What does poetry add to the ideas or responses to your work?

NT: What interests me most about poetry is the elegant envelope of form and the kind of density and compression that a poem demands. Because of those demands, I think I get to work more with silences than if I were writing prose. The silences are as big a part in my poems as what is being said. I believe my poems do a lot of work with what is implicit, rather than what is explicit. I just finished writing a work of creative nonfiction, *Beyond Katrina*, and I noticed that even in prose I have a strong tendency to circle back; repetition is a thing that I make use of constantly. It seems to me to be more natural in poetry and yet it also appears in my other writing.

DCT: Yes, your poems often contain overlapping levels of repetition, in terms of individual words, but also structural repetitions: the re-use of similar poetic forms as well as rhythmic and metrical reiterations. Do these layers of repetitions connect to your concern with memory and history?

NT: Absolutely. The types of forms I use in *Native Guard* have everything to do with the idea of historical memory and reinscription. I decided that it was necessary to invoke forms that had repetition or refrain in order to reinscribe those things that had been erased or forgotten. The necessity of repeating them, saying it not once, but twice, to make such things become memorable.

DCT: Between your poetry volumes there is marked repetition of motifs as well as within the individual volumes. How does recurrence on the level of language play into your thematic concerns?

NT: I think that I am obsessed, and I trust my obsessions, meaning I allow them to guide me through poems. Those words that keep getting repeated, those motifs—cotton, ghost, cross, for example, in *Native Guard*—are also intertwined with that desire to constantly circle back. There is a kind of momentum that's gained because the repeated words are used in different contexts: they mean, then mean differently again when they reappear in other places. I see myself as trying to build, layer upon layer, this larger sense of fanatic reinvestigation and reinscription of the past. This is why it is often difficult for me to simply pluck out certain poems for public readings. I am so focused on the layering of images and ideas in my poems and volumes that it seems as if you almost need every single time that layering happens in order to construct the full sense of obsessive retelling. My friend and fellow poet Dan Albergotti was at a panel at AWP [The Association of Writers and Writing Programs] about Robert Frost's idea of the twenty-fifth poem, which is the whole collection itself. I'm always interested in the twenty-fifth poem in a collection. In order for me to make the whole collection seem as if it were one long poem, it seems absolutely important for those kinds of repetitions and echoes to work their way through the entire volume.

DCT: One might say that you work with "plain" language in your poems. There is also a sense that, as you describe difficult, even traumatic, personal and historical matters, you use a plaintive tone—never maudlin or melodramatic, always restrained and plain-sighted. Could you say something about the tension between the symbolic and what we might call the "real" in your poems, your use of language that is plain, but takes on symbolic resonances?
NT: Thank you for saying that. I think sometimes it can be hard for certain kinds of readers to see how some of the most accessible things are also doing another kind of work. But of course we know that poetry is the one way we have of saying what we mean and meaning something else at the same time, and that ordinary words do that work for us. Ordinary words are poems in themselves. That's one thing I love about poetry, that if I choose the right word, there are so many levels of meaning, especially for the person who hangs out with the *OED* [*Oxford English Dictionary*] as much as I do [laughs]. I want to find the best words that open many doors as you walk through the poem. There's something even in my personality that has to do with frankness and plainspokenness. Maybe I must work on it because I'm the type of person—I'm embarrassed to say—who tears up at sappy commercials, and it's so maudlin when I do it. And yet it is not at all what I do with my poetry; I don't want to ever wrestle a scene for overplayed emotion in my work. A reviewer once described my poetic persona as a kind of *sangfroid*. And I do think of myself as a little cold-blooded as a poet. I've had to be that way in dealing with personal tragedy. I've had to look unflinchingly at my own past, and I try to bring that sensibility into my poems.

DCT: The blood metaphor just now put me in mind of the "confessional" poetry of the 1950s and 1960s, where the raw emotionalism of the verse makes it seem as if the poet is opening up a vein and bleeding out interior turmoil onto the page. But there is a conscious effort on your part not to give your poems over to unfettered emotion.
NT: Yes, I do not want to give myself over to melodrama. And I became

this way because I did have such a sensational history, things that one might read about in the newspaper. I am much more interested in ordinary objects and the weight of meaning that they bring to bear, particularly in their juxtapositions. Like looking at that window over there, just describing the objects that are on the sill—their relationships to each other, the angles that they're in, the shadows—that's what I'm interested in. I am fascinated with the gestural. I remember studying Bertolt Brecht in graduate school and encountering his idea that gesture was the thing that really couldn't be faked. So I'm very interested in the gestures of human beings, but also the gestures that objects make in their juxtapositions to each other, how they can tell a good part of the story.

DCT: That's fascinating—exploring how objects and things "speak" to the cultural histories that inform them and that they inform. Would you connect that sense of gesturing things to your extensive integrations of photographic art in your poems?
NT: Yes, one of the first photographers whom I fell in love with for the narrative power of her images was Carrie Mae Weems. There is this domestic series that she did, *The Kitchen Table Series* (1990). It was a series of interiors, of black people in the kitchen in a house, a man and a woman, but sometimes the woman by herself. These images told such a story, they conveyed so much meaning about the lives of the people in the scenes and their relationships to each other and to things that were outside the frame. I learned a lot about writing the image by looking at photographic images like that. The positioning of the people, their gestures, their proximity to each other, the things on the table between them—there was meaning embedded in all of it, and all you had to do was simply look at it and see it. And so I always want my poems to work like that. If you just see the scene, I won't have to say much about it.

DCT: With regard to that kind of restraint—holding back both emotionally and in terms of the imagery you present—how does your use of form and formalism enter into these dynamics?
NT: A plaintive tone can arise through the notion of restraint because a poem that is restrained by form, where something is being held back, suggests the absolute struggle to say what is being said. In the struggle to be able to get out even the one thing that is being said, so much has been pared away. The silence is part of that tone and that sense of plain-sightedness: the struggle to find the one way to say a thing so that it need not be embellished.

DCT: Although your work contains a strong sense of realism, even down to the reality of things and objects, your images carry a rich range of figurative connotations. A number of your prominent motifs seem to serve as self-reflexive images for your own poetic processes. For instance, "crosshatching" appears as an important image throughout the sonnet sequence of the poem "Native Guard." In one of the sections, a former slave, now a black Union soldier, exposes the whip scars "crosshatched" into his back. In another sonnet, the black soldier who narrates the poem recognizes that his writing between the lines of a journal discovered in an abandoned white Southerner's home is an act of "crosshatching," as is his soldier's duty of composing letters home for illiterate Confederate prisoners-of-war. These acts potentially create some connection with white Southerners, his former and would-be masters—even if this impulse toward understanding others is not reciprocated by them—by relating their stories to others. Can "crosshatching" be read as metaphor for what your verse does?

NT: I believe so. It's the integration of my personal story, my history, crosshatched, written over and within the public histories and more dominant narratives I have received. I like the idea of how these strands are interwoven, because our stories are never simply two trains running on separate tracks. They are much more like the basketweave of that crosshatching. And the great thing about the idea of the crosshatching is that, depending on how you turn it, you can read one or the other narratives. It doesn't actually obliterate one in order to replace it with another; they both exist, and we only need shift our vision to see both stories. And so I've wanted my own story to be inextricably linked and crosshatched with larger American stories.

DCT: The poet and critic Susan Stewart has written about poetic intersubjectivity, that poetry offers a way for the poet to take on the Orphic task of drawing along the other out of the darkness, or sometimes just to share the darkness. Do you see that as operating in your own work, that sense of connectedness?

NT: I want the largest possible audience of people to be welcomed into my poems and to use the most important muscle human beings have, which is the muscle of empathy. I want a reader who might not have considered some of the issues my poems raise to feel themselves drawn in and to see the world themselves through a slightly different lens that allows for shared histories, instead of separate ones. This happens with the narrator of "Native Guard." He's the one with the documentary power. He's the one who has the pen and is doing the writing and, because of that, he's the one who has the power to shape the narrative, what gets recorded. And so he takes on that task, attempting to find a way to articulate what it is the white soldiers are trying to say. So there is a bit of empathetic revision on his part. He's not simply taking dictation. I wanted to show that he is in this role of writing history, of reinscribing cultural memory, which is of course a role reversal. And so he has to grapple with what this means, with what kinds of ethical obligations we have when we are purporting to speak for others.

DCT: Even on the level of form in "Native Guard" and other poems, your texts reflect a kind of chiasmatic structure, a crosshatched repetition with variation that crosses over between lines and stanzas. For instance, in "Native Guard," the last line of one sonnet is taken up as the basis for the first line of the next section.
NT: Yes, I wanted to show the interwovenness, the inextricability of their voices, and this happens also in the back-and-forth crossings of some of the lines themselves. This also has something to do with the feeling that in some ways these kinds of crossings and crosshatchings exist within my own blood. I think about Langston Hughes's poem "Cross" concerning mixed race experience. And here I have lived and grown up in a place and a time where I could feel as if whatever story I had to tell could link what seemed to some people very disparate stories. That I myself embodied that sense of crossing.

DCT: In all your volumes, there is a recurrent pattern of graves and grave-tending, on both personal and historical levels. Does this motif also serve as an image of what your verse does? Is poetry a form of grave-tending?
NT: I do feel that poets should take on the responsibility of recording or re-recording the cultural memory of a people, and tending the graves is a way of doing this. It means tending to the past, to those things that are not gone or erased or invisible, but are indeed enacting themselves in our daily lives. Countless writers have found a way to say this. William Faulkner says that the past is never dead, it's not even past. James Baldwin talks about how the past is literally present in everything that we do. Tending the graves to me is really a way of tending the present too, a way of being attentive to our everyday lives and interactions with each other. I use that epigraph from Charles Wright, which is so wonderful, to begin the first sequence of poems in *Native Guard*:

   [*Trethewey recites the passage from Charles Wright*]

I walk through the world thinking always of what has come before, that it's still present, and I think it's my job as a poet to tend to that.

DCT: Charles Wright's poems are always so brilliantly abstract—they rarely fill in the set-aside—but your poems flesh out the set-aside and the lost in remarkable ways. Sometimes this happens physically in images of decaying bodies on battlefields in "Native Guard" or of ants making a mound of dirt on your mother's grave in "Monument." That seems important in your work, this concern with a weightier realism, with the reality of objects in our worlds, and with bodying forth the set-aside and their histories.
NT: Yes, I think so. I'm so glad you mentioned that about the ants in "Monument." This is another example of how such plainspoken words can be so laden with symbolism. When I was working on that poem, I discovered, while hanging out with my *OED*, that an ant mound is quite literally a monument. And so I titled the poem "Monument" in hopes of directing the reader towards that other definition, which is how the poem tries to do its deeper levels of work beyond the very accessible surface of just watching ants building an ant mound. In seeing the ants going about their business I am reminded about how I have not gone about mine. That they are building the monument to my mother's memory that I have not yet built.

DCT: That might take us into another question: the status of "nature" or environment in your work. At times nature shows up in somewhat grim ways, as in "Monument" and in other images of human bodies breaking down into their thingness, the bare bones of their material structure. One might not immediately think of you as a nature poet *per se*, but there are repetitive instances of nature coming into the human world, sometimes clashing, sometimes converging. How would you describe the role of nature in your poems?
NT: That's such a good question. The poet Camille Dungy just edited an anthology called *Black Nature*. She and I were talking about the anthology not too long ago and she said to me, "I realize that I could have included so many of your poems" beyond the ones that she did include. And I talked to her how my father used to say to me over and over again when I was first starting out trying to be a poet that I should write a poem about nature. And every time he'd say it, I'd roll my eyes and think that I don't have the same relationship with the natural world that my father has. I grew up partially in Mississippi, a place where nature to me was always my grandmother's yard, the ditch that ran right beside it, and then right beside the ditch a big highway, new Highway 49, and looming above my grandmother's house, in

all its irony, a billboard that read "Marine Life on the Beach at Gulfport," a billboard about some dolphin show there. So for me nature was always cut through by a highway. Unlike my father, nature wasn't the rural experience. So I was wondering how I had anything to say about nature. And this is one of the things that Camille gets at in this anthology: often when black people have written about nature, somehow a tree seems to become a lynching tree. African Americans' relation to nature is often a dark one or at least a different one, a relationship rooted in hardship or toil or labor. That's what my relationship to nature often is. Which is not to say that I don't walk around and enjoy beautiful nature and the flowers blooming and the birds singing, but nature always is a gateway that leads to some other thinking about things. For instance, in *Domestic Work*, I have a poem called "Signs" in which I write about my grandmother leaving home to go to the home of her new husband, who has a family farm farther north in Mississippi. Being from the Gulf Coast, she had never seen cotton before. As she's riding in the car to her husband's farm, she sees cotton on the roadside for the first time—of course, again, there's that image of a road cutting through nature. The nature she sees is cotton fields, which represent so much toil for people both black and white at this time in Mississippi. She thinks that it's a field of gladiolas, that these rows of cotton are fields of flowers. I always thought that this was such a crazy story and yet it suggested to me something about the way we can be blinded by our own past and environment. Because she was on her way to this family farm with this new husband, my mother's father, a man whom she would later discover was a bigamist. There is a failure to see the signs for what they are. Instead, she sees what looks to be loveliness and flowers and it's really something completely different. The way that nature commingles the lovely with the grim also plays a part in my poem "Photograph: Ice Storm, 1971" from *Native Guard*. I remember how beautiful the landscape was the morning we walked out into the yard and saw all of the trees encased in this shining layer of ice. It was sunny and the ice hadn't quite begun to melt yet, so everything looked like crystal, sparkling. And yet I couldn't help juxtaposing that lovely image of the natural world and the vision of things being so perfectly enwrapped in the gleaming ice with the other dark side of things, the violence against my mother happening within the house.

DCT: The Gulf often becomes the physical embodiment of nature in your poems. "The Gulf" seems to bolster a good deal of symbolic force, on personal, historical, even existential levels.

NT: When I think of the Gulf, I think first of the physical space itself, the very coastline. Along the Mississippi Gulf Coast is what is known as the world's longest man-made beach, twenty-six miles of sand. To make this beach in the middle of the twentieth century, they had to dredge and bulldoze the mangrove swamps and then import all this sand and dump it on top of this indigenous shoreline. That is a perfect metaphor for a kind of erasure and rewriting. This is a coastline that has been revised; we've taken what was natural, bulldozed it and replaced it with another layer. And yet I always think that there are ways that nature—especially the nature of the Gulf Coast and along that shoreline—both conceals and reveals something about that buried past, about what has been overwritten.

DCT: There is so much crossing or attempted crossing, actual and symbolic, in your poems. And yet there is also the Gulf, which holds a sense of potential separation and barrier. Could you say something about how these tensions coalesce, or not, in your work?

NT: Well, yes, the Gulf is also interesting because it's hemmed in by a series of barrier islands and it's very shallow, and deceptively so. It looks like this calm surface, but you'd have to walk out really far before you'd even be waist-deep and the water is cloudy. Once you get to the other side of the barrier islands, the water is much clearer. I remember as a child standing on the beach. I would look out and see some of the trees of the closest barrier island. Before anyone told me better, I used to think I was seeing Mexico because I knew this was the Gulf of Mexico. The idea that there was this foreign place in such close proximity struck me. I had been to Mexico as a child and so I was looking across the Gulf and imagining that I could see the other country. With a child's imagination of borders and barriers and crossings, I believed that I could cross over and get to this other place.

DCT: Another strong motif in your work is the matter of attempting to "fix" memory in writing, to capture the past on paper, or in some cases, engraved in stone, to make lasting memories.

NT: For me, the act of writing is always public. I never think of writing as a private act and there are a couple of reasons that I must feel this way. When I was twelve years old, I was given a diary for the first time, the kind of diary with a little lock and a key. I was given this thing that was going to be the repository of my thoughts and I started writing in it. Not long after, I realized that my stepfather was reading it. He would pick the lock and read whatever I wrote. I knew that I did not have the privacy in what I was writing and I began to think of him in some ways as an audience, as my first audience. I actually carried on a very difficult conversation with him. I would write things to him and almost dare him to say anything back to me. Because I knew he wouldn't. I would write in the diary, "For you to say anything about this would be to acknowledge what you're doing." And he never did. A little before then, I had read the *Diary of Anne Frank*. Here is this young woman in some ways writing a personal account of her experience but also seeming to have a knowledge that it would be public. That became the way for me to think about writing, that it was for the public and that it should do important work. Even if this work were based in personal reflection, it should speak to and for more than the person writing it.

DCT: Drawing on that sense of public responsibility, of writing as both personal and public, do you feel that the pattern of writing memories in your poems is related to the African American cultural archetype of literacy? This is so prevalent, for instance, in slave narratives, like Frederick Douglass writing between the lines of a white child's lesson book and realizing that learning to read and write would provide the actual passage to his freedom.
NT: Yes, literacy, the idea of freedom, selfhood—all of that comes from the ability to write, to be literate and to write. That undergirded how I thought of Ophelia in *Bellocq's Ophelia*. I really did think a lot about slave narratives and neo-slave narratives when I was working on that book, and the kind of quests that we see in those stories. Literacy is certainly one part of the hero's quest. That is why I make Ophelia so concerned with education, with learning to write and being well read.

DCT: How about the nature of "Southernness" in your work? You often refer to models of traditional Southernism: the Vanderbilt Fugitives make an appearance in "Pastoral" and there are allusions to Allen Tate's "Ode to the Confederate Dead" at the conclusion of "Native Guard" and as the epigraph for "Elegy for the Native Guard." Faulkner's Joe Christmas from *Light in August* is mentioned by name in "Miscegenation." Why the concern with this traditional vision of the Southern past—"Southern" stereotypically meaning white, male writers of privilege? Do you consider yourself a Southern writer?
NT: [Laughs] I am the quintessential Southern writer! Quintessentially American too! Geography is fate. Of all the kinds of fate swirling around my very being, this place in which I was born and this particular historical moment matter deeply. The story of America has always been a story of misce-

genation, of border crossings, of integration of cultures, and again, I embody this in my person. To me, I fit in as the quintessential Southerner. Perhaps even now my role is to establish what has always been Southern, though at other points in history it has been excluded from "Southernness." We just hadn't found the right metaphor yet. Which is to me one of the reasons why *Native Guard* has been successful. People finally saw the American story. I think Mississippians see our story in that American story. I boldly think of myself as that native guardian. Not to mention that my name, Natasha, actually shares the prefix of words like "native" and "national" and "nativity." It's there in my very naming.

DCT: Would you say a few words about the new book of poems on which you are currently at work?

NT: Certainly. The new book I'm working on is called *Thrall*. I see this as an expansion and perhaps fine-tuning of my concerns in my previous works. When I was finishing *Native Guard*, I was looking up all these words in the *OED*, and I looked up the word "native." I was surprised to find that the definition was not what I expected. I would have expected the first definition of "native" to be in the sense that I am a native Mississippian or that a plant is native to the Southeastern United States. Instead what came up was "someone born into the condition of servitude, a born thrall." The word then carries with it a history of imperialism, of colonialism, the idea that when we go there to colonize someplace, those people are the "natives." And so I became enthralled, to use the pun, with that idea. The notion of what we are in thrall to. I have felt in thrall to language my whole life because language has been used to render me illegal or illegitimate, to name me as other, and in that way to shape my identity and place in the world. The new book begins with a series of poems about Mexican casta paintings, which illustrated the mixed blood unions in the colony and also defined their taxonomies, the ways in which the people had been labeled as a form of social control: to name them and thus to know them in the naming. In his fifteenth-century grammar book of the Castilian language [*Castilian Grammar* (1492)], Antonio de Nebrija [Bishop of Avila] says that language has always been the perfect instrument of empire. So I begin by considering the ways in which we have been enthralled to language. Again, this idea has been especially close to my own experience. "Miscegenation," for example, is a word that entered the American lexicon during the Civil War. These terms are invented to identify and categorize human subjects. I'm very interested in the eighteenth century for the way that natural philosophers then were classifying everything, the way that, with the emergence of Enlightenment thinking, we also have the classification and emergence of codified racial difference. I'm interested in the way that these kinds of taxonomies were a form of knowledge production that subjugated some peoples. In *Thrall*, I'm examining everything from the casta paintings to botany to anatomy in the eighteenth century. But I'm expanding these poems beyond this historical period because I'm also looking at ideas of otherness, racial difference, blood purity and impurity across time and space. So of course one can find these things in religious paintings, for instance, going back across many centuries and nations. I'm fascinated with how these ideas assert themselves, these notions of blood and purity, through varied histories, how these concepts are still affecting how we think about and treat other human beings around the world. I guess you could say that, in many ways, *Thrall* is the book that is actually most about race that I've ever written. Race always appears in my work because I have a racialized experience of America. But in this new book I'm fully examining race as such, as a category itself, and its relation to that vexed issue of blood.

DCT: Finally, what is the future, or futures, of poetry?
NT: The ways that we encounter poetry are changing. I suppose they had to change. I'm always going to be a fan of the book and hope that the world will continue to be a fan of the book. But I'm also interested in poetry as new media: online journals, the kind of video work that we do at *Southern Spaces* where we film poets on location in their spaces reading poems. These are different ways to bring poetry to audiences. These new media probably create a much wider net for an audience than even a book that someone might go into a bookstore or library and pick up. We can measure how many hits the website has gotten and we can see where those hits are coming from. A poet who might have simply been "regional" can become national or even international because of these other media. I like to think that this is a good thing. Any time we discover new ways of getting poetry out to the public, this helps complement and expand the more traditional ways of getting poems to audiences. Those people seeing a poet in a "rock star" documentary video type thing might well go seek out the text, the book itself, and therefore know the poet on the page as well as on the computer screen. So I very much envision new yet strong futures for poetry.

Jake Adam York Interviews Natasha Trethewey

Jake Adam York / 2010

From *Southern Spaces: An interdisciplinary journal about regions, places, and cultures of the American South and their global connections*, 25 June 2010. The interview was videotaped 13 May 2010 in Decatur, Georgia, for *Southern Spaces'* Poets in Place series. The journal is published online by the Emory University Libraries at http://www.southernspaces.org/. The seven segments of York's conversation with Trethewey are archived at http://www.southernspaces.org/2010/jake-adam-york-interviews-natasha-trethewey and also available on YouTube. Jennifer Hall transcribed the final two segments for this volume. Printed here for the first time with permission from Jake Adam York and from Allen Tullos, senior editor of *Southern Spaces*.

Part 6

Jake Adam York: So you lived in Atlanta, or went to school in Atlanta, from the age of six or seven?
Natasha Trethewey: Yes, six—first grade.

JAY: So you've lived in Atlanta probably more of your life than any other place, right?
NT: Yes.

JAY: I mean since you've been back here in Atlanta for what? Eight years? Ten years?
NT: Almost ten years now. Unbelievable.

JAY: Obviously your poems in some ways gave you a mechanism for returning to Atlanta. Do you feel in some ways that maybe you were writing back to Atlanta, which we see very briefly in that poem "Pastoral"?

NT: When my mother died, I was nineteen. And I said to myself, that I would never come back here. My grandmother said she would never set foot in this place again. Now we both have come back here. My grandmother died here, which is such a strange thing for a woman who said she'd never come to this place. To not only have had to come because of the hurricane, but then to die here. So I never thought that I'd want to come back, that I could come back. So there was a real need to make peace with the place when I came back.

And I came back obviously because I had to; I came back because I got a job worth coming to. It was at that time that I began writing all the poems that are in *Native Guard*, mainly the first section, which is comprised of the elegies to my mother. I think it has everything to do with coming back here. There was a convergence of many things. I mean, also, approaching my fortieth birthday and having gotten to the point where I had lived as many years without my mother as I had with her. But Atlanta was not just a physical geography, of course, for me. It was a psychological one. And so I did not want to enter the physical geography because I thought it meant coming back to the psychological geography. In some ways it did. In the ways it allowed me to write the poems. But at the same time I did not come back to the same place. I didn't come back to the same place for the same reason I couldn't go back to the same place in "Theories of Time and Space." Because I'm not the same. Not just that Atlanta had changed, that Decatur had changed. But because I had. And so I suppose that, it was right, it was the right time to return—if you can call it a return.

JAY: I've seen Atlanta change a lot in those intervening years.

NT: I say Atlanta, people say Atlanta, that's what we say; but it gets more specific than that. I actually lived in Decatur a good part of when I was growing up. I can walk to the courthouse where my stepfather was sentenced. I moved that close to the place that I had left behind. But it was completely different. I feel different in this place now.

JAY: You feel different. You felt that way when you moved here first, when you returned here for the first time almost ten years ago?

NT: I knew it was different, and I could avoid going to certain places. There are places that hold a little bit more of that past than others. And so I could avoid them for the most part. I do feel differently when I go to those places because they still hold a lot of that history the way a place does hold it. It doesn't hold it here so much in this house, in this neighborhood. Even at the courthouse. I think when I first came here, too, I liked to think of myself as just passing through, that I'm not going to stay here forever.

But the more I'm here, the more I feel like I'm rooted here too. My brother is from here. And when our mother died, he had to move to my hometown. And all he wants to do is get back here. Of course, I don't want to go to my hometown either. I don't want to live there. Because, going back to what you were saying, it's more of a psychological place. I like it in my mind. I don't like it when I go there. And not just that it's been destroyed, but you can't go back to those places. The place that I like existed when I was between three and twelve years old.

Part 7

JAY: I'm asking these questions because these seem to be the real questions of place. Not where it is geographically on a map, like what buildings still exist or have been torn down, but what does it really mean and what is its pull on you, what is its gravity?
NT: Well, I think it's about, for me—when I think about Mississippi, for example—I don't imagine that I will ever live in Mississippi. And yet, it is absolutely the place that I hold onto.

JAY: You won't live there, but you'll always live there.
NT: I'll always live there. Because it is, to me, who I am. More than this geography, as you have mentioned, that I spent most of my life in. Because, in my head, I am Mississippi. I feel like it's Mississippi that made me.

JAY: That's interesting. It doesn't take much. You know, the right geography at the right time becomes your primary geography.
NT: Do you feel that way? Did Alabama make you?

JAY: No doubt. I was born in Florida, but raised all my conscious life in Alabama.
NT: Where in Florida were you born?

JAY: Born in West Palm Beach, Florida. But all my conscious life, until I was twenty-two, in Alabama. And so I didn't even know there was much of a world outside of it.

NT: But you would live there again.

JAY: I would. For the same reason, I think, that we're talking about. Your places have this kind of hold on you. I wouldn't want to live in Gadsden again. What does a poet do in Gadsden? I don't know. As far as I can tell, most Gadsden poets drink themselves to death.
NT: We won't let you go back there.

JAY: Okay. But you feel that there's some sort of pull on you. Even once my grandparents are not there, which hopefully is another couple of years away, there still will be this weird gravity that makes me feel like I will have to go back there to keep an eye on it. Part of that, I think, is, and this is my question to you, both about Gulfport and Atlanta. I feel to me like I might be coming back so that I remember where I am.
NT: Well, I think coming to Atlanta was about that. I think I had started to say this, and I got sidetracked by my own tears; but, when I said I was never going to come back here, I also blocked out as much as one can do this, as much of those years that I had grown up in Atlanta as possible. Because they were just really painful to remember. The years of living here with my stepfather I wanted to erase from my mind. Of course, that's impossible, but I did a decent job of it for years, I guess, which is what allowed me to survive after that terrible loss. So I didn't want to come back because I didn't want to bring that back.

But not bringing that back means not only did I not have a bunch of me, but I didn't have my mother. Because she was a big part of those years. So in order to get her back in some ways, it meant getting back me in those years. And it meant getting back all the stuff that those years had with them. Which was this place. So even though I had never intended to do it at first, it became something I had to do in order to reclaim so much of myself and her that I had lost. Mississippi is about a reclamation too, though. Though I wouldn't live there, it is absolutely necessary for me to assert again and again that it's mine. And that has everything to do with being rendered illegitimate by the place. I mean, the place said, "No. You are illegal. We have a clause in the Constitution that's meant to keep you from existing." That's the place I'm going to own. Own it. Yeah.

JAY: In that last line of *Native Guard*, "native land, where they'll bury me." What more of an act of ownership can one imagine? To return to my original question about your having been aware of certain landscapes kind of being ablated in some way, but also clearly being engaged in the act of maybe writing your own landscapes over these geographies that you know very well. That seems to be what maybe you're doing there in the final poem of *Native Guard*.

NT: I think that it's just a poem where I'm stomping my foot and saying, "Mine! Mine! Mine!" Yeah.

JAY: You get to be the author of it, not just the owner of it, but the author of it.

NT: You know, I learned that in writing *Domestic Work* because, for example, a poem like the one you mentioned, with the records and the static, "Saturday Matinee," is a poem about watching *Imitation of Life*—seeing that movie for the first time, and also hearing in the other room this domestic violence that's happening [*editor's note: York and Trethewey discuss her mother's love of music earlier in the interview*]. The act of writing the poem for me really was an act of being the author of the past in some ways. The past that I felt powerless in. I don't feel so powerless writing it.

JAY: You said coming back to Atlanta in part was about reclaiming your mother, but also about reclaiming a part of you. And reclaiming Mississippi is also about maintaining a sense of wholeness, and that there's something empowering. Not just about putting yourself back together in that way, but owning that geography. What are the fruits of grasping that power? What new work becomes possible because you have new power?

NT: What I know is that, I think in many ways like you, my obsessions don't change. I'm still interested in all these things that we've been talking about. And I'm just finding, I think, other ways of answering those questions to myself, again and again. I don't think that the answers are ever the same. I mean, I ask the same questions; and I think I'm answering it, or I'm asking it at least, again to myself in the book I'm working on right now.

You know, this is sort of an aside, but I've been thinking about it. When I do pay attention to reviews or things that people say, and I try very hard not to do very much of that; but some things stay with me, and I remember reading that someone had made this comment, back about *Domestic Work*, that I seem really focused on the past, and that there's something really cagey about that. Like I'm being real secretive or something. And I want to go, well give me a minute, why don't you? There's an *oeuvre* coming. You know? There have been people who have come up to me after readings and say, "How come your father doesn't really appear in many of these poems?" My answer would always be, "Well, he appears to the extent that he appeared in my life." I have an answer for them, but it's just the next thing.

JAY: Yeah. I noticed in some of your recently published work, the "Elegy" poem in *New England Review* and then you also have this poem in *Poetry Northwest*. I think it's called just "Mexico." Right?
NT: Right.

JAY: Where your father appears. In fact, in the "Elegy" poem, it seems that you've imagined him, or maybe you're remembering him in a landscape that's a lot more like that natural landscape that you ascribed to him earlier in our conversation. You imagine that for him nature was what he would have known growing up in Canada. And you've kind of put him in that landscape in that poem. You're fishing together.
NT: Right. He is figuring more prominently in the book I'm working on, just because now is the time to turn my attention there. I never meant to be sort of cagey or leaving out certain things.

JAY: It takes a while to get it all in.
NT: It does take a while. And I never know, perhaps you're like this, but I never know what I'm really interested in until I sit back and look at it. I know the research I'm interested in. I know the surface. And I never know what it's actually leading me to. You remember we read together at Auburn, and I read those poems, the casta paintings poems? I didn't know where they were leading me.

JAY: And they led in part to these poems about your father, right?
NT: Right. But it makes sense because those images always begin with the white father, and devolve from there. That's where it begins. And the ones I kept focusing on mostly were the white father and the black mother and the biracial child. And it's silly that it didn't occur to me that—well, I knew that I was interested in that family unit, obviously—but I didn't know the ways that it would lead me to thinking about ideas of knowledge and dominion and colony and empire. But it has. That's not so far from me thinking about my relationship to Mississippi and its history. It's just a little bit broadening of the focus.

Report from Part Three: Rita Dove and Natasha Trethewey, Entering the World through Language

Rudolph Byrd, Rita Dove, and Natasha Trethewey / 2011

A program for *Creativity Conversations*, a Creativity & Arts Initiative of Emory University, this interview was videotaped 22 March 2011 and was closely transcribed by Shannan Palma of the Center for Women at Emory. The video is posted at the Emory *Creativity Conversations* site: http://creativity.emory.edu/programs/creativity-conversations/dove-cc-0311.html, with audio at iTunes: http://itunes.apple.com/us/podcast/rita-dove-natasha-trethewey/id422850039?i=93896685. A complete transcript, including poems and Dona Yarbrough's introductory remarks, is available at http://creativity.emory.edu/programs/creativity-conversations/dove-cc-0311.html. The dialogue printed here is a true transcript of a live unscripted onstage conversation, published in print in this volume for the first time, with permission from Rita Dove, Natasha Trethewey, and the *Creativity Conversations* series.

[*Note by volume editor Joan Wylie Hall: Former U.S. poet laureate Rita Dove was featured in three conversations for Women's History Month at Emory University between 20 March and 22 March 2011, including two programs with composers, a violinist, and a pianist. Recordings of these and many other programs are available at Emory's* Creativity Conversations *website, which features "distinguished visiting thinkers and creators in conversation with great Emory scholars." Dove's informal discussion with Trethewey was the last program of her three-part series, and Shannan Palma's transcript faithfully retains the oral quality of the occasion. Trethewey's Emory colleague, the late Rudolph Byrd, was moderator; Dona Yarbrough, director of the Center for Women at Emory, introduced the discussion and recognized the many campus sponsors. The large audience, including students and community members, responded warmly with laughter and applause throughout. Audience members asked questions toward the end of the hour-long event.*]

Byrd: Welcome to this dialogue, which we have called, "Report from Part Three." And "Report from Part Three" is a reference to "Report from Part One" and "Report from Part Two," the autobiographies of Gwendolyn Brooks, who was the first African American to receive the Pulitzer Prize for Poetry for her volume *Annie Allen*, which she received the Pulitzer Prize for in 1950. And "Report from Part Three" is a reference to the fact that there are only three African American poets who have received the Pulitzer Prize for Poetry. It's Gwendolyn Brooks, then Rita Dove for *Thomas and Beulah* in 1987, and then Natasha Trethewey for *Native Guard* in 2007, so in every way this is an historic dialogue. When you see the two of them together, you know that this is what we have. This is the richness that we have, and this dialogue is an opportunity for both of them to map an important friendship, as well as their very important and significant contributions to the body of American literature and to world literature as well.

And so as a way to begin, I'd like to begin at the beginning, and that is when they first met. If you could, describe for us your first memory of one another as poets? When you first met, was it on the occasion, Professor Dove, when you selected *Domestic Work*, Professor Trethewey's first volume of poems, for the Inaugural 1999 Cave Canem Prize? Did it begin there?

Dove: It did begin there, in the sense that I was judging the first Cave Canem Prize, and manuscripts were anonymous. There were no names on them. I was reading through these manuscripts, and you know, when you're judging a contest, you're—at least I am—I'm looking for something to just knock me over, to push my comfort level in different places and make me gasp, make me think, how did he or she do that? How did they get there? How did they get me there? And that's what happened when I read Natasha's manuscript. I had no idea who she was, and I didn't know until I'd given in the name, but it was absolutely clear for me—and I was hoping that would happen when I was reading through the manuscripts, but you never know—and it was absolutely clear for me that this was the winning manuscript. I was so anxious to find out who this woman was. It was obvious it was a woman, but that's all I knew, and—and was delighted to meet her. Now, we were just talking about how we first met, because it took a while, and it was at the Virginia Festival of the Book, which takes place in Charlottesville, Virginia, where I live, where the University of Virginia is, and we were scheduled to read together.

And I—since that time, we just figured that out, since that time, I had seen a picture of her because they had pictures in the program for the Festival of the Book, but we had not met, yet. Do you want to take it from there, or do you want me—?

Trethewey: Not yet. [*laughs; Dove and Byrd laugh*]

You may be embarrassed to tell that lovely story about yourself, so I'll tell it, but before I do tell that part, I have to tell, of course, how I first encountered Rita even before meeting her. And of course I encountered her poems long before I met Rita Dove.

Thomas and Beulah was the first book that my father gave me when, in 1990, I was on my way to graduate school. He put it in my hand, and I did not put it down for years after that. I literally carried it in my bag with me everywhere I went, and it was like a [*laughs*]—see, I told you you'd be embarrassed—it was like a Bible to me. And so, that's why it's actually, if I get choked up it's because I couldn't have imagined all those years ago that I'd actually be sitting right here having this conversation.

I guess, early in 1999, I was at an AWP convention, the one that was in Albany? And I met this woman named Crystal Williams, who is a poet. She was sitting in the bar, and I walked in there and sat down and started having a conversation with her, and I had not, you know, had a book published or anything yet, and Crystal had a couple, and she told me about the Cave Canem Prize. She was the one who actually told me that they had started a prize, but the magical thing that she said was that Rita Dove was judging it. And all I could think was that, perhaps, if I could get my manuscript into her hands, maybe, just maybe . . . And so I sent it off to the competition.

The day that we met was when, of course, I was invited to the Virginia Festival of the Book to give a reading with this poet who I had admired for so many years, and there was a Cave Canem reading, and I was late getting there, so I went into the back of the room, and Rita was sitting on the front row, and I could see her and recognized her, and so immediately following the reading, I ran down to say hello, and of course, like she always is, she was swarmed by a group of people, and I just sort of slipped into an empty spot there, and it was at that moment, she looked at me, and her face just lit up.

And she opened her arms—

[*Dove says, "I—" and stops. Trethewey pauses, choked up. They begin to laugh.*]

Dove: [*choked up*] Yeah, we're gonna cry all day. I know. I know.

[*Audience laughter*]

Trethewey: I just—I fell into them. I fell into them, and I said, "Oh, thank you. Thank you." And she said, "It was all you."

Byrd: [*murmurs*] That's lovely.

Dove: [*to Trethewey*] I know.

Byrd: Anything you'd like to add? Comment on?
Dove: Not—that's exactly—that's how it happened. [*laughs*]

[*Audience laughter*]

And it was all her.

Byrd: We're all tearing up. We're all tearing up.

Trethewey: I can actually add something. I can actually add something to that. And I wonder if you remember this.

I got to spend a little time talking to Rita. Perhaps, if not at that moment, then the next day at our reading, and one of the first things I wanted to ask her about was, when she was reading my manuscript, if she recognized all those Rita Dove imitations in my first book?

[*Audience laughter*]

'Cause I tell all my students, I mean, I, you know, I really believe in it. I'm not the only one. Mary Oliver talked about it when she was here, about how much we learn from imitation. And Rita's book, I wasn't kidding when I said it was like a Bible for me. Not only did it show me that the stories of my grandmother, my maternal grandmother, could be the stuff of poetry, but it also showed me a way into it. And there were many poems of Rita's that I loved, and often in order to start a poem of mine, I would take a line from Rita's poem, and just change it ever so slightly to find my way into a poem. And I showed her all these lines, and I said, [*laughing*] "Didn't you see that that was just like this? Didn't you see?"

[*Audience laughter*]

Well, the great thing is, fortunately, she did not see that.

[*Audience laughter*]

Which means I wasn't as derivative as I thought I was. [*laughs*]

Dove: Well, you know, the thing, too, and we were talking about this yesterday at the panel, that everybody steals. There is no stealing, it's just who's the best theft, thief. And also if you make it your own, then it isn't stealing. I mean, there're, what, thirty plots in the world, basically? Probably only two I can think of—love and death. Now, so that means that—and I have read things which were imitations, and I kind of go, ohhh—

So that means you did something different with it. Yes, I could see. Yes, you know, it's about your maternal grandmother, but your life is so different from my life, and where you grew up was so different from where I grew up and where my parents, grandparents grew up, and so to me that is not—it's not, you know, just imitation. You just, it's something else. You take it; make it your own. So, hey—[*laughs*]

Trethewey: I'll share some lines with you guys later on, and you can judge.

[*Audience laughter*]

Byrd: All right.

In *Report from Part Two*, Gwendolyn Brooks makes this observation about what she terms her book story, her book story, "My own book story begins with my father's wedding gift to my mother. He gave her a bookcase, dark, dark mahogany, departmental. It was, is, rich with desk drawers, glass, friendly knobs, and it was filled with the Harvard Classics. I shall never forget visiting it as a little girl. Over and over selecting this and that dark green, gold lettered volume for spellbound study. The Harvard Classics were not the only transports. We had all of Paul Laurence Dunbar's books from which my father read to us in the evening after dinner. We had a famous black magazine, *The Crisis*. We had art, too. We had volumes of art much valued by my brother Raymond who wanted to be a painter. And as soon as we were old enough, our mother saw to it that we had library cards to the Forestville Branch Library. The Forest Branch Library was Enchantment Land. I was allowed to check out four or five books at a time. In a few days, I'd bring them back and take out more."

Could you share with us your particular book story? And is there any aspect of Brooks's book story that resonates with your own in Ohio and Mississippi respectively?

Dove: The bookshelf at my parents' home—there were two that were important. One of them was the bookshelf that had everything in it, you know, everything. And my father is a retired chemist, so there were science books and chemistry books, but there were also, it was also *The Complete Shakespeare*, and that was a very important book. It was huge, and I wanted to read the biggest book, so that was the one I started with.

[*Audience laughter*]

There was also *The Treasury of Best Loved Poems* was there. It was a very eclectic group of books. The other bookshelf was the Great Books of the Western World, that, I thought, well, if I read all of these, I'll know everything.

[*Audience laughter*]

Right. And I, of course, never made it through all of them, but I did start with the first literature book there, which was *The Iliad*, and I was ten. No one told me that it was hard.

[*Audience laughter*]

I'm glad they didn't tell me it was hard, because you just, you just start reading, and like a child figures out adult speech very quickly if you just let them hang around, I figured it out, and the stuff that I didn't get, I just let drop by, but I got the story. So I got the music of it. That was really important. And that *Best Loved, Treasury of Best Loved Poems* was really important because I could just—I got the music of it. Then there was the library card, and it does resonate with me. I was given a library card, and we got to take out six books.

Byrd: Oh, wow.

[*Audience laughter*]

Dove: So. And, but what I did was, you know, I would just take them out. As soon as I finished them, I'd take out some more, so I discovered my passions and the things that resonated with me on my own and that also meant a lot of poetry, because I loved the fact that poetry made language sing. So, but no one told me who was in or who was out and who was good and who was not, and that meant that I read Langston Hughes and Gwendolyn Brooks, and I also read, you know, I also read all of Shakespeare's sonnets and thought they were amazing, and Emily Dickinson, and it was all part of this amazing, beautiful thing we call the English language.

Byrd: So you were reading without judgment?

Dove: Yes. Reading without judgment. Making my own judgments.

Byrd: Professor Trethewey?

Trethewey: Well, there was also a bookshelf, but this one was at my grandmother's house, where I spent all the summers of my life, and on this shelf, there were lots of books that had been my mother's schoolbooks. All throughout college she was English and drama, so I remember the Chekhov. My father's books were also there, both of—and I knew they were their books because they had their names in them—but of course there were also things like the set of encyclopedias that they had bought the year that I was born, and so there were all these books that they had bought for me, thinking that this is where I would begin, and I have a memory of trying to teach myself Greek from—with the Greek alphabet—and of course that didn't work for me, but—

[*Audience laughter*]

Byrd: It's a great effort.

Trethewey: I really—I enjoyed doing it.
    What I think about more than that, however, is spending the summers with my father in New Orleans. He was a graduate student at Tulane at the time, writing a dissertation, but also writing his poems, and I would spend the whole day in the stacks at the Tulane Library, and what I loved about it was that not only did all the people who worked there call you "honey" and "baby" and point you to wherever you needed to go, but that I could roam

the many floors and just pick out anything, and I would pick out books and lie down there right between the stacks and disappear for hours until I knew that my father was no longer in a class or teaching a class.

I think in some ways the books also were about a relationship I think I was building with my father through language, through poetry. There are some early photographs of me pulling books off of his shelf and really destroying the shelves in so doing, because he didn't actually have real shelves. He made them with boards and, you know, a cinder block, and I would take them out, and he'd have to stack them and arrange them again and again, but it was also something that got his attention.

Dove: Yes.

Trethewey: And so, me picking those books up was a way to have a conversation with my father as well.

Byrd: Who was also a published poet.

Trethewey: Right.

Byrd: Let's turn now to *Thomas and Beulah* and *Native Guard*, and *Thomas and Beulah* closes with "The Oriental Ballerina," and Professor Dove, could you read the poem? And I'd like you to comment on why you chose to end the Beulah section of this two- part meditation on marriage with this particular poem, and could you comment on the relationship of "The Oriental Ballerina" to the other poems in the volume?

Dove: You see, well he didn't tell us these questions beforehand—

[*Audience laughter*]

This poem is the last poem of the book. In this poem, Beulah is an old woman. She is lying on her deathbed. My grandmother, in the last years of her life, she had glaucoma, didn't believe really in medicine, and so she was gradually going blind, and she took to her bed. As people used to do, she took to her bed. And my mother would come to bring her food, to try to make her take the drops, and to talk with her, and I would go along and see her sometimes. This bedroom, which had been a room of wonder to me, because it had all of these things in it—jewelry and the things of a woman—

became a place of real sadness. So this is a poem where Beulah is lying in bed, and she's looking at a jewelry box, which I used to love as a child. I used to look at it all the time. It was one of those ones where, you know, you open it up, and there's a little ballerina twirling around. You know . . .

[*Dove reads "The Oriental Ballerina"*]

In the book, Beulah is always—she wants to travel. She's dreaming of travel, she wants to get away, and that was really what my grandmother talked about—other places. I think she hoped that we would get there someday, and so it was really important to end the book not just with the biological facts, the facts that she was going to die, that she was going blind, but that in the reverie of this woman, in this room papered with those, you know, that old wallpaper, that still she could fantasize about the other side of the world, what they were doing there.

Byrd: Thank you.

Dove: You're welcome.

Byrd: And for Natasha, Professor Trethewey, in *Native Guard*, which is a meditation on the Civil War, and also on domestic violence as well, you end with the poem "South." Could you read the poem for us, and then also tell us why you made the choice of ending *Native Guard* with that particular poem? And could you comment on the relationship of "South" to the other poems in the volume?

Trethewey: Well, I think that the whole of *Native Guard* is an elegy. Elegies for my mother; elegies for those forgotten black soldiers who manned the fort off the coast of my hometown; elegies for my own relationship to my South. The title of the poem is "South," and I'm happy to get to tell this story again when my colleague, dear colleague, Ron Schuchard is sitting here, because I must have told Ron at some point that during the time that he was working to help secure Seamus Heaney's papers for MARBL that I had been reading again, Heaney's *North*, and in particular, the title poem, "North," and I was really moved by a part of the poem that seemed to suggest to me the moment that Heaney felt a calling, perhaps from the sound of the ocean, to deal with this particular history that he'd been given, and when I told Ron that I was struggling to deal with my South, he gave me a Xerox of all of the manuscript draft pages that Heaney had written while working on "North," so I had not only the finished poem, but I also had all of the markings, and all of the various drafts that Heaney made, and I think this is one of the things that really helped me, so thank you, Ron, to make my way through the poem "South," which is in many ways the answer to my calling to write about my particular South.

And my South, of course, is a difficult South. It's a South that has created in me a sense of psychological exile. It's a place that I am both of, but a place that has rendered me illegitimate in the eyes of the state. When I was born in Mississippi in 1966, miscegenation was still illegal, as it was in about twenty states in the rest of the nation, so the poem begins with an epigraph from E. O. Wilson that reads, "Homo sapiens is the only species to suffer psychological exile."

[*Trethewey reads "South"*]

I think I surprised myself when I ended that poem because it seemed to me that, in the past, I wouldn't have said anything in that way, and I even remember sort of being taken aback that I finally said it, that this place made a crime of me.

Byrd: Thank you.

Dove: Great line.

Byrd: Let's turn now to *Sonata Mulattica* and *Beyond Katrina*. I'm curious about your choice of epigraphs for the volume. Epigraphs are a way into a work, and so Professor Dove, would you read the epigraph for *Sonata Mulattica*. It's right here.

Dove: Oh, well, there are many epigraphs in *Sonata Mulattica*—

Byrd: The first one.

Dove: —but yes, I'll read the first one. There are ones for every section. The first one for the prologues is from Alice—*Alice's Adventures in Wonderland*: "'Begin at the beginning,' the King said very gravely, 'and go on 'till you come to the end, then stop.'"

[*Audience laughter*]
[*Dove laughing*] Oh—

Byrd: Why did you select that wonderful monograph—epigraph?

Dove: Why did I select—? Well, there are a lot of reasons.

[*Byrd laughs*]

    First of all, it's an unusual length for a poetry book. It's—it's—I can imagine someone would feel daunted by saying, "Poetry? Oh my gosh, I can't read that much poetry." And I wanted—and also, we tend to take ourselves so seriously. We should. But you can really drown under that seriousness, so I wanted to inject—catch people off-guard a bit by having something amusing as an epigraph, but also I wanted to—just—it's a certain kind of warning. It's like, well, if you think this is a story that has a beginning and an end, think again. I mean, by—you know, you begin at the beginning; you stop at the end—but who's to say where that end is? Who's to say where it's going to stop?
    So by saying—having that epigraph, I was kind of warning you that in a way this story began long before that little boy was born of the Polish mother and the African prince, and it is still going on today through our, you know, biracial president and beyond. So, it really doesn't have an end.

Byrd: Okay. Professor Trethewey, you begin your new book, *Beyond Katrina*, with an epigraph from Flannery O'Connor, which is repeated throughout the volume at key moments. Would you read that?

Trethewey: I have it.

Byrd: Oh, great. Would you read the epigraph and then provide us with some sense of why you chose to set the stage with O'Connor's words?

Trethewey: Yeah, it—actually, this is the only epigraph that I have in this book, but as Professor Byrd said, I pull lines of it out throughout the book and use them again and again. And now that I've had to say this, what I don't recall is which story it's from. Perhaps some of you hearing it will remember. "Where you came from is gone; where you thought you were going to never was there; and where you are is no good unless you can get away from it."

[*Audience laughter*]

Dove: So good.

Trethewey: I had been thinking about those words actually when I was writing *Native Guard* because I'd been thinking about the impossibility of returning home, and of course, as the epigraph suggests, not because home is changed, but because we change when we go away from a place, and it makes it impossible to go back. The idea of nostalgia, the love of a place or a time that never really existed, and so I think she really hits it, you know, in that epigraph, and I was thinking about that writing *Native Guard*, and there's a poem that's the first poem in *Native Guard*. It's also the first poem I used to begin *Beyond Katrina*, because the poem means something different in both volumes. In the first volume, it was simply this figurative thinking about that impossibility of returning home, and I turned in that book to my publisher in March of 2005, and by August 29 of 2005, this poem that had been a figurative meditation had become quite literal, as my hometown in the Mississippi Gulf Coast was destroyed. And it was actually forever changed. And so I use it here in this book because of what it means literally, but again also because this book is, again, one of my obsessions about historical memory and erasure and how things will be recalled in the rebuilding effort on the coast. It also suggests that impossibility, the impossibility that is rooted in my own nostalgia from my home.

Byrd: There's going to be an opportunity for a dialogue with all of you. And it's now just about time for that, and so I'd like you to begin thinking about the question or comment that you'd like to pose to Professor Dove and Professor Trethewey, and while you're thinking about that, I'll pose one more question to them.

Dove: We don't get to ask . . .

[*Audience laughter*]

Byrd: As you dare to pose your own questions and comments, and apropos of your observation, Professor Trethewey, regarding history and erasure, I'd like both of you to comment on the importance of history and memory and place as defining themes in your work. And treating these themes in your most recent books of poetry, what were some of the questions that were most important to you? And did the subject matter, the new subject matter, create new opportunities for you? Did it open up new vistas in your exploration of history, memory, and place?

Dove: Whew. I have to go first.

[*Audience laughter*]

Trethewey: I thought you were doing that thing.

Dove: Yeah. You know, well . . . history . . . has always been the core, I mean, of how I'm working—out of my work. It was there when I read *The Iliad* and when I read Shakespeare and all of these things because I wasn't there.

What—when I mean, me, I mean that little black girl was nowhere in the picture, and it began as a kind of, just a sense of absence. I mean, it wasn't that I got outraged, and I noticed it right away, but I began to get a little antsy, I mean, where was this chance for a woman or for someone of my race to impact history? And when I began to write, I began to write—I wrote science fiction, first of all, when I was ten, but the protagonist was always a little black girl on the moon or wherever she was.

[*Audience laughter*]

So that means that, you know, already there was that kind of sense of there's one History, History with a capital H, the printed History, and then there're all sorts of other histories. And I think I began to get haunted by the fact that there were histories we would never know, that when someone dies, there's, you know, there's another history that we never know, so it's been throughout the work. Obviously, with *Thomas and Beulah*, what I was really concerned about was or wanted to do was to show everyday life, ordinary black people, the history of a marriage, and give them a whole humanity, a full humanity, a humanity that was, of course, impacted by their race, but also impacted by their gender, and also impacted by the fact that one liked to fish and the other liked to sew, and these are important. That makes up a whole human being, and if someone insists that you only be looked at through one lens, they're insisting on another part of you being invisible. This is something that's always been my concern.

This last book, *Sonata Mulattica*, though, gave another twist to the notion of history, and that is that there is even written history that gets changed by whims, and we also tend to look at history through the lens of ourselves, of our contemporary times, and put the sepia lens over it regardless. I was concerned in this one with not only recovering the story of Bridgetower, but to remind people that those musicians running around, playing around in England and in Vienna were every bit as contemporary as we were, that they were every bit as conflicted and cool or not cool or, you know, nerdy or not, but they were not to be assigned only to the History book with a capital H, but they were living, breathing people, and I'd bring back their humanity—that was one of my concerns that made it slightly different. It was interesting.

Trethewey: Well, like Rita, I feel like I began getting interested in history because of what I saw as those glaring absences and omissions. I also wanted to use history as a way to understand my place in the world. One of the things I did early on with those encyclopedias that my family bought me to recognize the year of my birth, was to try to read them and to understand how they said something about who I was, or where I was, and there was a particular section on "Races of Man," and so at this point, this was 1966, so it was as if this was all the thinking that there was on races of man, and there were three, you know: Mongoloid, Caucasoid and Negroid. And in this description in the book, one of the things they talked about was actual, the physicality of race, the bodies, and there was a description of how—I never remember which it was, but that if you were black, you had—you were longer from your hip to your knee, or no, maybe it's if you're white—I know you're all going to go home and check this out—

[*Audience laughter*]

Dove: No, I think it's—

Trethewey:—because I did, but if you measured—but blackness meant you were longer from there to there, and so I actually did sneak into my grandmother's workroom and get out her tape measure to measure myself, because I thought that somehow using that knowledge that was combined there would help to tell me something about who I was, because I was fated to Mississippi. I was born to this crazy, violent history of a place that is also beautiful and is a place that made me. So, Heraclitus's axiom, "Geography is fate," made sense to me, that I was not simply adrift in the world, but that I was a product of a place and its history.

And that's the thing that I had to make sense of, and so for me, any question I ask myself is about any moment in history. There's always that question, always why? Why has this happened? Why am I a part of it? What does it say about who I am?

Writing the most recent book was different for me, of course, because it wasn't poetry, it was nonfiction, and so I had to deal with questions of history in a slightly different way than I had before, and because I was dealing with the history being made, it seemed, right at that moment, being made and unmade at the same time, because I had just seen the landscape of my coast sort of wiped clean, and I was very concerned with the narratives that were going to be reinscribed onto it. People there were very concerned with it, too—the worry that what story would be told would not be a story that represented them. People on the Mississippi Gulf Coast were rightfully worried that the story of New Orleans was taking over as the story about Katrina, and I was watching it happen. I was watching everything that I had worried about the farther distant past, those absences and erasures, taking place right now. And so I felt like I was writing feverishly into a historical moment that was otherwise being erased before my very eyes.

Dove: Yes.

Byrd: Now it's time for this dialogue to expand and to include all of you, so are there questions and comments from the audience? Yes—in the back. Thank you.

Audience Member 1: I'm familiar with the work of both of you wonderful poets, and I would like to hear a little bit of the role of myth in your writing. I know that you both call on myth. It was interesting to hear Professor Dove talk about *The Iliad*. I certainly encourage my students to become familiar with mythology and fairy tales, and how they can enhance our own poetry, so if you could just address that issue. I'm sure you both have some interesting things to say. Thank you.

Dove: Myths are stories that have been made to make sense of the world and ourselves, and they're highly ritualized constructs, I think, that allow us to hang on them like caps on a hook, all of our fears and things that don't quite make sense. And so that's why I think I was always really fascinated with them. It's—they're so useful for penetrating into the deeper psyche. For instance, one of my books is called *Mother Love*, and it deals with the Demeter and Persephone myth, and I entered into the book knowing the story, knowing the myth, and going into it deeper, but there are things about it that always bothered me. You know, like why did she eat if she wanted to go back? And by going into the myth deeper, I suddenly realized that it was not merely a story about kidnapping but it was also a story about growing up. It was a story about moving away from your mother and your family and eating because you really do want to get away, but not knowing quite what you're getting into. All of that stuff would not have been possible, I think, for me in terms of self-discovery—and every poem is a self-discovery in some way, I think—if I had not had the crutch, you could almost say, or the framework, of that myth to kind of work through it. So I find that—and there are all sorts of myths, it's not just the Greek myths or the Roman myths, but there's a myth of the encyclopedias. This is another myth, you know?

[*Audience laughter*]

I used to collect encyclopedias, old encyclopedias, and I would collect them so that I could see what they said about negroes or—in what year, and it's fascinating how the myths shift, so they're all coded ways for us to address all that squirrely stuff, I think.

Trethewey: You know, I was just thinking that some of the Greek myths are the earliest stories I actually know, because my father would tell me those myths as bedtime stories, and I think he was—it was always a cautionary tale.

Dove: Yes.

Trethewey: It was always the way that my father was trying to say, "Listen to me," you know? "I'm your father." And so the ones that I remember the most, he always told the story of Icarus, and of course you know why he would tell me that—

Dove: Oh boy.

Trethewey:—because you've got to listen to your father.
[*Audience laughter*]

Dove: Yeah.

Trethewey: He also told me the myth of Narcissus and, you know, warned me about, you know, falling in love with my own face in the mirror. And he told me, I think this must have been one of his favorite myths, and that is the moment that—from *The Odyssey*—of Odysseus being in the cave, blocked by the Cyclops, and I know that my father must have loved it because of Odysseus's cleverness. I remember the relish that he would have in telling the part about when Odysseus kept answering "No one"—

Dove: [*whispers*] No one.

Trethewey:—so that the Cyclops was saying, you know, when he was asked who had injured him, he would say, "No one! No one has injured me," because this is the name he had.

But what I've taken from it now, and I've been thinking about it a lot lately, was that, you know, image of Odysseus in there having to sharpen that stake in order to blind this big giant that stands in the way of him, you know, not only attaining his freedom, but whatever stands at the other end of that cave, that bright light into which he will emerge from this darkness of the cave. And that seems to me the way that my father was suggesting how I would think about, you know, sharpening my own stake, my pencil, perhaps—

[*Audience laughter*]

—to write my way past that big old Cyclops that would keep me in darkness.

Byrd: Another question or comment? Right there.

Audience Member 2: Thank you, Professor Trethewey and Professor Dove, for your moving and enlightening words today. I'm a senior here at Emory University and a writer myself. The both of you have written very much within the genre of poetry. I'm wondering if there was ever a time when you wrote very much in another genre or thought about, perhaps, attempting to delve more within a different genre? How you dealt with that?

Dove: Well, I've—I think that all, I really think that the separation of the genres is sort of like the separation of Church and State. I mean, it's silly.

[*Audience laughter*]

It's silly. It's silly to separate them, and I think that writing is writing. Language is language. It's just different timbres and different weights. I've written short stories. I've published a book of short stories. And I've written a novel. It's a—the novel, in language, I learned something different about the way you stretch perception in a novel, how you build the world of a novel, and how you move through it, and then—but the thing that I think informs me the most, I love poetry. I really am biased. I think it is the greatest of the literary arts, and it's only because it's the most rigorous, and it gets down to the bones of the language. That's where I like to be. But I also know that there are certain topics and things which just beg to be written in a different form and can only come to fruition in that way.

I had a play produced, and that was for me, I knew it was going to be a play before I began it, when I had the idea. I thought I don't know how to write a play, and I wrote the first draft, put it away. My husband kept pulling it out of the drawer every two years and saying, "Are you going to do something with this thing?" And it's to me the closest to poetry, because there's so much you have to do without, and it sounds odd, but you see people are talking all the time in plays, but they're concealing all the time in plays, because they're talking. Whereas in a poem, you're right in there and, you know, there's so much you can't say. I don't know. They're very similar. And I found that I learned so much about speech and what we don't say when we talk, and I learned so much about silence by doing this play where people were talking all the time.

Derek Walcott helped me a lot on the play because he—first of all, he encouraged me to finish it. Then he also told me at one point—he did a staged reading of the play at the 92nd Street Y—they wanted it cut down to an hour and a half. At that point it was three hours long. He said, he said, "Don't whimper, just cut it down."

[*Audience laughter*]

He was right. He said if you want—he said, just cut it. It's good for you, he said. And that's how it—

And he was right. It was good for me. It was good for me to cut it down like that, and he said you can always plump it back up, and he also—I said, well, how do you get the innermost thoughts out, you know? People—and he said, "They're arias. Think of them as arias." You know, the soliloquies, they're arias. So he went to another medium, yet, to explain it. And we've been talking about collaboration all weekend long, but that—that helped me so. But in the end, I always come back to my first love, poetry.

It has everything.

Trethewey: You know, I actually was in love with story, so I was in love with narrative, I suppose. And I might have just been temporarily misguided, but when I first went off to graduate school imagining that I was on my way to becoming a writer, I wanted to write short stories, and I got into a graduate program to write fiction, and within a month or so, realized that that was completely wrong for me, and that, like Rita, I was drawn to poetry for a different reason. And when I realized that a poem could also have its story—it's funny that I didn't quite see it like that at the time—then I turned my attention toward that. I don't know that—and like Rita said, she's published in all those genres—I've not published any fiction or a play, but I can see myself continuing to write prose. And I think it is because of the thing that you just said, that some things need a different treatment. Still, though, in writing *Beyond Katrina*, I couldn't completely leave poetry alone. I still needed it to tell the parts of the thing that couldn't be told simply in prose, and so I returned to it again and again, and see myself as a poet, though someone who needs to explore certain things in prose, occasionally.

Byrd: We have time for one more comment. Only one more. I'm sorry.

Dove: [*whispers*] Oh dear. I'm glad I don't have to choose.

Audience Member 3: Just, another question about crossing genres, but this time in a slightly different direction. I—it was fascinating to hear both of you talk about history and how you've used it, and I actually am a historian and a poet, so I see a lot of crossover between them, but I wonder if you see your work as a form of historical writing, or if you see it as in conversation with historical writing, or arguing with it, or challenging it, or just having some kind of larger conversation with it?

Dove: I certainly see the work, my work, as having a conversation with historical writing, and I guess it would all depend on how you would define historical writing. To me, history is composed of story, and it is composed of narrative, and so if you're talking about—well, from, yeah, obviously it is a historical writing of some sort. It's not necessarily the scholarly type of historical writing. The last book that I did, *Sonata Mulattica*, had a lot of research, and I found myself having to do historical, scholarly research, you know? Something that I swore I must never do—

[*Audience laughter*]

—but I had, I mean, I had to find out. The question became how do you translate that, or does it become transformed or transmogrified into something else, and I discovered there's quite a difference between what—the facts, and what I discovered, and how I'm going to render that into this other version of narrative.

Audience Member 3: Which is something that historians do, also.

Dove: That's true.

[*Audience Member 3 continues to respond, but her comments are inaudible without the mic.*]

Yeah, you always make these choices, right? So what story are you going to tell? What are you going to leave out? And I found myself actually leaving things out. I, who swore I would never leave out anyone's story, left out Napoleon's. I thought it'd been told enough, you know? But it's because you are shaping a version of a life or lives, always.

Trethewey: Always.
Several years ago, I participated in a roundtable discussion for the *Journal of American History* called "Genres of History," and it was a fascinating discussion because they—I was there as the poet. There was a novelist who does—My first moment of really thinking about it in this way, the kind of borrowing across the line between imaginative literature, fictions made from history, and the work that historians do, even to speculate a little bit, and to fill in those spaces where the documentary evidence has slipped away, and what I decided then was that in the aggregate of those two things, we can get a fuller version of the story; that sometimes imaginative literature about history can help fill in those gaps that—where we have no documentary evidence, and so I've been happy to see the ways that scholars, for example, have used poetry to understand certain periods of history. I know not only *Native Guard*, but also my book *Bellocq's Ophelia*, has been used

in history classes. So it's a way of also understanding, and you know, and having that conversation that Rita was talking about, that engagement about what to tell, what to leave out, but how to move beyond the facts of it and to find, to use Ezra Pound's phrase, the luminous details that allow a history to come alive in a different way.

And also to map a kind of emotional geography that maybe historians aren't able to go for as much in their work. Lots of historians have told me that—I don't know if you'd say this, but, since you also write poems—but that they envy, you know, the moments when it can be all speculation, where you can let all the research fall away and use whatever else you've gleaned and how you've made sense of the story and what's not said.

Dove: Right. Yeah.

Byrd: Professor Dove and Professor Trethewey have agreed to close this historic dialogue with reading a poem from their luminous body of work, and so, Professor Dove, if you could introduce the poem and explain why you selected the poem for this particular occasion.

Dove: Oh, I—well, this poem—I couldn't make up my mind. It's not that long, don't worry—

[*Audience laughter*]

—but I decided on this one because it's called "Reunion 2005"—that's the year of a family reunion that we had. I grew up in Ohio, and my family pretty much came up from Georgia. My father's family, one piece, part of the Great Migration, they were, you know, came up for jobs in the North. Rubber factories were the thing in Akron, Ohio. And some went to Cleveland; some went to Akron, but the whole neighborhoods, whole towns kind of went up and settled in one place.

The result of that, and my mother's family came from Washington D.C., and the result of that was when we have reunions, everybody slips back into a Southern accent and Southern attitudes, and it's just—we brought it with us. And because of that, because well—I am a Midwesterner. I grew up in the Midwest—the connection is still there. It's still always there.

[*Dove reads "Reunion 2005"*]
[*Audience laughter and applause*]

Byrd: Professor Trethewey?

Trethewey: I, too, could not decide what to read, but I think because we were just having this conversation about writing about history and what I learned in writing this book of prose that couldn't be done still without a few poems, scenes that I did not think could be matched by prose, and so I'm going to read the very last page of my most recent book, *Beyond Katrina*. It's a poem. The whole book is, as I said before, not only about historical memory and the rebuilding and recovery effort on the Mississippi Gulf Coast, but it's also about my family story, the way that my family story is entwined with the history of the Mississippi Gulf Coast, its development, and in particular, the story of my brother, who lost everything during Hurricane Katrina, and like the coast itself is struggling in the wake of this devastation to rebuild his life.

[*Trethewey reads "Benediction"*]
[*Applause*]

Byrd: Before we turn to the book-signing and to the reception, on behalf of all of the sponsors for "Entering the World Through Language," I would like to thank you for the gift that you have made to all of us in this dialogue and also through your luminous body of work. Thank you so very much.

[*Applause*]

An Interview with Natasha Trethewey

Jocelyn Heath / 2011

From *Smartish Pace*, 16 February 2012. The interview was conducted in August 2011. The poetry journal's website is http://www.smartishpace.com/, and the interview is archived at http://www.smartishpace.com/interviews/natasha_trethewey/. Reprinted by permission.

Jocelyn Heath: *Beyond Katrina* blends personal and collective memories of an event that is not too long gone from the public eye, and is still current for those living on the Gulf Coast. What are the challenges of writing about something topical, even if it has personal resonance for you the writer?
Natasha Trethewey: I think the biggest challenge that I faced with writing *Beyond Katrina* and that particular topic was that, as you said, it is in many ways ongoing for the people who are there, and it is also a thing of contested memory. Contested memory is the hardest part of it, because I found that I was dealing with people who wanted not only to be remembered, but people on the Mississippi Gulf Coast who felt like their story was being forgotten or being subjugated beneath the other story of New Orleans and the levee break. But I was also dealing with narratives from folks who wanted to remember the aftermath in different ways, I think, for political purposes. And so there was often a narrative of Mississippi as being the place where everything worked out and the government very quickly handled its problems unlike—they would say—in Louisiana, which was still very troubled. Except that wasn't exactly true, because just last year the *New York Times* reported on how many poorer people in Mississippi still had not benefitted from the money for recovery that should have gone to them, but was instead directed toward wealthier citizens, businesses, and projects that were already in the works before the hurricane.

JH: What you said about contested memory—memory for different purposes and subjugation of memory—made me think of the fact that we're coming up on the tenth anniversary of 9/11, which is quite publically memorialized. How does it compare with Katrina—how could Katrina be memorialized fairly? It seems that, although Katrina didn't start an international armed conflict, there are still conflicts to be resolved.

NT: One of the things that people have talked about, that Katrina revealed, was the depth of ongoing injustice in the United States. We witnessed it again and again on TV as we anticipated aid going to the residents of those places who were stranded on the tops of their homes, who were without water, who were without other kinds of resources. And it was broadcast around the world. I think there were many people in the United States who were embarrassed that, all of a sudden, the world was seeing one of the ways in which the U.S. is still struggling with equality and justice. That's one of those difficult things that you can imagine some people would rather sweep under a rug, just like some of the atrocious civil rights violations, murders that went unprosecuted for so many years for which they've just now gotten some convictions. There are many people who will write to the newspaper or call in to radio shows or find other platforms in which to say that we're dredging up old stuff, opening up old wounds that should've just been forgotten and allowed to heal. Except that they weren't wounds that could heal, because they were festering. It's only with a true reckoning—a true and honest recognition of what happened—that we can begin to have healing. So to me, that seems like the only way that the memory and memorializing of Katrina can be fair: to acknowledge all of those stories, all of the difficult parts of the story that show us ourselves in the mirror in ways we might not like seeing.

JH: In paying tribute to these stories, in *Beyond Katrina*, you write both poetry and prose. Did you find it more difficult to articulate your concerns in one genre, or was it a challenge all around?

NT: It was a challenge all around, and I think that's why, in many ways, I end up having a little bit of both in the book. There were things that needed the space of prose to consider. But then there were things that I felt could not be rendered most effectively without the language and imagery, the density and compression and music of poetry.

JH: You describe yourself in "Why I Write" as "tethered" to your native soil, yet in your upcoming collection, *Thrall*, you're traveling beyond these borders—through Mexican casta paintings, among other elements. What moved you to explore this new geography?

NT: I think of it less as a physical geography that I'm exploring and more of an intellectual geography that allows for a widening of the lens, a broadening of the field of vision. And so for me, leaving the physical boundaries of Mississippi to consider history elsewhere was about expanding that vision to think of the Americas—to think of the project of empire, of which Mississippi is deeply part and entwined. And yet, I needed to take those concerns that had always been my focus in my home state and expand them to the project of empire, to the histories of race across time and space.

JH: As you were widening the lens, did you find that changed the experience of writing, whether for individual poems or sequences?
NT: I still rely heavily on the same kinds of things that I always rely on: photographs, or in this case, paintings, visual imagery that I can research and discover, and also histories that I read. And so I find that I really enjoy researching material for the poems; I enjoy looking at paintings from particular historical moments that help illustrate the history of that moment.

JH: When you step into these historic moments, you sometimes do so by way of a persona—Ophelia, for instance. At other times the painting or the photograph comes into the poem, giving an added remove. What governs your choice to inhabit a point in time rather than study from a distance?
NT: Two things must be going on at once for me when I am trying to write about history using one of those objects, using a painting or a photograph. What happens is that I'm at once looking at it as a piece of material culture to see how it reveals something about the moment in which it was created; at the same time, I'm certainly responding to it out of my own contemporary moment. And I think if all goes well, in that space between the two perspectives, there's a kind of frisson as I try to understand the thing of the past as material culture, and bridge the distance between that and my own response, based on my own experience of the world. In between those two things, something interesting can happen.

JH: When trying to bridge that space between, what are the considerations for the reader? Or do you tend to focus on what you, the poet, need to accomplish in this poem?
NT: My exploration of history and these historical objects—these documents or photographs or paintings—is always about an exploration of the self, and the self in this contemporary moment. That's why I always choose to investigate things that allow for that kind of integration, that intersection of public and personal history. These histories that I look at help to illumi-

nate, for me, something of my own contemporary experience and place it in context along the web of history, such that I don't have to see my experience with my father, with American ideas of racial difference, as unique to me, but instead as part of the thread that holds our nation together and helps to shape it. So these things are never just about history, nor are they ever just about me.

JH: When you're writing about your childhood and family, it reads to many as autobiography: intimate in tone and dealing with difficult subject matter. How do you determine what's the moment to be shared and placed in the web of history, and how do you decide what to keep back for yourself?
NT: That's an interesting question. I think you're right that people always do read my poems as very intimate and autobiographical. And I think I am very interested in having a tone that suggests that intimacy, because for me it is a way to invite the reader in as closely as I can to share in that experience with me, as opposed to immediately putting up a kind of barrier to what's being revealed. Of course, any time we sit down to write a poem, whether it's a poem that's ostensibly in the first person and from the actual experience of the poet or if it's a persona poem, there is still a mask that we wear. And because of that, I think that I am allowed to take a few risks that I might not otherwise take in terms of what is revealed, but also to edit what seems less important for the overall emotional truth of the poem. I don't want to sound cagey, or that I am deliberately guarding or hiding certain things, but instead creating a thing that is just as true as anything I might not reveal.

JH: Would it be fair to say that what you're trying to present is not the "sincerity," to use Louise Glück's term for the actual lived moment, but the truth of the moment?
NT: I'm always interested in an emotional truth, and staying very true to that. In personal poems, I think that there is a way to stick to an emotional truth even if facts are manipulated, molded, or shaped. And I don't mean huge things; I mean if I've got to change the color of the dress my mother was wearing, because the color I can change it to gets closer to the emotional truth that I'm trying to convey than the actual dress she was wearing, I might do that. I'm not willing to make up events that didn't happen, because then that to me feels like I'm playing with history. And so in writing about history, I do try to use the facts of history in order to shed light on the emotional truth of the personal experience.

JH: Relating to the ideas of history and personal experience, much is made of the racialized experiences present in your poetry. There is far less discussion of the fact that your first two books were populated largely by women, their lives, and their experiences. What impact do concerns of gender have on your writing?

NT: I think they have a tremendous impact. I feel as a writer that I can never cast aside all the things that, historically, have shaped me, and made me the thinker and the writer that I am. And gender is a huge part of that, and the experience of race in America is a huge part of that. What I think is odd, and it's what you just pointed out, is that in the past, there has been much more made of the role of race in my books than the role of gender—particularly because I never thought that I was writing about race. The experience of race is my everyday experience, and if it's there, it's because it is there, again, in the fabric of our nation. This is a little off of your question, but it leads me to say that because I heard that again and again, I decided, when I began writing *Thrall*, to actually look at the question of race head on: to actually make it my subject, whereas it never had been. It was just there, just as my gender is there, just as the fact that I was born in Mississippi is there. It just is. And it was a different thing for me to actually decide to look at it as a subject.

JH: It seems that, by virtue of the experiences you were writing about, women's history became the subject of *Domestic Work*. Have you considered, then, investigating it as a subject, as you have done with race?

NT: I was very specifically writing about these women: in *Domestic Work*, thinking about the work that my maternal grandmother had done, and in *Bellocq's Ophelia*, thinking about the work and the life of Ophelia. But maybe this is something about what it is to be a black woman, and a biracial woman. I can't separate, either in *Domestic Work* or in *Bellocq's Ophelia*, the experiences of those women into their experience of gender and their experience of race. I can't disaggregate them.

JH: In her essay "Playing in the Dark," Toni Morrison talks about "the habit of ignoring race [as] a graceful, even generous liberal gesture"; "Southern History" and "White Lies" present a different kind of complicity with injustice through silence. How much responsibility for breaking through silence lies on the poets who speak out and how much on the readers who hear the story?

NT: It seems that the responsibility is pretty hefty on both sides, although

I'm completely happy for people to write about whatever it is they have to write about—and so those people who don't feel compelled to address the subjects head on in their work are completely justified in doing that. I'd like to think that they're aware they're making that decision, though, because I'm always conscious of the ways that other writers' experience can be looked at through a lens of race, which usually means that anyone is an "other" of some sort. But I'm troubled by the idea that some people's work is "normal" and can be looked at through a neutral lens. The lens is never neutral for any of us. The experience of being a particular race happens to us all, whether we acknowledge it or not. Blackness is not the only racialized experience. Whiteness is also a racialized experience, whether people choose to write directly about it or not. And I think that readers should be conscious of that when they read something, as opposed to simply making normative or neutral the experience of whiteness, and making "other" the experience of blackness. This goes as well for how we read the work of people with various, often "othered" racial designations, gender, and sexual orientation.

JH: So in a way, we can't ignore the label, and we shouldn't—the label can be used derogatorily, but it can also be used to represent a different view of life, and a different richness brought to the poetry.
NT: Right.

JH: I also wanted to ask you about form. When writing a longer sequence—such as "The Storyville Letters" or the title poem of *Native Guard*—how does the narrative help or hinder what you seek to do lyrically? For instance, a novelist may make a discovery about a character partway through a book or add in an unexpected plot development that changes the tenor of the narrative and the whole work must be revisited; have you, as a poet, encountered parallel concerns?
NT: I think that in *Bellocq's Ophelia*, for example, I was still making discoveries that you suggest as a novelist might make about a character halfway through the book, or three-quarters in, because I never was quite sure where she was going. And I think that form, particularly, is actually the thing that allowed for me to make discoveries about Ophelia and about the character of the Native Guard as well. In that sequence, because I was driven by the form of the crown, there were lyrical things that had to happen that often made surprising narrative things happen. I do find that my own narrative impulse can be a hindrance, which is why, in *Native Guard* and to an extent, in *Bellocq's Ophelia*, I followed a nonlinear way of telling the story by

using forms that required repetition, that made me circle back to a line that had been uttered before and needed to be said again in a different way. In a pantoum, for example, the form subverted the narrative impulse and led to a much more interesting direction for the poem to take. Likewise, in *Bellocq's Ophelia*, this kind of circling back occurs when I explore, in a series of unrhymed sonnets—Ophelia's diary—the same period of time and narrative ground covered in the form of her letters.

JH: Similarly, a number of your poems have rhyme schemes, and others employ poetic forms—"Miscegenation" is a ghazal, the title poem in *Native Guard* is a crown of sonnets—often so subtle that a reader may not pick up on them until after many readings. Does the choice of formal elements originate in the impulse toward a "pleasing pattern of sounds stretched along a line," as you described in your lecture "Why I Write," or does a different instinct inform it? I think of Rita Dove's remark: "If you can get the edges into the form, then that form becomes transformed—it hurts much more, it's much more disturbing."

NT: Well I think a good example of that in my own writing is a poem in *Native Guard* called "Myth," which is a palindrome. It's a poem that I wrote the first half of unrhymed and in free verse, and then I began to see the edges of possibility that Rita described. When I could see that with some wrenching and other painful things, these lines might also rhyme and mean differently, I began looking harder at the half that I had written, reading the lines separately, divorcing them from their rhetorical position in the stanza, divorcing them from their syntactical position within the sentence. And that's the moment that I realized there was yet another formal option available to me and that was that the poem could read backwards line by line, and thus enact in an even more painful way for me what it is like to have a dream in which I don't know that my mother is dead, and wake up to realize that she is—and that I am like Orpheus trying to lead Eurydice out of the underworld, then turning around and seeing her vanish.

JH: I keep coming back to the geographies you say you're exploring, the sort of emotional terrains, the intellectual terrains, and wondered how do you bring in the natural world, how do the physical geographies and emotional and intellectual geographies work together—if they do?
NT: I was just reading some essays by Mark Doty that reminded me that precision is beauty. And I think that trying to get that precise observation of something in nature is what can render even difficult things beautiful. And of course that goes back to something Shelley said: "poetry is a mirror

which makes beautiful that which is distorted." I keep that in mind because it helps me to think about writing those very difficult things that one would not necessarily think were beautiful, but that, if done with precision, are made beautiful.

JH: That brings me back to *Beyond Katrina* because the poems and the prose are rich with historical detail and descriptions that are so precise. And it is something of a hybrid of genre. As a poet, when you have the opportunity to use more words, how do you maintain that precision?
NT: I think it's so much harder. I think I certainly could've labored over it much longer, and had much more precision than is actually there—a deeper, even lengthier meditation that the subject seems to demand.

JH: Likewise, poetry is beginning to metamorphose, being integrated with prose, transforming from print into electronic media. Do you see the blurring of such boundaries as a fruitful development for poetry? Could it harm the precision and beauty?
NT: I like thinking of the possibilities of creating literary hybrids. When I was working on *Beyond Katrina*, I kept returning to Robert Penn Warren's *Segregation*, which doesn't have any poems in it, but I think of it as a literary hybrid nonetheless because it involves a blend of investigative reporting with interviews, blended with a kind of travel narrative, blended also with personal narrative—not a memoir, but somehow clearly an investigation of the self as well. That was my model for writing *Beyond Katrina*. And it seemed to me I needed all of those pieces in order to tell that particular story. So I don't think that the creation of literary hybrids is going to weaken either genre. And I can barely say this to you with a straight face because I just heard myself talking about literary hybrids in the same way that, across time and space, hybrids—or mixed-race people—have been talked about: all those eighteenth- and nineteenth-century arguments about how amalgamation or mixing would diminish both the white race and the black race. But then there came later this idea of "hybrid vigor," which asserts instead that the hybrid is much better and stronger than either of the parents. It's crazy to think about that in light of your question! But you can see clearly what my obsessions are.

JH: Maybe the truth of the matter is that it doesn't matter what our parts are, what a text's parts are, as long as the emotional truth is there?
NT: Right. I think that's true.

Index

Aberdeen, Miss., 51
Agee, James, 119, 120; *Let Us Now Praise Famous Men*, 119
Agni Magazine, 64
Albergotti, Dan, 158
Alexander, Elizabeth, ix, x, 57, 126
Alexander, Lindsey, xviii, xix
Ali, Shahid, x, 55, 67, 83; *Ravishing Disunities*, 55, 67
Alice in Wonderland (Lewis Carroll), 183
Allen, Mike, vii
Allison, Dorothy, xxivn19
Appalachian State University, 18
Atlanta, Ga., xii, xiii, 33, 34, 48, 88, 122, 126, 142, 143, 168–72
Auburn University, 46, 173
Auden, W. H., x
AWP (Association of Writers and Writing Programs), 31, 158, 176

Baldwin, James, x, 30, 161; *Notes of a Native Son*, 108
Barthes, Roland, xvi, 19, 37, 68
Begiebing, Robert, xxvn29
Bellocq, E. J., xv, xvi, 18, 25, 26, 27, 35, 42, 68, 69, 150
Beowulf, 62
Best American Poetry, 76, 149
Black History Month, 133
Blight, David, 28; *Race and Reunion*, 28, 30
Boland, Eavan, viii, 41, 116

Boston, Mass., ix, 16
Bread Loaf Writers Conference, 101, 147
Brecht, Bertolt, 159
Brewer, Joel, 30, 110
Brooks, Gwendolyn, x, 106, 113, 175, 178, 180; *Annie Allen*, 175; *Report from Part Two*, 178
Brown v. Board of Education, xi, 117, 118
Browning, Maria, xii
Bunting Fellowship, 47, 134
Bush, Laura, 31

Callaloo, ix, xiv, 11, 61, 66
Canada, 9, 31, 52, 97, 125, 128, 173
Capone, Al, 46
Carver, Raymond, 83
Cave Canem Book Prize, 61, 65, 76, 175, 176
Chace, Bill, viii, x
Charleston, S.C., 91, 103
Chekhov, Anton, 180
Chicago, Ill., 6, 82
Collier, Michael, 58, 67
Collins, Billy, vii
Collins, Martha, 148; *Blue Front*, 148
Constance, 23, 24, 28
Crampton, Nancy, xxii
Creativity Conversations (Emory), xxivn19, 174
Cullen, Countee, 91, 103; "Incident," 91, 103
Cyclops, 190

Daniels, Colonel Nathan, 53, 59, 90
Danticat, Edwidge, ix
Dargan, Kyle, xxii–xxiiin1
Dark Room Collective, ix, x, 16, 17, 64–65
Daughters of the Confederacy, 29, 117
Daughters of the Revolution, 29
Davidov, Judith, 69
De Cenzo, Giorgia, xxiiin10
Debo, Annette, xxivn17
Decatur, Ga., 33, 45, 48, 169–70
Demeter and Persephone, 189
Dickinson, Emily, 180
Dixon, Son (great-uncle), xiv
Dixon, Sugar (great-aunt), xiv, 6
Doty, Mark, x, 59, 104, 108, 202
Douglass, Frederick, xi, 24, 72, 165
Dove, Rita, viii, x, 8, 9, 15, 45, 49, 57, 63, 76, 100, 106, 134, 174–94, 202; *Mother Love*, 189; "The Oriental Ballerina," 181–82; "Reunion 2005," 194; *Sonata Mulattica*, 183–84, 186–87, 193; *Thomas and Beulah*, viii, 8, 63, 76, 100, 134, 175, 176, 181–82, 186
Duke University Center for Documentary Studies, 54
Dumas, Major Francis E., 53, 71, 72
Dunbar, Paul Laurence, 178
Dungy, Camille, x, 162–63; *Black Nature*, 162

Eady, Cornelius, 17
East Carolina University, 106
Eastern Connecticut State University, xx, xxiiin5
Elam, Angela, xiv
Ellis, Thomas Sayers, 16, 17, 64
Emerson, Claudia, 73, 100
Emory University, xiii, 18, 41, 61, 88, 99, 122, 126, 143, 174

Enlightenment philosophy, xix, 107, 124, 166–67, 203
Eurydice, 83, 202
Evans, Walker, 119; *Let Us Now Praise Famous Men*, 119
Everett, Steve, xvi

Farm Security Administration (FSA), 69
Faulkner, William, xi, 20, 60, 67, 68, 116, 161, 165; *Light in August*, xi, 165
Foner, Eric, 30, 60; *Who Owns History?*, 30, 60
Fort Massachusetts, xi, 45, 87
Frank, Anne, x, 78, 165; *Diary of Anne Frank*, 78, 155, 165
Frost, Robert, x, 48–49, 158
Fugitive poets, xi, 29, 45, 60, 141, 165

Gadamer, Hans-Georg, 20
Gadsden, Ala., 171
Gadsden, Brett (NT's husband), 33, 49
Genoways, Ted, 85, 147
Georgia, 34, 73, 78, 90, 117, 126, 155, 194
Gibson, Margaret, xv, 81, 101, 134–35; *Memories of the Future: The Daybooks of Tina Modotti*, 134
Gingher, Marianne, 95, 144
Glück, Louise, 199
Great Migration, xv, 6, 82
Greek alphabet, 180
Grimmette, Joel (NT's brother Joe), xii, xvii
Grisham Visiting Writers Series, xxi
Gross, Terry, xiii, xxivn20, 61, 92
Gulf Coast. *See* Mississippi Gulf Coast
Gulfport, Miss., xii, 6, 28, 34, 35, 46, 51, 61, 67, 73, 74, 75, 87, 119, 128, 130, 145, 150, 171
Gunn, Robin Wright, xiii

INDEX

Hall, Joan Wylie, xxivn15
Hass, Robert, x, 68, 82, 131; "Meditation at Lagunitas," 68
Hayden, Robert, x, 116
Hayes, Terrance, x, 73; "Postcard from Okemah," 73
Heaney, Seamus, viii, x, 41, 116, 182–83; *North*, viii, 41, 116, 182–83
Hegel, Georg, 130
Henninger, Katherine, xxivn18
Heraclitus, 187
Herrick, Robert, x
Highway 49, 8, 35, 128, 162–63
Hine, Lewis, 54, 69
Hollandsworth, James G., 46, 53
Hollins University, vii, 12, 61, 91, 95
Holocaust, 71
Hudgins, Andrew, 30; *After the Lost War*, 30
Hughes, Langston, x, xxivn20, 161, 180; "Cross," 161
Hugo, Richard, x, 5, 14; *The Triggering Town*, 14
Hurricane Katrina, xi, xvii, 58, 73, 74, 75, 85, 118, 120, 144, 145–46, 147, 169, 185, 188, 195, 196–97

Icarus, 189
Iliad, The (Homer), 179, 186, 188
I'll Take My Stand, 118
Imitation of Life, 172
Ireland, 103

James, Henry, 151
James Weldon Johnson fellowship, 126
Jay, Martin, 19, 20
Jim Crow South, xv, 8, 82, 107, 156
Johnson, Clifton, xv, 82, 134
Johnson, Robert, 10

Journal of American History, 193
Jumpin' Jim Crow (ed. Jane Dailey), 30

Keats, John, 116
King, Martin Luther, Jr., 52, 60, 90
KKK (Ku Klux Klan), 148
Komunyakaa, Yusef, x, 59, 63, 100; *Magic City*, 63
Kooser, Ted, 103, 111
Kundera, Milan, 139; *The Unbearable Lightness of Being*, 139

Lanier, Sidney, 30
Laubenthal, Penne, xix–xx
Lehrer, Jim, 61
Let Us Now Praise Famous Men (James Agee), 119
Levine, Philip, vii, xviii, 31, 50, 70, 77, 93, 100, 105
Library of Congress, 37, 72, 146–47
Lincoln, Abraham, 134
Louisiana Native Guards. *See* Native Guards

Maimie Papers, The, 24, 25, 35
Malcolm, Janet, xvi
Mallarme, Stephen, 70
Manet, Edouard, 27; "Olympia," 27
McCombs, Davis, 30
McGrath, Charles, vii, viii, xi
McHaney, Pearl, xiii
McPherson, Sandra, 7
Merwin, W. S., vii
Meurent, Victorine, 27
Mexico, 57, 124, 151, 154, 164, 166
Middle Passage, 107
Millais, John Everett, xv, 26, 27, 114; *Ophelia*, 114
Mind of the South, The (W. J. Cash), 30
Mishol, Agi, x, 57

Mississippi, xi, xiii, xix, 24, 34, 43, 82, 94, 99, 105, 106, 107, 112, 116, 118, 120, 125, 132, 133, 146, 155, 162, 163, 166, 170, 173, 187, 196, 198
Mississippi Governor's Award, 94, 133
Mississippi Gulf Coast, xi, xvii, 28, 73, 74, 75, 85, 86, 118, 119, 128, 142, 145–46, 147, 163, 164, 185, 188, 195, 196
Mobile, Ala., 73
Monticello, 26–27
Morrison, Toni, x, 200; "Playing in the Dark," 200
mythology, 188–90

Napoleon, 193
Narcissus, 190
National Book Festival, ix
National Public Radio, xiii, 92, 119, 147
Native Guards, ix, xi, xii, xiii, 28, 45, 46, 47, 48, 53, 54, 57, 59, 88, 89, 90, 104, 108, 141, 146, 147, 150
Native Son (Richard Wright), 108
Nebrija, Antonio, 125, 166
New Deal, 38
New Orleans, xv, xvi, 35, 40–41, 52, 91, 118, 119, 125, 129, 139, 145–46, 180, 188, 196
New York City, 92
Nietzsche, Friedrich, 77
Northern Ireland, 69, 116
Notes of a Native Son (James Baldwin), 108

Obama, Barack, 95, 112, 184
O'Connor, Flannery, 130, 184
Odyssey, The (Homer), 190
OED (*Oxford English Dictionary*), ix, 54, 80, 86, 108, 158, 162, 166
Oklahoma City University, 150

Olds, Sharon, x, 9
Oliver, Mary, 177
Ondaatje, Michael, 77; *Diversidero*, 77
Ophelia, xv, xvi, 18, 21, 22, 25–27, 30, 45, 46, 47, 69, 129, 130, 138, 139, 140, 156, 165, 198, 200, 201–2
Ophelia's Gaze, xvi
Orpheus, 83, 202
Orwell, George, 119–20, 123; *Road to Wigan Pier*, 119

Padgett, Ron, 99
Parks, Suzan-Lori, ix
Phillips, Carl, 65
Piazza, Countess Willie, 22, 23
Pinsky, Robert, vii, 103
"Poor Wayfaring Stranger," 60
Pound, Ezra, 37, 80, 136, 194
Pulitzer Prize, vii, xiii, 45, 52–53, 61, 75, 76, 77, 86, 87, 91, 92, 103, 106, 126, 150

Radcliffe, 88, 134
Rankin, Tom, 54
Redneck Riviera, 75
Rindge, Debora, xxivn17
Roach, Joseph, 22
Roethke, Theodore, x, 65, 113; "My Papa's Waltz," 65, 113
Rosen, Ruth, 24
Rowell, Charles Henry, xiv

Schuchard, Ron, 182, 183
September 11, 2001, 63, 196–97
Shakespeare, William, xv, 27, 179, 186; *Hamlet*, 27, 69
Shelley, Percy Bysshe, x, 78, 202–3
Sherman, Cindy, 69
Ship Island, Miss., xi, xii, xiii, 28, 45, 46, 58, 71, 74, 87, 89, 130

Siena College, 156
Simone, Nina, x, 112; "Mississippi Goddamn," 112
Solomon, Deborah, xxiiin2, 71
Somers-Willett, Susan, 119, 148
Soniat, Katherine (stepmother), 63, 95
Sontag, Susan, 3, 4, 19, 54; *On Photography*, 3
South Korea, 120
Southern Agrarian poets, x
Southern Spaces, 167
Stasio, Frank, xvii
Stewart, Susan, 160
Stieglitz, Alfred, 69
Storyville, xv, xvi, xvii, 22, 68, 150, 151, 201
Strange, Sharan, x, 16–17, 64; "Still Life," 17

Tannen, Deborah, 11
Tate, Allen, x, xi, 60, 165; "Ode to the Confederate Dead," xi, 165
Tate, James, x, 50, 69, 88
Thomas, Erika, ix
Tolstoy, Leo, 78
Trethewey, Eric (NT's father), vii, xx, 49, 124; "Her Swing," 124, 127, 153
Trethewey, Gwendolyn Turnbough (NT's mother). *See* Turnbough, Gwendolyn Ann
Trethewey, Natasha: on absence, 3, 9, 10, 38, 145, 188; on accessibility in poetry, 14, 100, 158; on aesthetic considerations in poetry, xvi, xx, 31, 32, 100, 102, 130, 201; on African American women writers, 75, 76, 106, 175; on African American workers in her poetry, ix, xiv–xv, xvi, 3, 6, 20, 28, 38, 82, 116, 129, 130, 134–35, 163, 200; on agency, 24, 25, 139; on Alzheimer's, 7; on the Americas, 198; on art, xx, 26, 27, 30, 76, 77, 78, 81, 114–15, 137, 151, 154; on her audience, 13, 43, 79, 98, 111, 115, 138, 160, 165, 167; on her Aunt Sugar, xiv, 6–7, 11, 49, 80, 135; on autobiographical aspects of her poetry, xv–xvi, xix, 4, 15, 25, 44, 46, 48, 49, 50, 51, 138–39, 141, 143, 154, 158, 163, 199; on avoiding interpretive mistakes, 110–11, 114–15; on the ballad form, 113; on the beauty of precise observation, 6, 73, 159, 202; on becoming a writer, 190, 192; on being biracial, vii, xv, 8, 22, 26, 44, 48, 49, 53, 69, 87, 89, 146, 173, 200; on being black, 8, 12, 22, 32, 76, 89, 116, 132, 139, 187, 200; on being mixed-race, xiv, xvi, xviii, xix, 8, 30, 44, 80, 109, 127, 128, 131, 150, 152, 153–54, 161, 203; on being "old-timey," 4–5, 100; on being a southern writer, 7, 44, 82; on her birth in Mississippi, 133, 183; on her birthday on Confederate Memorial Day, xviii, 105, 133; on black English, 13, 25, 153; on black essentialism, 17, 107; on the black mother, 124, 127, 173; on black soldiers, 58, 89, 108, 121, 122, 133, 137, 146, 150, 160, 182; on black southern history, 13, 90; on "blackface," x; on blood, xviii, xix, 5, 53, 58, 107, 124, 158, 166, 167; on blood memory, 107; on blues music, 8, 10, 128; on blues poems, 57, 66; on the body, 11, 40, 42, 124, 127, 128, 131–32, 153, 154, 161, 162, 187; on her book titles, xiii, xiv–xv, 28, 53–54, 70, 108, 119, 146; on breaking rules of poetry, 14; on her brother, xvii, 5, 42, 52, 58, 73, 74,

87, 89, 122, 131, 145, 147, 170, 195; on the burden of history, 110, 116, 123; on buried history, xi, 34, 44, 75, 90, 91, 105, 128, 137, 145, 164; on call and response, 55, 98, 111; on the canon of southern poetry, 60; on captivity narratives, 108; on casta paintings, xviii, 57, 58, 124, 126, 127, 151, 154, 166, 167, 173, 197; on her changing focus, 136–37, 156, 198; on changing times, 4–5, 8, 74, 94, 95, 128, 169; on character development in poetry, xvi, 129, 138, 201; on cherishing artifacts, 5, 6–7, 68; on chiasmatic structure, 161; on her childhood, xvi, xx, 5, 8, 9, 22, 52, 62–63, 67, 78, 90, 93, 95, 108, 109, 112, 124, 128, 132, 133, 139, 142, 152, 153, 154, 164, 168, 170, 180–81, 189–90, 199; on circling back in poetry, xiv, xvii, xviii, 56, 59, 66, 67, 83, 84, 138, 157, 202; on the civil rights movement, 105, 117, 148, 156, 197; on the Civil War, ix, xi–xii, xiii, 28–30, 37, 45, 47, 57, 58, 87, 106, 116, 121, 122, 125, 133, 137, 146, 166, 182; on clarity in poetry, 14; on class status and race, 118, 132; on code-switching in language, 153; on colonialism, xviii, xix, 57, 107, 108, 124, 125, 154, 166, 173; on the Confederacy, xi, 28, 35, 45, 46, 53, 72, 87, 117, 119, 133, 151–52, 160; on Confederate monuments, ix, 28–29, 34, 47, 89, 90, 116–17, 131, 132, 140, 151–52; on confessional poetry, 121, 158; on connections among her poems, xx, 40, 47, 48, 88, 104, 108, 137, 141, 154, 173, 182; on connections with her subjects, 4, 93; on contemporary poetry, 30, 100, 103–4, 110, 115–16, 148; on contested memory, 196; on creating monuments in poetry, xiii, 52, 59–60, 75, 92, 108, 121, 140; on cropping in photography, 54, 68, 151; on the "crossbreed child" in her father's poetry, xix, 124, 127, 153–54; on crosshatch imagery, 48, 53, 73, 90, 101, 160, 161; on crossings, xi, 53, 161, 164, 165–66; on cruelty of poetry, 4; on cultural memory, 28, 39, 47, 75, 76, 85, 86, 104, 107, 130, 145, 150, 151, 154, 156, 157, 159, 161, 185, 195; on dates cited in her poetry, xiv, 38, 39, 51; on determining the subject of her poetry, 105, 109, 110, 121, 123, 134, 137; on diagramming sentences, 63; on diaries, 23, 25, 28, 46, 53, 59, 72, 78, 90, 133, 138, 155, 160, 164–65, 202; on diction in poetry, 25, 71, 72; on the dictionary, ix, 54, 80, 81, 86, 108, 125, 133, 158, 162, 166; on diversity of voices, 17, 107; on documentary work, 54, 79, 81, 105, 119, 141, 147–48, 151, 160, 167, 193; on domestic violence, 121, 163, 172; on early reading, 78, 155, 165, 180–81, 187–88, 189–90; on education, 24, 72, 165; on ekphrastic poetry, 25, 76, 114, 151, 198; on elegies, xi, xiii, xix, 44, 47, 49, 50, 59, 68, 74, 82, 105, 121, 123, 131, 137, 143, 169, 182; on emotional truth, 15, 51, 94, 122, 199, 203; on emotions in poetry, xiv, xix, 50, 90, 99, 102–3, 112, 123, 144, 158–59, 194, 202; on empathy, xx, 76, 78, 79, 93, 94, 120, 123, 130, 144, 148–49, 155, 160–61; on encyclopedias, 180, 187,

189; on the environment, xvii, xviii, 8, 34, 75, 128, 130, 145, 162–63, 164; on the epistle form, 79–80, 107, 138, 202; on ethical action, vii, 75, 118, 161; on evolution of the volumes, xi–xii, xviii, 59, 60, 87, 98–99, 104, 108, 121–22, 124, 127, 137, 143, 173, 201; on exclusions from history, viii, ix, 29–30, 43, 44, 50, 65, 104, 132, 141, 150, 151–52, 187, 193; on exploring the self, x, xv, 165, 187, 198, 203; on family history in poetry, viii, xviii, 45–46, 49, 63, 65, 70, 82, 97, 98, 108, 112, 124, 134, 163, 173, 177, 195, 199; on her father, vii, xiv, xviii–xix, 8, 9, 15, 29, 31, 35, 40–41, 45, 49, 51, 58, 62–63, 65, 91, 93, 94, 97, 98, 100, 102, 108, 109, 110, 111, 113, 122, 123, 124, 125, 128, 133, 139, 142, 150, 162, 163, 176, 180–81, 189–90, 199; on feminists, 13, 26; on finding a home in language, 43–44, 132, 185; on her first critical creative moment, 134; on her first encounter with poetry, 62, 142; on the flag debate, 117; on form in poetry, xii, xiv, xx, 20, 24, 40, 54, 55, 57, 59, 65, 66, 71, 78, 90, 101, 112, 113, 114, 123, 138, 141, 157, 159, 161, 201, 202; on formal experimentation, 113; on formalism, 66, 71, 113, 202; on found language, 58, 59; on framing in photography, 19, 37, 54, 151; on free men of color, 53, 72; on the future of poetry, 167; on the gaming industry, xviii, 145; on the gaze, xvi, 3–4, 23, 26, 38, 139; on gender and race, 200; on gender concerns, 10, 11, 26, 27, 44, 153, 154, 200, 201; on geographies, 41, 88, 102, 123, 132, 150–51, 163, 165, 169, 170, 173, 187–88, 194, 197–98, 202; on the gesture, 20, 42, 139, 159; on the ghazal, 55, 66, 67, 202; on graduate school, x, xv, xvi, xx, 12, 13, 15–16, 34, 39, 41, 63, 69, 70, 76, 81, 88, 95, 97, 109, 110, 113, 115, 121, 134, 142, 144, 153, 159, 176, 192; on her grandmother, ix, xiv, xv, xvi, xvii, xx, 4, 5, 6, 9, 10, 14, 35, 38, 46, 49, 51, 67, 68, 82, 87, 88, 94, 128, 129, 132, 134, 135, 153, 156, 162, 163, 169, 176, 177, 178, 180, 187; on grave-tending, xi, xii, 51, 122, 141, 161, 162; on haiku, 24; on hands in her poetry, 6; on herself as native daughter, 85, 104; on herself as native guard, xiii, 29, 54, 70, 89, 104, 140, 141, 166; on herself as southern writer, xi, 29, 89, 165, 166; on the hinge in a poem, 83; on historical erasure, xii, xvii, 20, 27, 28, 34, 37, 39, 46, 47, 52, 57, 58, 59, 66, 68–69, 72, 74, 75, 85, 87, 89, 104, 106, 107, 110, 114, 116–17, 120, 123, 130, 140, 141, 145, 146, 147, 150, 151, 154, 156, 157, 164, 185, 188; on historical writing, 193–94, 195, 198; on history, xv, xx, 20, 26, 30, 37, 44, 45, 53, 58, 60, 76, 106, 107, 112, 114, 115, 116–17, 121, 123, 125, 136, 137, 150–51, 187–88, 198, 199, 200; on her husband, 33, 49, 58, 74, 91, 100, 103, 104, 131, 142; on hybridity, 57, 107, 124, 127; on iconography, 107, 108, 115, 124, 127, 167; on identity, 27, 106, 124–25, 127, 138, 153, 166; on illegitimacy, 125, 132, 171, 183; on imagery, xx, 18–19, 21, 25, 27, 38, 62, 79–80, 84, 90, 96, 114, 136, 137, 142, 143, 151, 154, 157, 160, 162,

190, 197, 198; on imperialism, xviii–xix, 124, 125, 154, 166, 173, 198; on the impossibility of a neutral lens, 22, 201; on injustice, xix, 117, 132, 148, 149, 196, 197, 200; on intersections, 53, 119, 128, 133, 157, 202; on intersections of public and personal history, viii, xv, xix, 47, 48, 49, 52, 59, 82, 85, 89, 110, 124, 125, 127, 128, 137, 156, 160, 163, 165, 196, 198–99; on interwoven history of races, 53, 90, 106–7, 119, 124, 126, 127, 133, 160, 161; on investigative reporting, x, 123, 203; on Irish poetry, viii, 116; on jail writing classes, 31; on journeys, 58, 165; on juxtaposition in poetry, 7, 8, 11, 73, 80, 128, 141, 159, 164; on labor history, 130, 132, 163; on lack of a common language, 10–11; on landscape, 34, 35–36, 48, 50, 52, 75, 80, 89, 108, 116–17, 122, 127, 128, 163, 171–72, 173, 188; on language in poetry, 12–13, 25, 27, 55, 57, 82, 83, 92, 96, 98, 101, 142, 143, 197; on language of communities, 12, 152; on language of empire, xviii, 57, 107, 124, 125; on language of her father, xx, 127, 152, 153, 181; language of her grandmother, 13, 152; on language of her mother, xx, 25, 152; on learning rules of poetry, 14, 96; on Lincoln as president of amalgamation, 134; on her linear impulse in narrative, xvii, 56, 66, 84, 138, 201–2; on literacy, 24, 28, 72, 165; on her literary awards, vii, xv, 45, 47, 61, 64, 76, 88, 92, 126, 133, 144, 155; on literary hybrids, x, xvii, 203; on literary modernism, 111; on loss, xiii, xiv, xv, xvii, 18, 44, 67,

68, 75, 83, 84, 93, 108, 109, 121, 123, 128, 130, 131, 141, 143, 144, 162, 171, 185, 195, 202; on her love of story, 192; on her love of words, ix, xix–xx, 93, 98; on loving and hating the South, x, 43, 50, 90; on luminous details, 37, 68, 136, 194; on lynching, 73, 148, 163; on manipulating facts in poetry, 199; on the marginalized, 120; on masks in poetry, 46, 49, 199; on material culture, 151, 198; on her matrilineal family, 8, 9, 11, 156; on memorializing, ix, xiii, xvii, 47, 52, 54, 63, 89, 104, 131, 196–97; on memory, xi, xiv, xv, 5, 28, 49, 51, 54, 65, 68, 85, 88, 91, 110, 117, 128, 129, 131, 137, 140, 157, 164; on men in her poetry, 10; on miscegenation, xi, xviii, xix, 8, 29, 55, 82, 87, 94, 105, 106, 112, 124, 125, 132, 133, 134, 165–66, 183; on missing markers, xi, xii, xiii, 44, 51, 52, 86, 89, 104, 108, 121, 122, 140, 141, 161; on monuments to the forgotten, xiii–xiv, 108, 140; on her mother, x, xi, xiv, xx, xxivn20, 5, 17, 29, 42, 44, 45, 47, 49, 54, 59, 93, 129, 133, 141, 162, 163, 173, 182; on her mother's death, xii, xiii, xiv, 3, 45, 47, 48, 50, 51, 63, 69, 70, 75, 76, 81, 87, 88, 89, 93, 104, 108–9, 116, 120–21, 122–23, 137, 140, 142–43, 150, 169, 170, 180, 202; on motifs in her poetry, xix, 84, 86, 157, 160, 164; on the mulatto, 124; on her muses, x, xiv, 6; on musicality of poetry, xx, 41, 54, 96, 98, 197; on mythology, 9, 188–90; on the name Natasha, 55, 166; on national identity, 110, 156, 165; on national stories, 160, 166,

199; on Native Americans, xii, 34–35, 108; on nature, 8, 11, 34, 35–36, 127, 128, 145, 162–63, 164, 202; on new media and poetry, viii, ix, 167, 203; on her nonlinear strategies, xvii, 55, 56, 66, 138, 201–2; on nostalgia, 5, 18, 74, 86, 130, 131, 185; on objectification, 139–40; on observation, 21–22, 159, 162; on her obsessions, xx, 3, 30, 32, 39, 40, 42, 49, 59, 104, 107, 108, 123, 156, 157, 173, 185, 203; on the octoroon, 22, 108; on origin of a poem, 136; on otherness, 120, 154, 167, 201; on outsiders, 120, 156; on paintings, 81, 114, 115, 124, 127, 151, 198; on palindromes, 83, 202; on the pantoum, xii, 55, 56, 65, 202; on her parents' divorce, vii, 9, 122, 139; on passing for white, xv, 22; on the past, viii, ix, xviii, 20, 105, 116, 131, 151, 157, 161, 163, 165, 169, 173, 188; on her paternal grandparents, 52; on the persona in poetry, xvi, 69, 79, 85, 138, 198, 199; on photographs, xiv, xv, xvi, xviii, 3, 4, 5, 6, 9, 10, 18–19, 20, 25–26, 35, 37, 38, 42, 56, 67, 68–69, 81, 82, 93, 114, 129, 130, 131, 134, 135, 138, 151, 159, 181, 198; on photography theory, xvi, 19, 37, 38, 54, 68; on place, 41, 74, 150–51, 168–73, 185, 188; on her place in the southern literary tradition, x, 7–8, 89; on the poet laureateship, vii, xx, 175; on poetic intersubjectivity, 160; on poetry as performance, 111, 113; on poetry as social practice, xvi, 130, 148, 161, 164; on poetry contests, 43, 175; on poetry outreach, 31; on poetry readings, vii, 77, 98, 99, 111, 121, 124, 153, 157; on the poet's work, 130, 131, 198, 200; on point of view, 3, 8, 14, 30, 45; on poverty, xiv, xvii, 118, 196; on the power of words, 90, 91, 131, 158; on prosody, xii, 38, 40, 41, 157; on prostitution, xv, xvi, 18, 21, 24, 35, 69, 138, 139, 150; on psychological exile, xix, 43, 82, 90, 116, 131–32, 133, 141, 152, 183; on the punctum, xvi, 19, 37, 67, 68; on race, ix, xi, xii, xv, xvi, xviii, xix, 8, 11, 12, 22, 24, 28, 29, 30, 31, 44, 65, 69, 108, 124, 152, 167, 187, 198, 200, 201; on racial difference, xix, 68, 69, 152, 167, 187, 199; on racism, 12, 106, 187, 197; on the reader, xx, 13, 14, 32, 44, 48, 79, 84, 100, 111, 138, 141, 149, 158, 189, 199, 200–201, 202; on reading poetry, 62–63, 78, 91, 97, 103, 136; on reclamation, 171–72; on relationship between photography and poetry, 18, 41–42, 54, 82, 134, 151; on remembering, xii, xiv, xvii, 20, 52, 66, 67, 71, 75, 84, 105, 116, 122, 131, 141, 145, 154, 157; on repetition in poetry, xii, xiv, 55, 65, 84, 90, 114, 157, 158, 161, 184, 202; on research, xvi, 24, 26, 30, 31, 35, 37, 38, 39, 46, 47, 59, 69, 72, 80, 81, 89, 105, 107, 108, 110, 129, 134, 136, 138, 141, 146, 173, 194, 198; on resisting stillness, 20, 40, 68; on restoring lost narratives, 20, 28, 38, 50, 70, 76, 85, 114, 116–17, 118, 156, 157, 188; on restraint in poetry, xiv, 21, 55, 70, 73, 98, 112, 120–21, 158–59; on reviews of her books, 25, 112, 131, 140, 158, 172; on revision, xix, 38, 80, 102, 127; on risking sentimentality in poetry, 5,

63, 98; on role as poet, 85, 89, 116, 149, 158; on rural settings, 8, 25; on self-discovery, xv, 23, 27, 47, 188; on sequences of poems, 84, 127, 137; on sexual orientation, 201; on shared history, 115, 160; on significance of poetry, 111, 158, 165; on signifiers, 22, 23, 27, 82; on signifying, 11; on silences, xiv, xv, 70, 85, 157, 159, 200; slave narratives, 165, 166; on slavery, 53, 71–72, 107, 108, 117, 139, 152, 160; on social concerns, vii, xi, xii, xviii, xix, xx, 26, 31, 32, 130, 156, 160, 166; on sonnets, xii, xvii, 13, 41, 57, 58–59, 66, 72, 113, 114, 161, 201, 202; on sounds in poetry, 84, 96, 112, 202; on the South, 34, 37, 45, 50, 82, 90, 106, 116–17, 132, 134, 156, 166, 182; on the southern literary tradition, x, 29, 45, 59, 165; on her Southernness, xi, 44, 50, 69, 89, 90, 141, 152, 165–66; on speakers in the poems, 3, 25, 39, 45, 57, 72, 138, 140, 160; on spectatorship, 3; on the state of poetry in the U.S., 103; on her stepfather, xii, xiii, xiv, 42, 52, 87, 88, 122, 164–65, 169, 171; on her stepmother, 63, 91, 95, 109, 142; on storytelling, 5, 62, 65, 67, 76, 94, 96, 98, 100, 138, 156, 160, 192; on submitting poetry to journals, 42–43; on symbolic resonance, 158, 159; on syncopation, 57; on systems of knowledge, 124, 125, 153, 166, 187, 203; on the *tableau vivant*, 19, 22; on taking risks in writing, 17; on taxonomy, 57, 108, 124, 125, 126, 127, 166–67; on teaching creative writing, vii, 6, 13, 14, 16, 31, 46, 55, 78, 91, 96, 97, 100–101, 102, 136; on theories of hybrid vigor, 203; on tone in poetry, 65, 158, 199; on tourism, xvii–xviii, 128; on travel narratives, 108, 118; on her Uncle Son, 9, 49; on understanding her place in the world, viii, ix, 187; on Union soldiers, 28, 46, 53, 57, 59, 70, 71, 72, 87, 89, 116, 133, 160; on variety of black experience, 17; on victimization, 24–25; on the villanelle, xii, 40, 55, 56; on visual art, xv, xvi, 114, 124, 127, 151, 198; on voice in poetry, 12–13, 25, 27, 39, 45, 59, 99, 112, 137, 138, 148, 149, 161; on the white father in her poetry, xviii, xix, 45, 124, 127, 139, 172–73, 199; on whiteness as racialized experience, 12, 44, 69, 199, 201; on women in her poetry, 10, 20, 68, 124, 134, 200; on women writers in the 21st century, xix, 76; on women's history, 200; on the word "guard," 54; on the word "native," 86, 108, 125, 166; on the word "thrall," 86, 108, 125, 166; on work, 131, 132, 134; on workshop communities, 16, 101, 102; on writers who influenced her poetry, viii, 8; on writing books of poems, xx, 25, 39, 46, 47, 84, 87, 105, 108, 137, 158; on writing habits, 99; on writing poetry, xviii, 5, 8, 49, 54, 55, 62, 78, 81, 83, 90, 93, 94, 95, 96, 97, 99, 103, 109, 120, 137, 138, 142, 144, 157, 192, 193–94, 197, 198, 199; on writing prose, xviii, 12, 20, 54, 75, 95, 109, 117, 129, 142, 144, 157, 188, 192, 197, 203

Works: "Accounting" (poem), xiv; "At the Station" (poem), 10; "Bellocq's Ophelia" (poem), 26; *Bellocq's Ophelia: Poems*, xv–xvii, 18, 19, 20,

22–28, 31, 35, 37, 38, 39, 42, 45, 46, 47, 49, 59, 61, 67, 68, 71, 113, 114, 126, 127, 129, 134, 137–38, 150, 151, 156, 165, 193–94, 200, 201–2; *Beyond Katrina: A Meditation on the Mississippi Gulf Coast* (non-fiction), vii, x, xvii–xviii, 117–18, 119, 126, 130, 142, 144–45, 146, 147, 157, 183, 184–85, 192, 195, 196, 197, 203; "Beyond Katrina: A Meditation on the Mississippi Gulf Coast, Present, Past, and Future" (Page-Barbour Lectures), 85, 117–18; "Blond" (poem), 60; "The Book of Castas" (poem), 107; "Cameo" (poem), 73; "Collection Day" (poem), xiv; "Domestic Work" (poetry sequence), 49, 82, 137; *Domestic Work: Poems*, x, xiv, xv, xvii, 18, 19, 32, 38, 40, 41, 46, 49, 50, 57, 61, 65, 67, 82, 93–94, 113, 120, 126, 127, 130, 137, 143, 150, 151, 156, 163, 172, 175, 176, 200; "Drapery Factory, Gulfport, Mississippi, 1956" (poem), 64; "Early Evening, Frankfort, Kentucky" (poem), 50–51; "Elegy" (poem), 173; "Elegy for the Native Guards" (poem), 60, 141; "Flounder" (poem), 11, 80, 113; "Gathering" (poem), xiv; "Genus Narcissus" (poem), 70, 71, 80; "Gesture of a Woman-in-Process" (poem), 20, 40; "Give and Take" (poem), xiv; "Glyph, Aberdeen, 1913" (poem), 51; "Graveyard Blues" (poem), 48, 70, 89, 122; "His Hands" (poem), 11; "History Lesson" (poem), 128; "Hot Comb" (poem), x, 17; "Incident" (poem), xii, 40, 55, 56, 65–66, 90, 91, 103; "Knowledge" (poem), xix, 113, 153–54; "Letters from Storyville—October 1911" (poem), 68; "Limen" (poem), xiv, 143; "March 1912—Postcard, en route westward" (poem), 24; "Mexico" (poem), 173; "Miscegenation" (poem), 45, 48, 51, 55, 67, 165, 166, 202; "Monument" (poem), 48, 51, 141, 162; "My Mother Dreams Another Country" (poem), xxivn20; "Myth" (poem), 70, 71, 83–84, 202; "Naola Beauty Academy, New Orleans, 1945" (poem), 64; "Native Guard" (poetry sequence), 39, 57, 59, 72, 90, 113, 141, 160, 161, 162, 201, 202; *Native Guard: Poems*, vii, ix, x, xi, xii, xiii, xiv, xvii, xix, xxivn20, 28–30, 37, 38, 39, 41, 42, 43, 44, 45, 46–48, 49, 50, 53, 57, 58, 59, 61, 65, 67, 70, 71, 73, 74, 75, 84, 85, 86, 87, 92, 98–99, 102, 104, 106, 108, 110, 112, 113, 114, 116, 119, 120, 121, 122, 123, 126, 127, 128, 130, 131, 132, 133, 134, 137, 140–41, 142, 146, 147, 150, 151, 154, 156, 157, 163, 166, 169, 171–72, 175, 182, 185, 193–94, 201; Page-Barbour Lectures, xviii, 74, 85, 117–18, 147; "Pastoral" (poem), x, 29, 60, 141, 165, 169; "Photograph: Ice Storm, 1971" (poem), 163; "Photograph of a Bawd Drinking Raleigh Rye" (poem), 19, 25–26; "Pilgrimage" (poem), 110, 116, 195; "Saturday Matinee" (poem), 172; "Scenes from a Documentary History" (poetry sequence), 51, 55, 56, 57; "Self Portrait" (poem), 23; "Signs, Oakville, Mississippi, 1941" (poem), xiv, 9, 163; "South" (poem), viii, 41, 43, 102–3, 182, 183; "Southern History" (poem), 58, 84–85,

200; "Southern Pastoral" (poem), 29; "Speculation, 1939" (poem), xiv, 38; "The Storyville Letters" (poetry sequence), 201; "Tableau" (poem), 49; "Target" (the poem titled "Incident"), 55; "Taxonomy" (poetry sequence), 126; "Theories of Time and Space" (poem), 58, 74, 130, 169, 185; *Thrall: Poems*, xviii–xix, 106, 107–8, 110, 153, 166, 167, 172, 197, 200; "Three Photographs" (poetry sequence), 3, 134; "Vignette" (poem), 25; "White Lies" (poem), xxivn16, 200; "Why I Write: Poetry, History, and Social Justice" (lecture), 197, 202; "The Woman" (poem), 20
Tucker, Memye Curtis, 60
Tulane University, 35, 52, 91, 180–81
Turnbough, Gwendolyn Ann (NT's mother), xii–xiii, 45, 52, 60, 89, 122
Turnbough, Leretta Dixon (NT's grandmother), xii, xiv, xx, 49
Tuskegee, 24

University of Georgia, xii, 61, 63, 150
University of Georgia Press, 147
University of Massachusetts at Amherst, x, xv, 14, 16, 50, 54, 61, 64, 81, 83, 115, 134
University of Missouri, 136
University of North Carolina at Chapel Hill, 55, 74
University of Virginia, xviii, 74, 85, 117–18, 147, 175
University of West Florida, 77

Venetian Hills Elementary School, 62, 95

Vietnam War, 52
Voigt, Ellen Bryant, x, 99, 100, 101, 112

Walcott, Derek, 191
Wall, Ezra, xviii
Warren, Robert Penn, x, 30, 60, 118, 203; *Segregation*, x, xi, 30, 118, 203; *Who Speaks for the Negro?*, xi
Watkins, Billy, xviii
Weaver, C. P., 46
Weaver, Teresa K., x
Weems, Carrie Mae, 159; *The Kitchen Table Series*, 159
Weigl, Bruce, 73
Wheatley, Phillis, 155
Whitman, Walt, x, 28, 60
Wideman, John Edgar, 15, 50
Williams, Carrie Mae, 20
Williams, Crystal, 176
Wilson, August, 5, 107
Wilson, E. O., 60, 82, 183
Wine, Charlie, 150, 151
Woodward, C. Vann, 29
Wright, Charles, x, 60, 91, 149, 161, 162
Wright, James, 63; *Collected Poems*, 63

Yale University, xv, 126
Yeats, W. B., x, 73, 120, 140
York, Jake Adam, 148
Young, Kevin, x, 144; *The Art of Losing*, 144